IT WAS BETTER THAN WORK

To: Jerry Devine
        with
    Warm Regards
        and
    Good Memories

Bev Kelley

IT WAS BETTER
THAN WORK

F. Beverly Kelley

The Patrice Press
Gerald, Missouri

**Library of Congress
Cataloging In Publication Data**

Kelley, Francis Beverly, 1905-
    It was better than work.

    1. Kelley, Francis Beverly, 1905-
2. Press agents — United States — Biography.   3. Theatrical agents — United
States — Biography. 4. Circus — United
States — Biography. I. Title.
PN1590.P7K45 1983   659.2′97913′0924 [B]
82-24556   ISBN 0-935284-25-7

Printed in the United States of America

Published by
The Patrice Press
Box 42 / Gerald, MO 63037

To Ruth
who shared with me in person
and in spirit so many of the
adventures in this book,
all the while adding luster to my life.

Contents

Foreword

I only wish that the reader of this book might know the author personally. "Bev" Kelley has been my friend for many years and I've heard many of the thrilling stories related in his book from his own lips. He is unequaled as a raconteur and lends to the material the charm of an extraordinary personality.

Every American boy and girl has been thrilled in youth by the Circus coming to town. How stirring is the music of the calliope and the bands in the colorful and exciting parade up main street. And how many of us have dreamed of following the big tent on its romantic trail across America!

Well, we didn't, but Bev Kelley did.

And he loved it and loves it still in memory. Once, sitting with him watching the Circus in the old Madison Square Garden in New York and realizing his public relations and promotional responsibilities for the Circus, I asked, "How do you like this job, Bev?" His reply was instantaneous and unforgettable. "It's a lot better than working." That told the whole story; Bev Kelley is still circus-struck, still an American boy following the sights and sounds of the big show with stars in his eyes. No one in this country is better qualified to tell the story of this great American institution than he.

So if the years are adding up and life sometimes gets a bit on the dull side, tell you what you do; just read this great book and let Bev Kelley wave a magic wand which will make you feel young again.

I know of no more fascinating story for the nostalgic library of youthful memories. It brings to mind the romantic experiences of yesterday.

So, I salute my old friend Bev Kelley with admiring affection. Here is a great book for every American boy and girl from nine to ninety.

Norman Vincent Peale

Acknowledgments

I am especially grateful to Dr. Norman Vincent Peale and his associate, Myron Boardman, for their kindness to me in these past months. Those two were the first, after my wife and my agent, to read the completed manuscript. I am also warmed by the generous praise given to my effort by Dr. Peale in his Foreword.

I must offer special thanks to the distinguished author, artist and clown friend from our circus-trouping years, Bill Ballantine. Bill took valuable working time from a new book of his own so that he could design and execute the art which appears on the jacket of this book.

I am grateful for the efforts of Miriam Lane, my initial typist, amanuensis and abiding friend; and to Shirley Gregory, who typed the completed manuscript.

Robert and Gregory Parkinson are at the magnificent library of the Circus World Museum, in Baraboo, Wisconsin — they supplied many of the best photographs of our Big Top adventures which appear in this book.

A good many stage luminaries and other friends from the performing arts supplied blessings and encouragement during the preparation of this manuscript. A few of them, in no particular order: Lynn Fontanne, Signe Hasso, Lillian Gish, Sol Jacobson, Seymour Krawitz, John Kennedy, Gene Wolsk, Pat McDonald, Mae Mack, Madge Oliver, Mary Martin, Edwin Lester, Dorothy Callahan, Iggie Wolfington, Mary Wickes, Harry Davies, Tony Buttitta, Helen Brooks Rose, George Wilmot, Dave Lawler, Shirley Herz, Mary Bryan, Shirley Carroll, Parley Baer, Winthrop Partello, Anne Ford and Kathleen Anne Sullivan, the queen of the production stage managers. All of them loyally remained in my cheering section during the time required for writing this book. Thanks are due to my daughter, Kathleen Vogt, who was most helpful in proofreading.

A special note of appreciation is due to the distinguished ophthalmologist and staunch friend, Dr. Ronald Burde. He is the man who controlled the enemy of writers (and readers, too) — glaucoma — from the time of its first appearance several years ago.

And finally I want to thank my literary agent and good friend, Joyce Flaherty, who introduced me to The Patrice Press and its multi-talented owner, author-publisher-musician Gregory M. Franzwa. In him I have discovered not only a dedicated, patient, skilled and tyrannical editor, but a new friend as well.

He is the one who chose the pictures. I feel that some of his contributions tend to amplify the accomplishments and professional stature of the author. For example, he strongly suggested that newspaper articles about me be included in this text. He was also firm in his belief that inclusion of several of my poems would be helpful to the book.

I know my colleagues are going to accuse me of ''three-sheeting,'' but I suppose such condemnation is preferable to the complex of phantasmagorical horrors visited upon those authors who don't listen to their editors.

— F. Beverly Kelley
December 15, 1982

Other books by the author

Fun By The Ton
with Eddie Allen, Hastings House, 1941

Pink Lemonade
with Maxwell Coplan's photos, McGraw Hill's
   Whittlesey House, 1945

Circus Holiday
Harper Bros., 1942

Kathleen Visits The Fair
Little, Brown, 1952

Clown
with Emmett Kelly, Prentice-Hall, 1954

Denver Brown And The Traveling Town
Exposition Press - Banner Books, 1966

The Language of Show Biz
(principal contributor) Dramatic Publishing Co., 1973

The Great Circus Street Parade
with C.P. Fox, Dover Press, 1978

IT WAS BETTER THAN WORK

Troopers Retire

They saved enough to quit, live in a town —
Old troupers, leaving circus trails at last.
And yet, when evening's curtain has rung down
And silence cleaves the quiet, sheltered cove,
They hear the phantom wagons rumbling past.

The hollow sound keeps rolling through their dreams,
And when a storm knocks at the window pane,
And through each tiny crack the north wind screams,
They hear instead as on a canvas dome,
Drum-tight, the soft tattoo of summer rain.

Still, hoping with determination grim,
They vow to live the life that others do,
But when the organ peals a stately hymn,
Inspiring with majestic, solemn surge,
A ghostly calliope comes piping through.

This is the promised land, the golden day;
This is the bright mirage that blinds the eyes
Of circus troupers whose bright roadway lay
Beyond the boundaries of a village street —
Abreast Apollo's sun steeds in the sky.

The snorting, charging stallions of the sun!
The spinning, flame-flecked wheels that pace the dawn
Of seeming endless seasons never done;
Like winding spangled caravans that pause
In sunlit hours, then load and thunder on.

They saved enough and left the show, retired,
And built a house to hold them 'til they'd die;
They boasted they had all their hearts desired,
And never looked back down the winding road —
But in their dreams the wagons still roll by.

— Bev Kelley
1947

1

SATURDAY'S CHILD

I never have been able to recall exactly how old I was when I first heard that old birth days verse. The last line promises that anyone born on my natal Saturday may expect to work hard for a living. What I do remember, however, is that I never even dreamed that it could be so much fun!

I was born in the middle of July at St. Marys, Ohio, where my father owned a furniture store. At the age of six months our family moved to Delaware, Ohio, 75 miles away. That's where Leroy Pyke Kelley and Grace Adelia Brown had met while they were students at Ohio Wesleyan. Now my father would become a partner in a larger furniture establishment operated there by his brother-in-law, Sam Blair.

So my earliest recollections are not of St. Marys, but of Delaware, and of being taught to repeat from memory that I lived at 101 North Washington Street. I was about three years old at that time and seldom strayed further from home than the house next door. I could be attracted there irresistibly by the aroma of cookies freshly baked by Mrs. Dave Grube. Mother always knew where I had been — there was a smudge on my nose that came from Mrs. Grube's screen door.

One of my playmates, Virginia Moore, lived in a second-floor apartment nearby. I still have the book *Black Beauty* which she gave to me on Christmas Day 1913. That same day my Aunt Ruth came to visit from her home in Cincinnati. She taught school there.

My father kept a horse and buggy at a downtown livery stable. We went to meet his sister at Hocking Valley railway station in this rig. I was very excited that morning because I wanted to show Aunt Ruth that I had learned to whistle.

I suppose I have so much affection for that address because it is there that I have my earliest recollection of my mother. I had awakened from an afternoon nap in a big bed to discover that she had returned to us after having been hospitalized for surgery. She was lying there beside me.

My father was still an Indiana farm boy at heart. He kept a vegetable garden and nearby was a pen for my rabbit. My pet made me a firm believer in the egg-laying propensities of the Easter Bunny. Two beautifully colored eggs were in his pen Easter morning — that is what I would call hard evidence.

The bunny's helper in this delightful ruse was our good neighbor, Mrs. Otho Williams. For some reason she had not boiled them, and it was decreed that I could keep them no longer than Easter Sunday. They were much too valuable to me to discard so I hid them under some of my clothing in a dresser drawer. Mother Nature eventually blew the whistle on me and I was called on the carpet for disobedience.

Our street, with its tall elm and maple trees, was a favorite habitat of a flock of blackbirds. Dad saved some firecrackers from our Fourth of July celebration and declared war. At twilight, when our unwelcome visitors were among us in great numbers, he lit the fuses and threw his primitive grenades high into the branches.

That did it. They took off with a roar. They made one wide circle and landed in exactly the same place. The scenario was repeated time and again, but I never tired of watching the battle.

I remember looking out our second story west window one memorable night. A lady was staying with me while my parents were out for the evening. She showed me Halley's Comet. When my parents returned from their party they told us that they and all the other guests had gone out into the street to do exactly the same thing.

My mother read to me often. I can remember the excitement of *Teddy Roosevelt's Hunting Trip In Africa, The Little Lame Prince,* and later the nature stories of Ernest Thompson Seton. (He occasionally reversed his signature to Ernest Seton Thompson.) His books had such provocative titles as *Squeaks and Squawks From Faraway Trails.* Among the diversions shared with my parents and playmates were the popular ''Parchesi'' and a card game called ''Authors.''

One day my father brought home a sample ballot which had a

rooster atop one column and an eagle on the other. That was my introduction to the game of politics. He asked me which one I liked best. I chose the Republican eagle. That remains my preference to this day, but like my father, I usually split my ticket at the local level, because I usually am acquainted with the local candidates.

I'll never forget my first day at Sunday school. The teacher tried to put us at ease by asking if we knew any songs which we could sing for the class. Several small hands were raised. We heard a number of ditties of modest consequence, such as "Jesus Wants Me For A Sunbeam." Then it came the turn of my cousin, Helen Blair. The teacher's eyes grew wide as Helen belted out the popular tune, "I Wonder Who's Kissing Her Now."

In my first semester of public education at North School my teacher was the same lady who had been my mother's teacher. My stay with Miss Woodman was brief, because I contracted measles, mumps and whooping cough in rapid·succession. I was removed from school and began again at age 7 in another building. By then we had moved to Winter Street, which was served by the West School.

I had no enthusiasm for departing from this fond and friendly neighborhood. Never again would I see the old familiar faces of "Grandpa" Hart, playmate Mayrox Young, and especially Dave Grube. He had made a handsome toy airplane for me, propelled by rubber bands. This distaste for moving persisted, even though our new address was only two blocks away.

That all brings to mind the time we were trying to make our youngest daughter less unhappy about changing cities. Her mother told her that she would have a good time and meet many new friends, but Rebecca responded with impeccable logic: "I'm having fun right here and I already know enough kids."

There was an abundance of lilacs at our new address, then as now my favorite flower. Mother planted nasturtiums too, and sweet peas, spirea and hydrangea bushes. Geraniums flourished in porch window boxes and wisteria climbed a lofty elm tree on the property next door.

There was a large cherry tree in our backyard. Despite nonstop competition from our feathered friends I could pick enough cherries for home use and still have enough left over to sell. Grocers supplied quart-size boxes for that purpose.

Although I had seen some newborn babies, it remained for my first black cat, Fritzie, to provide my first witness to the miracle of birth. I was so excited I ran all the way to Gallaher's store to buy a basket big enough for Fritzie and her new family of six.

I spent considerable time with them in our basement nursery. After they were weaned they were allowed to grow up on their own outside the house.

When I was a boy I owned but one dog, a white fox terrier called Chummy. After traffic on our street increased alarmingly I gave him to a farmer. I didn't want him to be run over. Several of our cats had been done in by local speed demons, some of them traveling as much as 25 miles an hour.

When I was about 5 or 6 years old we took a winter trip to Florida. We visited an ostrich farm near Jacksonville, and I begged my father to buy a huge egg, which in fact was artificial. Nobody could convince me that it didn't contain a living embryo, and it certainly seemed logical to me that if we took home an incubator too I would soon own a baby ostrich. That is the only time I can recall crying for a pet — and it wasn't even mine.

I awakened one raw March morning to the news that there would be no school that day. Our town was in the grip of the devastating flood of 1913. Both the Olentangy River and its tributary, the Delaware Run, were out of their banks and inundating the entire lower downtown business area. Most of the stores had flooded basements; some had water on their main floors. Houses carrying people and pets were afloat on the river; more stable homes had water as high as their second floors. People were being taken through windows to safety by volunteers. Local lumber companies supplied the boats for that purpose.

It was a terrible disaster which saw a heavy loss of life and many instances of heroism. Dayton probably suffered more than any other Ohio city and soon began a flood control project which has remained effective to this day.

One of Delaware's industries which survived was our big chair factory. Delaware Chairs were widely heralded for their fine cane work. Their huge rockers graced the porches of America's finest hotels. Robert Lybrand headed the firm. He was a well-liked and amusing fellow. He received a telegram from an agitated Cincinnati customer about an overdue rail shipment, just as the flood waters crested. Lybrand studied the wire from the incensed customer and gazed at the ocean outside his office window. He decided he could answer truthfully in the 10 words alloted by Western Union: "Your valued order left factory today via Olentangy River. — Lybrand."

Our town was served by the Pennsylvania, Chesapeake & Ohio and New York Central railroads. The New York Central carried a sleeping car which was transferred in Cleveland and could be ridden all the way to New York City. I used this accommodation in later years with such frequency that my wife said she regarded the 9:14 train as a member of the family.

Delaware also enjoyed electric interurban service. The line connected Columbus, Delaware and Marion, and therefore was called the C D & M. In later years the C D & M carried a "palace" car with large swivel chairs and some other exceptional features.

By the mid-'50s electric interurban service had disappeared from most of the

I was about age 2 when my father, Leroy Pike Kelley, commissioned this photo.

nation. However, I discovered one line still operating between Cedar Rapids and Waterloo, Iowa. In those days I was traveling the Midwest for the show, *Mr. Roberts.*

The car looked awfully familiar. I asked the conductor where it had been built.

"I don't know that," he replied, "but the company bought it in good condition from a repair shop in Ohio — town by the name of Delaware, I think." Sure enough, I was being hauled around by a fine old friend.

2

IN THE GOOD OLD SUMMERTIME

Delaware's summers, which at school closing had seemed to stretch out endlessly, picked up an unwelcome tempo just prior to Labor Day. That's when the bells called us back. Still, the days of summer were fun-filled for a boy.

Frank Collins and I spent a lot of time playing soldiers. We exchanged mudballs with Harvey Mohn and his recruits. Collins, as it turned out, was not playing so much as he was practicing, for he became an Army career man. Frank had duty in Panama, in Italy during World War II, and served in Korea before retiring to make his home in Spokane.

I was 4 years old when I caught the malady which I have carried down through the years — Big Top Fever. My father and I boarded a trolley car and went out Lincoln Avenue to Euclid. There I heard the band playing star spangled music and the tents of the famous John Robinson Circus were billowing in the breeze.

When I returned home I aspired to emulate the wild animal acts. Our next door neighbors were the A.J. Willey family. Dr. and Mrs. Willey had three boys, Gene, Bob and Herb. We lived on Winter Street then, just across the street from the Jane M. Case Hospital, where Dr. Willey practiced.

My herd of cats showed absolutely no enthusiasm for circus stardom. I placed them in wood-barred, brightly-painted cages atop our coaster wagons. I wasn't about to be discouraged by their attitude. By the summer of 1918 this budding circus tycoon was old enough to mount a Red Cross benefit show. We even had a street parade, led by Frank Knight on his pony. The performance was in the backyard of Jim Campbell's home on North Washington Street.

In our troupe were two exotic lady aerialists, Ruth Thomson and Abigail Semans. Their trapezes were tree limbs, and from them they performed tricks that we males lacked both the skill and the courage to attempt. Jim's mother made a clown suit for him. For me she sewed a more formal costume — I was both ringmaster and clog dancer. The music for my act came through open windows from a phonograph in the house. Since we had a first class show we felt justified in charging a first class price — two bits. We grossed $15, a third more than we would have had not Dr. Semans paid $5 for his ticket.

Just as our performance ended we received some thrilling news, relayed to us from a letter received from Col. Kirk Campbell. The colonel was serving in France, as were

I was about 5 when this photo was taken with my mother, Grace Brown Kelley.

many others from our town. The news was of the smashing American victory at Soissons — an important contribution to the eventual German surrender on Nov. 11 of that historic year.

This wasn't exactly my introduction to the performing arts. A couple of years earlier Eugene Willey and Griswold Campbell staged a show in the latter's backyard on West Central Avenue. Edward Star, Chuck Bodurtha and other neighborhood lads comprised the performing personnel.

I happened to be the star of the thrilling finale. It was a leap to bare ground from a rather tall shed. I contributed the feat simply because nobody else could be found who was stupid enough to do it. The fact that I had a total lack of acrobatic prowess had no effect on my determination to rise to the top.

The show had several performances, one of which was attended by my mother. That evening my father persuaded me to discontinue my Leap for Life act. At that moment the circus world lost one of the great daredevils of all time but the pain was eased considerably by an understanding dad. He gave me the princely sum of 50 cents. I was making absolutely nothing in the show, so that turned out to be a pretty good deal. And anyhow, I needed a new squirt gun.

It was about this time that my mother told me some things about our ancestors. My great-grandfather, Rev. Jacob Anson Brown, served several local and rural churches. She described him as a circuit rider. Those words aroused both my curiosity and my pride in my dedicated and hard working ancestor — not because he was a member of the cloth but because I thought she said he was a circus rider.

In later years, much of the furniture which came to our store was shipped in large corrugated containers but when I was a boy it all arrived in crates. So the days of summer included the building of backyard shacks from those discarded crates. Paul Clark, a classmate, was a good carpenter. We hammered and sawed our architectural masterpieces. One was a skyscraper, towering two stories high. We used linoleum scraps for roofing. Paul's yard had one with a window of real glass.

My own backyard turned out to be something of a midway. I built a roller coaster, and guided my coaster wagon over the dips and rises. Then I made a ramp, and left a gap to be jumped by those hurdling down on roller skates. Actually this saw only one performance. When I landed, my skates broke in two at the instep. My interest in the performing arts was greatly dimished in that one fell swoop, so to speak.

We kept active in more conventional summer games. There was no softball in Delaware in those days, but we did play baseball with a conventional ball. We didn't have a golf course but croquet and tennis were popular. Francis Marriott, president of the Delaware Tennis Club, gave Jim Smith and me a job lining the clay courts. They were on West Central Avenue, at the foot of the hill near the sanitarium.

We mixed our white lime solution in a barrel inside a tiny shed, frequently ducking outside to cough and to inhale some fresh air. The pay was modest, but with this job came permission to use the courts, and tennis became my game. Among the better players were Drs. Will Borden and Rees Philpot, whose family had a private court which they generously made available to us. Most of our games were played nearer home on North Franklin Street, where Dr. Ed Semans had built a court for his daughters, Anne and Abigail.

Actually I played fairly well. However, Abigail Semans, who was my age within a week, could take me almost any time she felt like it. I never resented this; she was a natural athlete, a good friend

This is the first grade of West School, Delaware, Ohio, in 1912. I am fourth from the left in the top row. Our teacher was Miriam Brown. Ruth Stephens would join that class the following year. She would become Mrs. F. Beverly Kelley some 18 years later.

Photo courtesy Mildred Haynes Gorsuch

and a good teacher who helped me improve my game. Ab went on to a social service career in New York City. Years later she came home to head the Red Cross office and to lead the Delaware County Chapter with its water safety program. That program won national prominence and she was able to bask in a little limelight before she lost a long and heroic fight to cancer.

I had some yard chores to do and spent some time playing outside. But a great deal of time was devoted to summer reading. I especially remember *Beau Geste,* Jules Verne's exciting *From The Earth To The Moon,* and *The American Boy* magazine. It contained fascinating stories by Clarence Buddington Kelland. His hero was a fat boy named Mark Tidd.

Our West Winter Street home faced south. On hot summer days my mother kept the window shades drawn. The living room seemed almost cool when I came in from the hot sun. The parlors of some homes of that era served as galleries for a popular photographer named Wallace Nutting. His tinted landscape artistry was favored by home decorators prior to the boom in oils by Maxfield Parrish.

Mother was a fine pianist who could have pursued a professional career. To this day I have never heard anyone with her gift for improvising; I can still see her beautiful hands on the keyboard. She would play the songs of the great balladeers: Ernest Ball, Oley Speaks, Carrie Jacobs Bond, Ethelbert Nevin, Victor Herbert and Charles Wakefield Cadman, who composed songs about the American Indians.

It was pleasant, growing up to the sound of such memorable musical poetry as "The Sunshine Of Your Smile," "In The Garden Of Tomorrow," "Little Gray Home In The West," "The Road To Mandalay," "Land Of The Sky Blue Water" and "The End Of A Perfect Day."

When the ukulele became popular I acquired one and took two 50-cent lessons from Nancy Campbell. She taught me four chords and two songs: "Castle On The Newport" and "That's Where My Money Goes." Soon I was playing and singing tunes learned from phonograph records. I guess I posed no great threat to the careers of the recording artists of those songs — people like Eddie Cantor, Ted Lewis and Al Jolson.

Broadway's Tin Pan Alley was the source of most of the popular songs of that day. The sheet music was priced at 35¢ a copy; phonograph records ranged from 35¢ to the 50¢ figure commanded by Victor's "Gold Seal" recordings of famed vocalists and symphony orchestras. Our furniture store sold Pathe phonographs and records. Customers could sample them in private listening booths. Our best customers were the newly arrived Italian-American families whose tastes leaned to the classics, especially grand opera.

Before we owned a good phonograph I invested $4 of my allowance savings for a toy model from a mail order house. It worked surprisingly well. It came with two little records, "Just A-wearyin' For You" and "Can You Tame Wild Wimmin?" The latter had growling lion sounds in the background and a conclusion which asked, "If you can, please tame my wife." I can remember my recently-widowed Aunt Addie listening to the former and recall that she had a hard time holding back the tears.

The Ouija craze finally found our community. Not many years ago Mamie Watson recalled that I was the kid who rang her doorbell to ask if I could borrow her Ouija board so that it might tell me where I had lost mine.

Jimmy McGuire had a newsstand on our town's main street and sold dime novels, the ancestor of today's paperbacks. He also handled some fireworks, chewing gum, snuff, cigars, cigarettes and a medicine called "Cubebs" for the relief of bronchial asthma.

Kids under the legal age for buying tobacco could buy Cubebs legally — they went up to these from corn silk and dried grape leaves. They tasted terrible but we felt important — just like the grown-up sports with their Camels, Fatimas, Sweet Caporals, Old Golds and Lucky Strikes.

We had such a smokeout one summer afternoon in the summer house of a neighbor (they call them gazebos now). Our grape leaf cigarette wrappers caught fire and we narrowly avoided having to call the fire department.

Summertime usually meant two weeks on my Aunt Edna's farm, where my dad had been born and raised. It was five miles south of Kokomo, Indiana. We traveled there by train and were met in town by Uncle Max Cammerer with horse and carriage. I loved that farm. There were eggs to be gathered, berries to be picked, sunfish to catch in a stream called the Little Wildcat, and livestock to feed. I welcomed waterboy assignments at threshing time.

Elizabeth and Margaret Cammerer, my young cousins, lived here, and half a mile east was the farm of my Showalter relatives. There was usually a family reunion there during our visit. I can remember a lively one — the year when we were playing in a hay-cock field and a swarm of bees got into Ralph Hutto's pants.

My Aunt Ruth was teaching school in California by that time, but every summer she would time her Indiana visit to match ours. It was a special occasion when my great uncle, Howell Pyke, a Methodist missionary in China, came home. He and his family had survived the infamous Boxer Rebellion.

We took our first trip to Indiana by automobile the summer after my father bought the first of his steady string of Buicks. It was about 175 miles to the farm and the preparations were almost as exciting as the trip itself. I can recall my parents donning the linen dusters, standard equipment for driving a roadster over the dirt roads of that day.

We were able to go about 75 miles the first day. That wasn't bad considering the type of road maps of those days: "Turn south at red brick schoolhouse corner," "Turn right at the hamlet store" or "turn north at the large pile of rock."

The Hoosiers maintained their gravel roads far better than the Buckeyes. My father gave me my first driving lessons on Indiana's gravel roads. Sometimes he let me take the wheel for a considerable distance. I remember well how proud I was the first time I drove up the lane at the farm. That particular trip was the first when we were able to cover the entire distance in a single day.

Cecil Shephard, the farm's hired man, was kind to this city boy.

He allowed me to sit with him in his buggy during the after-supper twilight while he practiced his trombone.

I also remember the hired girls with fondness. Those young ladies were hired to help out from time to time, especially when the arrival of visitors multiplied the daily chores. These included Naomi Rhea and Pearl and Ruby Frey. Those two sisters barely missed being struck by a falling iron farm bell. I rang it with far too much enthusiasm in anticipation of a carriage ride to the Russiaville Fair.

My friend George Noble was the first of our crowd to be permitted to drive his family car unattended. George occasionally drove his older sister and two of her attractive friends from Delaware to Olentangy Park in North Columbus, and occasionally took me along. There was a fast roller coaster there. Its dips and turns just demanded that protective males hold their arms tight around the older girls. They were able to convince us they were terrified. Whether they were or not was unimportant. I certainly was.

3

SEASONS AND HOLIDAYS

The willows are still wearing their green summer dresses but the oaks are ready to disrobe for slumber. The maples dance in their red and gold formals as the hour of their year strikes 11. The spruces and pines are like happy coeds awaiting their snowy ermine capes. Fat orange pumpkins wear funny faces and window panes suddenly become gossamer etchings. Porches stand empty after doorbells have been punched by young goblins, who now stand begging in the front halls.

Tonight I wonder if perhaps the restless wraiths of my past Halloweening may be mingled with the merry company come to celebrate the wake of October. Above their hoots, squeals and sepulchral tones I seem to hear the echo of a board fence protesting the wrench of a crowbar. Bob Borden and I were using it one night long ago.

That wasn't a "trick-or-treat." They didn't have that when I was young. Our night of excitement consisted principally of trick-and-run. Seldom was there any real vandalism. We observed "corn night" on the evening before the official mischief date. We threw kernels of field corn against windows. This seldom disturbed a resident enough to bring him to the door, but our window-soaping certainly did. There weren't many family cars that escaped.

Later we fashioned a simple device to draw more attention. It consisted of an empty thread spool with the edges notched by our pocket knives. We would wrap it tightly with string and put a 10-penny nail through the center of the spool. We held it against the window with one hand and pulled the string with the other and it caused an awful racket.

Sometimes we would rearrange peoples' porch furniture, to the extent of upending tables and chairs, or sometimes placing them in the yard of a neighbor. Once we pushed Howard Bryan's little shop delivery truck a half mile and parked it on the steps of the high school. It was found in good condition the next day.

I'm sure everyone has heard about pushing over outdoor privys on Halloween. It was always more enjoyable if the structure were occupied by someone who was disliked, but experienced pranksters were always careful to push occupied privys over on their doors. The perpetrators then could be a block away before the anguished resident managed to roll the structure off its door and prepared to pursue the tormentors.

Those of us who lived in towns of any size were denied this foolishness. By the time we were old enough to observe the holiday without adult supervision, central sanitary sewers had outmoded the outhouse.

So we went to Halloween parties. They usually took place in the homes of our playmates. The favorite beverage was apple cider and the usual game was bobbing for apples. We would kneel around a washtub filled with water and apples. We had to keep our hands behind our backs and snag an apple with our teeth. Sometimes it was a costume party and we came as witches, goblins or ghosts.

Back to the crowbar. Bob Borden and I decided to topple a back fence owned by an ill-tempered neighbor. He had chastised both of us in times past when he caught us climbing that fence — it was on the shortcut to another friend's house. That night the barrier gave us a lot of resistance and the noise of the operation eventually exposed our mission. The complaint came to my father and my partner and I were the pictures of wide-eyed innocence as we denied any knowledge of the dastardly act. My father then taught me a lesson in truth telling. He knew we did it, and we knew he knew we did it. Nevertheless, he quietly restored the fence to its upright position and we never climbed it again.

In my day November 11 was Armistice Day, not Veterans Day. I wonder if Bob Bordon remembers that historic day in 1918. We were Boy Scouts then, selling Liberty Bonds on the home front. Bob was in my cheering section when I won a citation for being the first to sell five $50 bonds. Bayard Ehnes was second and our pictures appeared in the *Gazette,* a rare distinction in those days before small city dailies carried numerous pictures with regularity.

My friend Borden now lives in Missoula, Montana with his own family, but in 1918 he was my next door neighbor. When the great news of the war's end flashed authentically (after a premature announcement some days earlier) Bob and I led a makeshift parade.

It was one of many in town that morning. Ours differed in that our only musical instrument was a big metal washtub.

We were quite young and it seemed like a long time since our nation had been at peace. It was a year and a half earlier. In that time we learned an entire new group of songs, all inspired by the World War. None of America's other military involvements seemed to spawn so many. Now they come marching down Memory Lane every November: "It's a Long Way To Tipperary," "Pack Up Your Troubles In Your Old Kit Bag and Smile, Smile, Smile," "There's a Long Long Trail A-Winding," "Keep The Home Fires Burning" and "Rose of No Man's Land."

That war spawned some tear-jerkers too: "Hello Central, Give Me No Man's Land" was about a child trying to telephone her soldier-father. We heard "Just A Baby's Prayer At Twilight For Her Daddy Over There," "The Little Gray Mother Alone" and "My Buddy."

There were funny tunes too: "K-K-K-Katy," was about a stuttering volunteer bravely trying to sing a farewell to his sweetheart. There was the sleepy doughboy's lament, "Oh, How I Hate To Get Up In The Morning." That was written by a young recruit at a boot camp in New Jersey. He was Izzy Balane then, but the world would come to know him as Irving Berlin. There was "Hinky, Dinky Parlais Vous" with a martial tempo, and the lively "Dixie Doodle" that I like to hear our friend Robert Eichhorn play on the piano.

And who could forget "Over There," written by the immortal George M. Cohan? His Broadway musicals invariable reflected his patriotism with flag-waving finales. He wrote "Over There" in less than an hour on the morning America entered the war. Within moments he showed it to New York's reigning thrush, Nora Bayes. She introduced it that very night to a theater audience whose spirits may still be cheering.

That song made its composer the only civilian to receive the Medal of Honor. It was presented some years later by President Franklin D. Roosevelt.

In remembering the musical giants of those days I almost forgot an eminently forgettable ditty: "Would You Rather Be A Colonel With An Eagle On Your Shoulder Or A Private With A Chicken On Your Knee?"

In those days Thanksgiving was not swamped by the over-commercialization of Christmas. We had a Thankgsiving play at my West School, in which I was cast as the despised British monarch responsible for the flight of the Pilgrims. I'll never forget my introduction: "He stoned them and put them in prison and beat them with cruel blows; they said they would find a new country and worship God as they chose.''

Many years later my wife and I were shopping in a big city department store at Christmas time. She asked me if this merchandising behemoth impressed me as much as The New York Cash Store. At the mention of that name more than a half century fell away and we were kids again on a shopping expedition. The New York Cash Store was our town's tabloid edition of the big city stores. It occupied most of a three story yellow brick building on East Winter Street. Born out of its time, it lasted only a few years but it brings back memories of lady clerks in starched white shirtwaists and black skirts.

The store featured a huge variety of toys but the principal attraction to us was the change making contraption. This consisted of a small container like a mason jar. The currency was placed in it, the container was fastened to a carrier on a wire, and a lanyard was pulled. The container was propelled by a spring along the wire to an elevated central position where the change was made. We all stood awestruck as this moving miracle flew back and forth over our heads.

I can remember during my years at Ohio Wesleyan that my father and my uncle Sam Blair had nicknames fashioned from their home towns. They were called ''Kokomo Kell'' and ''Sycamore Sam.'' They both had to work until noon on every Christmas day, to help deliver the gifts ordered by our customers. Before the store had motorized delivery they had an aging delivery ''boy'' named Nelson Anderson. He had a big wagon and a white horse named Dolly, and they were indispensable to the performance of the holiday obligation.

Before the coming of electified Christmas lights the trees were decorated with candles. This caused many tragic accidents; by the time Christmas came the trees were like tinder.

The first string of electric Christmas lights was such a novelty that it brought a steady parade of people to the home of the owners, the Willey family. They were our next door neighbors at that time.

It seems as if there were more white Christmases in those days. I can't recall lacking enough snow to launch a magnificent new Flexible Flyer. On that magic Christmas morning I couldn't have taken more than a few seconds for breakfast before bolting to the nearest slope with the sled.

One Christmas I received a wind-up train, but a year or so later there was an electric model under our tree. And I remember a "stereopticon," or opaque projector, that flashed images of even colored postcards onto a wall or a sheet. Another Christmas brought me a snare drum. And I remember the Christmas I received my first Boy Scout uniform, and that marvelous December 25th when a shiny new bicycle was under the tree.

No Christmas surprise was more enjoyable than one staged by our youngest daughter Becky. We were celebrating Christmas in Philadelphia more than a half century after my youth. Becky had worked secretly with her mother for a long time and assembled all kinds of toys that I had owned 50 years earlier. There was a length of track supporting the engine from that old electric train. There was my circus parade wagon, my stuffed lion, an elephant and a monkey I had called Jocko. There too was a smaller one that my mother had said I should name "Brother." And best of all, there in the arms of our grandson Michael was my old teddy bear, satisfied now after waiting a half century to be hugged again by a little boy.

Delaware has the reputation of being a community of many churches. Religion had a substantial impact on young people in the years when I was growing up. It was felt acutely as the yuletide approached.

My family belonged to the Methodist church, but the first Sunday school I attended was Presbyterian. Most of my friends went there, including the Willey boys from next door. Phil and Max Wylie went there too — they went on to become famous novelists. There was another brother, Ted, and a sister, Verona. Their father was minister at that church.

My first Sunday school teacher was Julia Campbell. Later, while I was attending the William Street Methodist Sunday school, my teachers were Fannie Clark and Adam Baumgartner. Baumgartner once generated some excitement among several of us. George Noble, Charles Morrison, Ted Canright and I were invited to his home for a "groundhog" dinner. Of course the main course was soon recognized as waffles and sausage, which was indeed ground hog. Our popular teacher's joke was greeted with a good laugh.

Our church, located on West William Street, was nicknamed the "Bill Street" church. It had two top choir soloists in soprano Mrs. Ashton Conklin and Mrs. John Pfiffner, who was an alto. Mrs. Pfiffner's annual selection for Mother's Day was "Rock Me To Sleep," and it always brought tears among the congregation. Mrs. Conklin's nephew, Horace Russell, had a good high school tenor voice. Roscoe Klee and I sang bass. If I live another 100 years

I won't forget those days when I sang in the choir.

Delaware's streets and store windows were always decorated lavishly for Christmas. Walter Pollock, our popular mayor, liked to drive his horse and cutter through the neighborhoods at Christmas time with the sleighbells jingling. He stopped frequently to thrill children with short but long-remembered rides. Our children still recall him as "Mister Jingle Bells."

The old familiar Christmas carol, "We Three Kings of Orient Are," was on one of the Christmas programs at the Bill Street church. Horace Russell, an older college-age student named Jim Simester and I were scheduled to sing the well known solo verses.

I guess I was a little late in arriving and in the rush I tripped at the top row of the choir and tumbled all the way into the banked evergreen boughs at the lectern. Had it not been for the rail I would have fallen into the front row of the congregation. I returned to my position among the singers and found Russell laughing uncontrollably. When it became time for his solo he was unable to sing a note. So I sang his part, as well as my own. As far as I know it all went unnoticed, except by his Aunt Loma. She had come especially to hear her nephew perform.

When the program was finished our boy tenor was well on his way into Franklin Street and gaining speed all the time. I felt it necessary to face his perplexed aunt, and explained to her that the incident was entirely my fault for having fallen. She went away scratching her head.

That wasn't my only embarrassment as part of a singing group. A few years later several of us town members of the Ohio Wesleyan Glee Club were recruited to augment the choir members at St. Peter's.

There I learned two things: the music of the Episcopalian church was much more difficult than the sacred music I had been singing, and the Episcopalians served real wine to the choir as well as the congregation during communion.

I expected grape juice, to which I was accustomed at Methodist services. When the chalice was passed among the choir I swallowed enough wine to start me on a coughing fit. It persisted long enough to amuse some of the regular choristers; certainly not my mother and our next door neighbor, Fausta Borden, who were seated down front.

4

IT WAS A GRAND OLD OP'RY HOUSE

Not long ago I was in Lexington, Kentucky, heralding the coming of a handsome touring revival of *My Fair Lady*. I much admired what this history-minded city had accomplished in restoring its vintage opera house to the grandeur that the grand dame had paraded in 1875.

I reflected on how appropriate this elegance was, in serving as a frame for our beautiful show. I proceeded to arrange for newspaper and television interviews to take place a month hence with our stars, Ann Rogers and Edward Mulhare. My mind kept flashing back to the long-gone opera house in my home town and to the enchantment it had held for this stagestruck kid growing up in Delaware, Ohio.

Delaware's town hall had a tall clock tower and a red beacon that signaled patrolmen to report to the police station. It looms large in my memory not so much because it contained the city offices but because of the opera house. It was on the second floor, reached by a wide flight of stairs.

The more I worked for touring shows, throughout the United States and Canada, the more I realized what an architectural gem we had in our hometown opera house. The auditorium was designed in the French and German tradition and had boxes on both sides of the proscenium opening, extending over the stage apron and even a little over the stage proper.

Like youngsters who hurry home from a circus to pretend that the backyard fence is a tightwire, I would come from the opera house to my own "theater" made from an open-front box. There were toy figures for actors and scenery painted from one of those old Devoe watercolor sets. It had a front curtain carrying advertisements which could be raised or lowered by a mechanism I had copied from the roller shades on our porch.

I could recall dialogue and songs from shows I had just attended and duplicated the performances as best my limited resources would allow.

My initial audition for a hometown production of *Snow White* ended in disappointment. I wanted to be one of the dwarfs but had to settle for the role of a brownie because I happened to be the tallest kid there. But it was a start and marked my debut on that glorious opera house stage. I made no further theatrical appearances there until a couple of decades later. Then I was cast as the interlocutor for a minstrel show staged by our Kiwanis Club, and I also led a robust male chorus in the old rouser, "Stout Hearted Men."

Our opera house had a seating capacity of a little over 600, including the balcony. Delaware's fire engines and the horses that pulled them were kept one story below the stage until they galloped off down Memory Lane, replaced by motorized fire trucks. Harnesses hung directly over them, ready to be dropped onto their backs at the sound of the fire bell.

The scent from those noble equines rose abundantly through the big trapdoor through which we hoisted the scenery of traveling attractions. Often the entire auditorium was flooded with this unexpected bouquet.

Most of the traveling companies carried their own scenic effects to augment standard opera house equipment. These usually consisted of a street scene, a woodland dell and a parlor setting which showfolk referred to as a "center-door fancy." That is because it had double doors that could be opened at the back. I always looked forward to seeing the scenery and recall being bitterly disappointed if a second act rang up on the same set that had served the first. And I still like a lot of scenery; it is an important dimension of the total theater.

There were two seats dead center behind a cross aisle on the main floor of our opera house. This location was favored by Jim Smith and me when we attended home talent shows which starred our friends. On occasion we would borrow opera glasses from his aunt or my mother.

One such attraction was a revue labeled *Fads and Fancies*. It was produced in a brave (and futile) effort to raise enough money to save the home of Rutherford B. Hayes, Delaware's contribution to the United States presidency. The house was to be demolished for a filling station.

The performance had a musical exercise entitled "Oh Skinny,

Come Out and Play With Me,'' featuring a chorus of high school girls. They tossed wrapped candy kisses into the audience. There was also a scenic "spectacular" consisting of Christmas tree lights strung on latticework and connected to ladies gowned in vintage costumes. They sang the popular new melody, "In An Old Fashioned Garden."

Our town was an occasional one-night stand for touring shows from before the turn of the century on into the mid-1920s. The shows usually were enroute from Newark or New Philadelphia, Ohio, to engagements of a week or more in Columbus.

The renowned United States Marine Band came to our stage once, and many of those lucky enough to have 75 cents skipped school for their marvelous matinee performance.

Sometimes a Broadway touring company would pay us a brief call. Two performances I especially liked were a drama called *Fine Feathers* and a show named *Robin Hood.* In that one a tipsy Sheriff of Nottingham said, "The next time that door comes around I'm going through!"

Several years ago in Chicago I looked in on a revival of a 1927 musical comedy, *Very Good Eddie.* I first saw it in Delaware and wondered if the new edition still contained a hotel lobby scene with a comedic desk clerk. Sure enough, there was not only the same setting and typecasting; the one joke I remembered was still alive and well. The clerk answered the telephone to hear an irate guest complaining. He replied, "A couple of rats are fighting in your room? What do you expect for a dollar and a half, a BULLfight?" A joke like that, good once, is good forever.

The asbestos fire curtain at our opera house carried skillfully-painted advertisements of local merchants. One was on the back side, visible only to the performers, and probably pulled better than any of those on the front. There in big black letters was some advice to the thirsty: "Go to Holtzmiller's and Hannings After The Show."

Traveling minstrel show companies and shows like *Uncle Tom's Cabin* had street parades. A good "Tom Show," as they were known in the trade, featured a small marching band and a horse-drawn carriage carrying its lady principals. These included, of course, Topsy and Little Eva. There was a flatbed wagon, also pulled by steeds from local livery stables. It had a portable cabin, in front of which sat the man playing Uncle Tom. Bringing up the rear were the dogs led by the villian, Simon Legree, and Lawyer Marks, the comedian. Bloodhounds were not very impressive so they used giant Great Danes. It was quite an honor for this town boy to be a part of this parade, as leader of two or more of the huge dogs. It was also something of an achievement if the march could be completed without the animals pulling the boy off his feet.

Theater tickets could be purchased downtown at Joyner's Drug Store, which was across the street from the opera house, or at the box office. Busy Billy Woolheater was the stage boss and billposter for the operation.

Delaware's opera house was closed for several years. When it reopened it became the showcase of the drama department of Ohio Wesleyan. The university spent about $30,000 to refurbish and remodel it. The initial production was the famed old melodrama *East Lynne*, directed by Roland Clarence Hunter. He was the distinguished mentor of the college dramatic department and my drama coach there during four interesting years. The second show after the restoration was *Uncle Tom's Cabin*, an excellent town-and-gown presentation that included the popular citizen, Bruce Burgess, in the role of mean old Simon Legree.

The municipal building, including the opera house, was destroyed by fire in the early 1930s and university and town theatricals returned to schoolhouse stages. One of the best local shows I ever witnessed was directed by Mrs. Vincente Minnelli at St. Mary's Auditorium. To the lively music of ''Pony Boy'' she both staged and starred in as superb a western dancing number as ever lit up a stage.

At the famous Lambs Club in Manhattan more than a quarter century ago I asked Leonard Long, an aged character actor, where he had begun his memorable career. ''In a place you never heard of,'' he replied. ''It was a town in Ohio called Delaware. The Minnelli brothers hired me at age 19 to be their leading man for a traveling dramatic tent show.''

Then I told him that his springboard to theatrical eminence was my old home town. He said he remembered the college campus and its sulphur spring, and then went on to tell me that Vincente Minnelli's wife was a talented New York professional with the stage name of Mina Gennell. She was the mother of my high school classmate, Lester Minnelli, who later took his dad's first name professionally. He achieved fame in stage design and in motion picture direction in Hollywood. There he married Judy Garland, the young luminary of *Meet Me In St. Louis*. Their daughter Liza Minnelli carries on their long family tradition.

The Ohio Minnellis, headquartered in Delaware, fielded a summertime tour that played a new town every week. There was a dif-

The Delaware Opera House, shown during a production of H.M.S. Pinafore, featured magnificent architectural ornamentation. Lester Minnelli played the role of "Dick Deadeye." He is the last sailor on the right in the front row.

ferent play nightly and a matinee for children on Saturday. Similar companies toured in numerous states in that golden era before the motion picture discovered its voice. That erased these touring tent attractions along with vaudeville, the tented chautauqua companies and the silent films.

In the early days everybody on the show doubled in brass and overalls, presenting their formal stage roles and contributing novelty numbers between the acts.

When they retired, Mrs. Minnelli operated a dancing school and occasionally her husband resumed his stage career as director of musicals sponsored by lodges in eastern and midwest cities.

I had composed a number for an Ohio Wesleyan homecoming show, and I recall how flattered I was that this courtly showman asked to use it in a minstrel show he was staging in Pennsylvania. Then I felt I had to forgive him for a disenchantment he caused me when I was 10 years old. I attended an opera house performance of *Bringing Up Father* by the Minnelli Brothers troupe. It was a welcome-home-from-the-tour matinee treat for school kids and cost five cents a ticket.

I had expected the characters to look **exactly** like Jiggs and Maggie and other characters looked in the newspaper comic pages. Years later I was in Dinty Moore's Restaurant in New York and met the famed cartoonist George McManus. I told him this story and we both agreed that, despite an imperfection in the Minnelli edition of his cartoon masterpiece, at a nickel a ticket the price was right!

5

QUEENS OF THE SILVER SCREEN

A dinner date with our friend and fellow Ohioan, Lillian Gish, can really stimulate the memory. We recently had a good talk about the adventurous early movie-making days, when Lillian and Dorothy Gish and Mary Pickford were directed by the great D.W. Griffith. My mind refused to leave the subject. It flickered like an old-time silent film and led me again down memory lane to the magic of the movies.

The silver screen and its theaters held a strong attraction for me, especially in the early '20s when Delaware's Strand was still new. Its owner, Henry Bieberson, gave me a job as an usher. It was my first employment in show business. It not only paid a full 50 cents a night, but when I was not occupied with a flashlight escorting customers down the darkened aisles, I could stand in the back of the house and watch the silver screen work its magic.

At that time I was in love with Constance Talmadge and Marguerite Clark. They shared stellar billing with the likes of Bessie Love, Blanche Sweet, Anita Stewart, Norma Talmadge, Mary Pickford and the Gish sisters, Lillian and Dorothy.

Many years later, when Mary Pickford and the Gish girls became friends of mine, we talked a lot about the early days of history-making films. The movies were the fastest-growing phenomenon ever to become an established part of the entertainment field.

Several years prior to being employed at the Strand I attended the new theater's auspicious opening. That was the biggest crowd I had ever seen in Delaware. There was a new film every other day.

The first one starred the popular Francis X. Bushman and Beverly Baine in *His Choice*. Next we enjoyed Mary Pickford in one of her early triumphs entitled *Rags*. (That was the name of her pet dog in the story.)

Our town had three other motion picture houses in those halcyon days: the Star, the Superba and the Grand. The Grand had an outer lobby slanting so steeply that a customer had to get a running start to get to where he could buy a ticket.

This film house was owned by a prominent Delawarean named Park Byers, who had been a skilled tightwire performer in his younger days with the circus.

This was the era of the movie serial. The exciting weekly chapters always had cliff-hanger conclusions calculated to bring the eager viewer panting back for the next episode.

The undisputed queens of the serials were Ruth Rowland and Pearl White. Pearl's *Perils of Pauline* even inspired a popular song entitled "Poor Pauline." The lyrics, as I recall, went like this: "Bing, bang, biff; they throw her off a cliff; they dynamite her in a submarine. In a lion's den she stands with fright, the lion goes to take a bite; zip goes the fillum; Goodnight, Poor Pauline!"

There were other serial thrillers, including *The Million Dollar Mystery* and *The Mine With The Iron Door*. My favorite was a wild animal entry starring Kathleen Williams in *The Adventures of Kathlyn*. It was at the Grand, where I was occasionally invited to sit in the choice, 'way-down-front seats with a classmate named Helen Oviatt. She attended as the guest of the management because her father was the film projectionist. That could lift a person's social standing considerably.

A youngster in those days could attend a matinee for five cents and a night showing for a dime. That meant that he might take his date to a movie, stop on the way home for an ice cream soda or a sundae and feel like Diamond Jim Brady — all for a total of 50 cents or less.

On one occasion the price soared to a half-dollar for all customers, regardless of age, but that was when the Star showed *The Birth Of A Nation*. Despite the bitter winter weather, it was a bargain at any price.

Occasionally small-time vaudeville acts were seen on the small stages of the early-day motion picture houses, and I remember that the Star once featured a trainer with his educated male lion in a circular cage barely big enough to accommodate both man and beast. At the Superba there were vocalists who, standing in the boxes beside the orchestra pit, sang the latest songs that could be coupled with colored slides for such renditions as "Apple Blossom Time In Normandy."

Colored slides were used also for local advertising, and between these commercials there might be slides asking ladies to remove their hats so the row behind could see the films, and admonitions against throwing peanut shells on the floor, and also against smoking.

Movie houses all had pianos. The musicians matched the mood of the film story with imagination and tireless skill. The Star's owner, George Buchman, had a sister named Rose, who was one of the best.

A few of the early film palaces installed electrically-operated player pianos. The music rarely matched the action. The Strand became the only theater in town to acquire a full-sized organ, which was manned with picture-matching authenticity and for audience sing-a-longs by Delaware's fine talent, Frank Hyatt. He later was replaced by another professional, Harry Stewart.

These kings of the motion picture keyboard reigned for a period as the small town equivalent of the famed Jessie Crawford, of New York's Paramount Theater. He was known on Broadway as the "Poet of the Organ."

Unsung heroes of the early movie days were the projectionists in their hot little booths. There they cranked the reels by hand with endless patience at a prescribed slow and steady tempo. They changed reels regularly and quickly. Sometimes they had to splice a broken section, or cut out a strip that had burst into flame. It was a dangerous place to be if fire started in those close quarters.

A single reel of movie film ran for 15 minutes, the usual length of a newsreel or an animated cartoon, and a two-reeler consuming half an hour was likely to be a comedy or a travelog. A full-length feature film would unroll its enchantment for a full 90 minutes.

Long before the silver screen found its voice, the Superba Theater featured very briefly a simplified forerunner of sound on film — a phonograph recording was used, reasonably synchronized with the action on the screen. The sound track on the film itself was invented some time later.

Before the reign of Tom Mix, Hoot Gibson, Ken Maynard and singing cowboys Gene Autry and Buckeye-born Roy Rogers, we watched such heroes of the silent screen as William S. Hart, William and Duston Farnum, Thomas Meighan, Wallace Reid, Douglas Fairbanks Sr. and Richard Dix. An early comic was John Bunny.

We saw lots of slapstick comedians: a western funnyman known only as Alkali Ike, Chester Conklin with his walrus mustache, and the ever-bumbling policemen in the Keystone Comedy car chases over Hollywood streets and into the nearby mountains.

I can remember watching cross-eyed Ben Turpin and stuttering Roscoe Ates as they ground out a lot of mileage from their simulated handicaps. The comely foils of such funsters included two young women who in time were covered with starshine: Gloria Swanson and Joan Crawford.

We laughed at Charles Ray, Harold Lloyd and "Snub" Pollard, who had a short Irish nose to match his nickname. These folks often shared the celluloid with such comediennes as Louise Fazenda, a boisterous type; and fluttery Zasu Pitts.

Movie sirens back then were labeled vampires and then simply vamps, because of their skill in preying upon the gullible male, and of this sorority Theda Bara and Pola Negri were the headliners. Soon there was a popular song, "The Vamp," to salute their winning wiles. I can remember seeing the first silent picture to cause a song to become popular nationally — Mabel Normand's *Mickey*. During that same era there was a Russian-born classic actress named Nazimova. She was destined to be called Nasty Mova by young movie fans who couldn't pronounce her name.

In the silent film days movie stars were expected to perform their own stunts, no matter how dangerous they were. Frequently this included actresses as well as actors. Lillian Gish once told me of an incident which took place during the filming of her powerhouse feature, *Way Down East*. They were on the turbulent White River during New England's rugged winter weather, and she was required to lie on a patch of ice so long that her hip froze. She was at the very brink of a rushing waterfall, awaiting heroic rescue by her leading man, Richard Bartholmess.

Not long ago, while I was working a publicity assignment for a touring Noel Coward play entitled "Present Laughter," I discovered that our leading man, Douglas Fairbanks Jr., has a World War II record that is simply amazine. This modest man seldom speaks of it unless pressed to do so. He has numerous decorations and citations for Navy exploits and commando valor. His real-life wartime exventures match his distinguished father's swashbuckling swordplay and acrobatic prowess in the make-believe world of the silent screen.

In Delaware's summertime the only air conditioning came from electric fans. However, the Star management put together an "airdrome," an outside theater on a vacant lot along East Winter Street. It had an elevated projection booth and a screen and stage big enough to accommodate small vaudeville turns. It came complete with a generous supply of mosquitoes and kindred summer visitors. They may have deceived the live performers into assuming that the almost continuous slapping of bugs by the audience was applause.

There was a sizeable popcorn machine in the outside lobby of our theater, the forerunner to today's elaborate lobby confection stands. The enticing aroma that was spread by an electric fan was indeed a strong commercial for the hot buttered popcorn. It was a bargain, too, at a nickel a bag.

I worked at the Strand, which had no goodies for sale. The management discouraged popcorn being brought in because the rattling of the paper sacks annoyed many who were trying to watch the show. The theater sold only entertainment and the affable wit of Kitty McAuliffe. For many years Kitty sold tickets from a roll in her tiny glass booth out front. She shared popularity laurels with the film queens on the silver screen inside.

Manager Bieberson owned an illuminated sign in a lettered frame inside a glass-front box. That was attached to a telephone pole on the southeast corner of Winter and Sandusky streets. It advertised the Strand's current attraction in small white letters fitted carefully into rows.

When I had been an usher for a suitable period I was promoted to the job of changing the corner sign. I carried a short stepladder. On one busy Saturday night, while the corner was crowded with shoppers, I managed to spill the tray of letters. It seemed an eternity to me as I kneeled on the sidewalk to put the letters back in their proper places.

I can remember the day my parents took me to see *The Last Days Of Pompeii*. I was about 6 or 7 years old, and this was a really big picture which I was anxious to attend.

During the course of the film I found I had other business to attend to. There were no public rest rooms in the Superba at that time, so my father called an usher to escort me to the rest room back stage, and gave me a quarter with which to tip him.

I returned to my seat and returned the coin to my father. I explained, evidently in more than a whisper, that "I didn't tip him because he had to go too." That turned out to be the best part of the evening for patrons in the surrounding seats.

6

HIGH SCHOOL HIGHLIGHTS

Some classmates and I were on the way home from the last day of eighth grade at West School. We were met by Mrs. Cyrus Austin. She told us how much we would enjoy high school and how quickly the time there would pass. Walking on West Winter Street and looking across at our new school, I thought, "Four years? That's forever!"

But the good lady was right on both counts. The tempo of our high school days was to be more like a march beat than a waltz. They contained a special excitement that not even the college days ahead would provide.

Best of all, we had exceptional teachers at Delaware High. All were good and some were great, considering the "material" with which they had to work. These educators, along with some grammar school teachers of whom I was fond, stamped me with a lifetime conviction that their's is the greatest profession.

One of the numerous exceptional teachers was Mrs. Dell McAfee Naylor. She taught English at the high school level, guided me when I was editor of the annual *Bulletin* in my junior year, and encouraged me generally in early literary efforts.

Thinking back on the high school years, I often wonder if some others from the French classes of Laura Schultz still keep in touch with pen pals acquired soon after World War I. We exchanged letters with French and Belgian children as part of a bilateral learning program. My Belgian counterpart was Lillian Hautrieve, who married a soldier named Jensen during World War II. We have exchanged Christmas greetings and family news without interruption for more than half a century, although we have never met.

Our high school had good athletes. Both football and basketball teams excelled in a league that included Marion, Bucyrus, Galion and Mansfield. In a state tournament our cage heroes came within five points of winning the title and lost only to Dayton Stivers. That team, Dayton Steele, Toledo Scott and Canton McKinley usually comprised the toughest competition. The final score of that crucial title game would be unbelievable in later years of non-stop action — it was 10 to 5!

During my high school years, I came no closer to gridiron or court action than in the role of cheerleader. I took that post so seriously that I'd mope for days after we lost a tight contest. The cheering, or "yells" as they were called, included several that began or ended with a prolonged Y-E-A! An example would be, "Fight Team Fight, Fight Team Fight; Delaware, Delaware, Y-e-a-a-a!"

The popular "locomotive" was performed by spelling out Delaware letter by letter, slowly at first, and then with accelerating tempo like a railroad train gathering speed. There were numerous quickies in the cheerleader's repertoire, exhorting the team to "Block That Kick!", "Get That Ball!", "Hold That Line!", and "We Want A Touchdown!"

A number that smacked of Ivy League origin was "High, High, Yigh, Yigh, Biff Boom, Sky High; Rah, Rah, Rah, Sis, Boom Bah; Delaware, Delaware, Y-e-a-a-a-a-a!"

And I never did know where this silly-sounding holler originated unless perhaps at Walla Walla, Washington: "Walla, Walla, Walla; Yip, Yap, You; Walla, Walla, Walla; Other Teams Skidoo! Tomahawk 'em, Tomahawk 'em; send 'em home to Ma; Delaware High School, Rah, Rah, Rah!"

Although there was no band accompaniment in those days, we would sing enthusiastically from the stands. We proclaimed that "We Love The Black-Eyed Susan" — our official colors were orange and black. Our music instructor, Elizabeth Sheen, provided an original song with intelligent lyrics and a melody I remember well: "Make all advances strong and sure today; take all the chances fate throws in the way; fight for the glory in which all may share; victory makes history, so fight for Delaware!"

Classmate Margaret Barrett wrote a lively paean of praise saluting our basketball team, to be sung to the tune of "Peggy O'Neal": "If they're big and strong and good, that's Delaware High; If they fight just as they should, that's Delaware High. If they come on the floor with a smile, and go off with a score that's worthwhile; Pep for their snappiness, rep for their scrappiness, That's Delaware

High!''

Abbreviations "pep" for energy and "rep" for reputation or renown, had only recently found their way into our vocabulary.

Our dedicated music mistress worked minor miracles with her glee clubs, so that from their ranks came both chorus and principals for the annual Gilbert & Sullivan operettas. I was privileged to appear in two of them: as British Admiral Sir Joseph Porter in *H.M.S. Pinafore,* and in the title role for a production of *The Mikado.* The real star of that show, however, proved to be Harold Stephens. He played the comedy role of the Lord High Executioner, Koko.

In a previous *Pinafore* presentation, Lester Minnelli was cast as Dick Deadeye. Later in the semester he starred in the title role of *The Fortune Hunter,* our senior springtime play that year.

I became a high school debator by substituting on short notice for an ailing member of the team. My ability to commit to memory rather quickly brought an invitation to attempt a principal role after the first-choice player departed town suddenly. He fled for no apparent reason unless, perhaps, from stage fright. This emergency casting meant learning, rehearsing and playing, within a day and a night, the part of Dick Donnelly in the 1924 senior class play *Nothing But The Truth.* It was a Broadway comedy about a man who made a bet that for all of 24 wide-awake hours, everything he said would be the truth.

Among special events on our high school entertainment calendar was the yearly appearance of Civil War veterans just prior to the May 30th official observation of what we then called Decoration Day.

The ranks of survivors of the great war between the states were thinning by the 1920s, but I remember R.K. Willis, who talked to us about the Battle of Atlanta, and a Captain Kellogg, who had written a popular book about his experiences while a prisoner of the Confederates at Andersonville.

There were memorial parades from the courthouse to Oak Grove Cemetery where, at its Soldiers' Circle, a veteran delivered a brief address. Flowers then were placed on the graves already bearing small American flags supplied by the G.A.R. In later years, that duty was taken over by the American Legion and the Veterans of Foreign Wars.

Veterans marched in these processions for as long as age and infirmities permitted, and then reluctantly rode in open-top cars.

As a participating Boy Scout, I looked forward to placing another and smaller flag at the grave of my maternal grandfather, Beverly Waugh Brown, who at age 16 left home sans parental consent to join the Union Army. So did my paternal granddad, Francis Asbury Kelley, who joined the Indiana volunteers at age 17.

I don't recall that there were street parades on July 4th. That holiday always began for me when my father and I went out onto the roof of our front porth to place Old Glory in its holder there.

Later in the day there would be a Delaware Club picnic complete with fireworks to celebrate the nation's birthday. The one I remember best took place at the Lester Riddle home, where the fireworks display carefully executed by our male parents included some items which were terribly loud. They scared us kids into running into the house where we crowded under a big bed, only to discover that a wise family collie had beaten us there.

At Delaware High School we received a visit from Ohio Wesleyan's dean, Dr. William Emerson Smyser. He also was the English department's wizard of words, and his recitations brought to pulsating life the verses of Rudyard Kipling.

Another distinguished author of "tone" poetry, to be heard as well as read, was Vachel Lindsay. He generously graced our stage at a matinee appearance prior to his official date that night at the university auditorium, where he appeared as one of the luminaries of the Concert and Lecture Series.

This American giant of his craft put so much enthusiastic action into his poem, "The Congo," that my seatmate, Ellsworth Sonner, began to laugh uncontrollably. I finally clamped a hand over his mouth, sensing that we just might be witnessing a performance that was culturally memorable.

A decade or so later, I often began my circus talks to service clubs and schools with that poet's verse: "Every soul is a circus and every mind is a tent, and every heart is a sawdust ring where the circling race is spent."

So I felt that the least I could do when we exhibited in Lindsay's hometown, Springfield, Illinois, was to invite him to attend a performance. This he was delighted to do because he loved the Big Tops. We had a good chat. I chose not to remind him of his lively reception at Delaware High.

Delaware High had no marching band in the '20s. This was before the remarkable organizer-trainer-conductor Clyde Fitchorn propelled our school bands to prominence in state competition. However, our physics and chemistry instructor, D.H. Leas, put together a small symphony-style group in which I played drums, chimes,

anvil and baritone sax. Not great, but busily. And this modest orchestra became one of the first attractions from Delaware to be
heard by its hometown boosters on radio from a Columbus station.

At West School I had played drums to Robert Smith's piano
music. The students marched to this music several times a day —
from playground to classes and to assembly hall. We performed
such heroic-sounding thunderers as "The Storm King" and "No
Surrender."

So, now in high school, pianist Dale Bartholomew and I put together a dance orchestra. It was during an era of such great popular
numbers as "Margie," "Avalon," "Whispering," "Love Nest"
and "Japanese Sandman."

And when I discovered that our anchor man's real first name was
Sidney, I labeled our group "Sid's Syncopated Six." John Conklin's
saxophone, Jim Smith's clarinet, Darwin Forsyth's violin, Hank
Thomson's banjo and my percussion were Bartholomew's musicians
until we lost Hank to Cupid.

Thomson and I invited our best girls to attend a performance at
the Hartman Theater in Columbus. The show was *Sally,* a touring
New York musical hit starring Buckeye-born Marilyn Miller. Tickets
were $4. It was touch-and-go for awhile as we tried to raise our total
requirement of $20 to go first class. Hank finally pawned his banjo.
Incidentally, it never came out of hock.

Syd's Syncopated Six proved popular with town dancers, so I
persuaded George Buchman, owner-operator of the Star movie
theater, to give us a try for one night at $2 a man. We briefly re-
placed his sister Rose, who was the regular pianist and a good one.

The film fare was a western thriller. Among my accoutrements
in the drum corner were cymbal, tom-tom, song whistle, cowbell,
a bird whistle that sprinkled my face some when it warbled, and a
Chinese wood block to simulate galloping hoofs. Also, I had a pistol
that fired blanks.

It was all rather on the melodious side until the cowboys and red-
skins began to mix it up. Then I let go with the ammunition, turning
to see how the customers down front were responding to the real-
ism.

What I saw were people with hands cupped over their ears and
theater proprietor Buchman hurrying down the aisle to tell me off
for shooting in what he called "a soundbox" auditorium. He remained unimpressed when I suggested that to his theater had come
the distinction of being absolutely the first to introduce "sound"
in films to Delaware.

At Delaware High we had a fraternity called Pi Gamma Pi. Earnest Pollock had organized it and written its ritual. Dale Bartholomew and I wrote its two songs. It flourished into the '40s, by which time some sons of its original members had joined it. Finally it fell victim to a state law holding such private groups illegal.

I have a favorite memory of the halcyon days at Delaware High in the terrific '20s. It is of seeing Ruth Stephens coming out of Norwood's music store carrying a copy of the new popular song, "A Pretty Girl Is Like A Melody." It was a perfect blending of my favorite girl with my favorite song, and that melody lingers on . . . and on!

I learned recently that back in my hometown the reigning Miss America had been booked to add luster to a reception saluting the opening of a new bank building. I then recalled another time when another Miss America had honored our community.

She had won the title at the first Atlantic City contest in the early '20s, and to this day is the only beauty queen to have worn that coveted crown twice, in two consecutive years.

Mary Katherine Campbell was the daughter of the Herman Campbells of Columbus, Ohio, and she came to our town soon after her initial triumph. She arrived without fanfare, to visit her paternal grandmother, Daisy Rhodes Campbell. Daisy was a distinguished novelist, one of whose books I recall as *The Fiddling Girl*. It was about a young violinist.

So, when I read in a town social column that the guest of the author was her famous granddaughter, I remarked casually to my good high school buddy, John Conklin, that I might have a date with Miss America. He offered to bet money that no such stranger as I could date this prominent personality.

We settled on a substantial sum without appointing a holder; it was, we said, a "gentlemen's agreement." What my friend did not know what that although I was unacquainted with Mary Katherine Campbell, her parents and mine were long-time friends. Of course, that improved my position. I was accepted.

The usual dating program was to attend a movie, to be followed by a stop at one of the ice cream parlors — Vatsures, Raljo's or Bun's. As we left the Strand Theater at the conclusion of the first show, the cashier and my friend, Kitty McAuliffe, whispered to me that my chum had dropped by to ask her if Kelley was inside with Miss America. She told him I was inside with a girl she hadn't seen before.

Later at Bun's, I could see John peeking through the balcony curtains to see if my date was the real article as our wager required. I suppose it would have served me right if he had come to our booth to say, "You win." But, being a proper gent, John Conklin performed no such embarrassment. Instead, he disappeared, but next day promptly paid off the considerable sum we big-time gamblers had bet — 50 cents.

7

NOW YOU SEE IT, NOW YOU DON'T

I once had a lively visit with the magician, Harry Blackstone Jr. I had just watched him perform his stage miracles, just as his famous father did before him. He left me with recollections of my own youthful fascination with the world of hocus-pocus.

At the age of 12 or 13, I was bitten by two strong bugs. While my mother nursed both my father and me through three weeks of influenza, the other "bug" arrived in the form of a Gilbert Beginner's Magic Set — a present from my Aunt Genevieve Blair.

This sparked a lively interest in a branch of the performing arts that lasted through more than a decade of practice and presentation. It gained momentum when another Aunt, Georgia Brown Allen, took me to see Howard Thurston, at that time the world's greatest magician. He was playing his annual engagement at the Hartman Theater in his home town of Columbus, Ohio.

Georgia Brown Allen in the 1890s.

Soon my parents, schoolmates and some relatives began showing at least polite interest. Red, white and blue silk handkerchiefs quickly became an American flag. A glass of bran became candy. Chosen playing cards rose mysteriously from an innocent container. A gold ball floated unassisted in midair. Live goldfish appeared in a bowl where none had been before. A marked card that had just vanished turned up in a freshly-opened hen's egg.

As a teenage magician I was my own booker and publicist, even to the shooting of my own photos. For this I used my "Brownie No. 2" camera and flash powder in small round containers. I used a short fuse. After setting my stage in my bedroom, I would place the camera atop some big books on a small stand. In the dark, I'd open the lens, light the fuse and step quickly into the scene, trying not to blink until after the flash came. It filled the small room with a descending haze, to the dismay of my tolerant mother. She often appeared in time to catch her young magician before he could make the smoke disappear.

I posed with fanned-out playing cards and a wand pointed at them, and with other paraphernalia from my act.

Finally I became skilled enough to mount a full-scale show. My equipment was bought by mail from the magic supply houses in Chicago with hoarded allowance money. I had built some of it myself. The rising young trickster printed a slightly less than modest business card proclaiming that this "Master of Mysteries" was available for party and club dates, and with "Satisfaction Guaranteed."

From these exposures evolved "The Twentieth Century Magical Revue," which was an enlarged edition of my single act. Now the act was double-size, inasmuch as it included the talent and paraphernalia of my cousin, Porter Shur Welch. He lived in Lakewood, Ohio, but spent his summers visiting his paternal grandmother in the same Winter Street block where we lived.

Port shared my enthusiasm for legerdemain. On more than one occasion, when his grandma was having a nap, we would convert her big dining room into a makeshift theater. We usually had her permission. We entertained her neighbors in a sort of trial run performance to try out some of our new effects.

Usually we practiced in a large corner bedroom left vacant for the summer by a roomer, Astronomy Professor Crump. He taught at Ohio Wesleyan. This spacious room contained a large mirror, such as all magicians need almost constantly during rehearsal times. At this address one warm summer afternoon a minor crisis

OPEN FOR ALL ENTERTAINMENTS

F. B. KELLEY, Magician

=======AND=======

Master of Mysteries

PHONE   -   -   -   -   -   -   2629

CLUB DATES A SPECIALTY

ROBERT SMITH, ASSISTANT

PHONE   -   -   -   -   -   -   2595

SATISFACTION GUARANTEED

The first business card.

occurred. While I rehearsed the sudden and mysterious appearance of a flaming nickel-plated bowl of fire from a scarf held over my arm, I managed to drop the bowl. Quicker than one could say "Abra Cadabra" or "Presto Chango," a very small burn spot magically appeared on the carpet.

Now, my friend's grandmother was a meticulous housekeeper. The only appropriate "magic" the young entertainers possessed was, possibly, ingenuity. In our favor was the size of the spot, plus some of my furniture store training in the moving of heavy household objects to permit rug-turning. So, with the use of considerable muscle, plus an occult incantation, the "evidence" of my accident mysteriously disappeared under a big bed. We never heard of its discovery.

One summer, when we decided we were ready for the big time, the great Kelley And Welch Twentieth Century Magical Revue opened at Robinson's Opera House in nearby Ostrander, Ohio. They had the dubious distinction of being the scene of our initial out-of-town engagement.

The theater's kindly owner set a record I never knew to be matched by any Broadway or other big-city operators of that kind of real estate. His rental price for our one-night stand was five bucks!

The posters we used were colorful, and are called "stock posters" by show printers. We obtained ours from the Donaldson House in Cincinnati. This meant that they would, with suitable dates and location, serve any magic show. It was not necessary to have every item appearing on the poster, such as comely young female assistants wearing tights. My assistant for magic show dates was Robert Smith, a close friend through elementary and Delaware High School years, and he most assuredly didn't wear tights!

Bob Smith suffered the ravages of ragweed fever every summer. Although he knew how all our tricks were accomplished, one feat of "magic" he never accomplished was the art of swallowing a pill. I can still see him tackling a series of asperin tablets while bending over a drinking fountain. He had non-stop determination and little success. We were at the town square in Mt. Gilead, Ohio, another city we honored with our extravaganza.

As an assistant, Bob Smith was unfailingly reliable. However, while we were entertaining at the Children's Home, he let our bunny escape and run up the aisle. That was just before it was due for a mysterious appearance in a Welsh rarebit cooker.

Bob's sole professional shortcoming was an inability to appear nonchalant in bringing something surreptitiously on stage or removing it. During such entrances and exits, he couldn't have looked more guilty if he had been caught robbing a hen house.

In Ostrander, there was a town pump in front of the theater. We carried two buckets of water up to the stage area, as there was no running water available. One bucket was for personal use, and the other for filling goldfish bowls and other water tricks. Included was an effect requiring my magician friend to drink some from a tall glass to prove it was there before glass and water vanished in a flash.

That night when my co-star had taken a strong sip to impress the spectators with the trick's authenticity, I lacked the self-control to resist murmuring quietly from the wings that he should not have drunk that water because Smitty, our assistant, had used that bucket.

A green color materialized on the entertainer's face so quickly that some of the audience must have thought he possessed the talent of a chameleon. For this brief departure from strict professionalism, Porter repaid me by keeping the theater's curtain going up and down through so many tailor-made encores that I must have come off as the worst applause-beggar extant.

In the summer of 1924, just before the college years began to occupy our time and interest almost completely, we had added the

This is my first professional publicity shot, used in the promotion of my magic act.

mind-reading act for our final date in Ostrander. It enhanced our
total performance considerably. Our mental marvel was described,
in my modest publicity effort, as "Sidney Dale, The Man With The
Miracle Mind; The Mystery Of Two Continents." We may have
exaggerated the geography a bit, but not the act, for indeed it was
a baffler.

This was called, in those vaudeville days, a Piano Mind-Reading
Act. We passed slips of paper to members of the audience. They
were invited to write the name of a song and to sign their name or
initials. The slips then were collected and put into a large transpar-
ent bowl on stage.

The audience was then enraptured with a two-minute lecture,
self-written, on the subject of the subconscious mind. It concluded
with a statement which may have stuck in my mind from having
heard the great Howard Thurston introduce one of his stage miracles: "Ladies and Gentlemen, we do not ask you to believe that we
are endowed with supernatural powers, but we now propose to show
you something that you will remember as long as you live!"

Then, our "seer of the century," who, on less formal occasions
was also my pal and fellow musician, Dale Bartholomew, appeared
on stage. He seated himself at the piano, affecting deep concen-
tration. In a moment or two, he would announce that a certain initial, or name, had come to his mind. Standing to one side of the
stage apron, I would then ask anyone answering to the labels to
please raise a hand. Then our mind reader would say, "I receive the
message that you are requesting me to play this." He would then
play the song, and it was always the right one.

This brief excursion into the occult was one of numerous musical
milestones in what was to become Bartholomew's lifelong love affair
with what he called the "Old 88." He went through college composing and playing as accompanist for our championship Men's Glee
Club. He went on to further study on scholarships in New York.
Dale enjoyed a distinguished career of teaching at prestige eastern
schools, and with all the personal concert appearances he cared
to give.

Reflecting upon his later triumphs, I recall how impressed I was
by an incident during our high school days. Dale was invited by a
college dance band to replace their regular pianist during a week-
long booking at a night club outside Pittsburgh. In those days, many
dance orchestras felt that because of the great popularity of Dixieland jazz, they should have a southern label, such as McKinney's
Cotton Pickers did.

So the group, who took our Dale to Pennsylvania, elected to call themselves the "Dixie Carols." It didn't matter that none had been farther south than the Ohio River. One musician quipped that he had played in South Bend, while another said that his room in the fraternity house had a southern exposure.

Bartholomew returned to tell two jokes on himself from that adventure, which we felt had initiated him into big time show biz. His band friends called him "Little Eva," because he still wore nightshirts rather than pajamas. He also was the victim of the Funnel Trick. In that one the intended victim watches a friend try to lean so far backward without falling that a coin atop his head falls into a funnel. The neck of the funnel is stuck into the back of the trousers, to hold it in place.

After seeing a couple of stooges accomplish this feat, it looked easy. Our friend allowed as how he thought that he, too, could do it. As he was bending back his head with the coin on top, a pitcher of water was poured into the funnel.

But back once more to the magic-making days. The only date Porter Welch and I ever played away from our home stage was in Bellaire, Michigan. That was during one summer while he, Henry Thomson and I attended the nearby Camp Fairwood.

A committee of Bellaire citizens had been trying to raise money to buy a big clock for the courthouse. Because we had brought some of our magic show equipment to camp with us, the camp's management suggested we volunteer a benefit performance in the town's opera house.

Appearing with Welch and me on this bill was a counselor named H. Leroy Butler. He taught school in Middletown, Ohio, and his hobby was magic. He liked to sing too, and so did I. That is why we threw together a short, between-the-acts specialty, in addition to the legerdemain. In that olio, Butler and Kelley, complete with straw skimmers and canes, sang a couple of numbers including, "I Want To Be In Tennessee." That probably was where we should have been, for in thanking us, the chairman of the Clock Fund stated that what we had thought to be straight warbling had been the "best job of comedy singing we've heard around here in a coon's age!"

My high school graduation picture.

8

YEARS OF CHEERS

I had no desire to attend any other seat of higher learning than the coeducational Ohio Wesleyan. After all, I had been reared in the town where it was founded in 1842. Our family had attended it all the way back to when my step-grandmother Nellie Norton saddled her pony to ride from the rural Welsh community of Radnor to Delaware. She enrolled there when it was called the Female Academy.

The transition from the high school academic and social climate was made easier than had I been "going away" to college. I knew some of the faculty members and numerous university students, both boys and girls. During our senior year in Delaware High some hometown pals and I had been pledged to Sigma Chi. That was my father's social fraternity affiliation when he became an OWU student, near the turn of the century.

Now we were traditionally worthless first-year collegians. We were watching the Harold Lloyd silent film comedy entitled *The Freshman* and hearing on phonograph records its theme song, which asked, "Why Do They All Pick On Freshies?"

There was a campus tradition that unless the freshmen boys won the tug-of-war across the Olentangy River on the Saturday of Registration Week, they must have their red and black frosh "beanies" with them at all times. Sophomore guards were at the exit doors after morning chapel services, and if we were caught without them the capless and hapless freshmen were asked to remove their coats, ties and shoes. They they were to be dunked in the nearby sulphur spring. The dunkees then would have to return to their residences for a change of clothing before attending their next class.

After more than an hour of steady struggle, our freshmen stalwarts pulled the sophomore team through the river. We wore our freshman caps anyhow, out of sheer pride.

Attendance at chapel was compulsory, five mornings a week immediately after our first class. I never objected to that. Instead, I found it to be a good feeling to be with the entire student body there in Gray Chapel. It could accommodate the total enrollment of about 1,500 students, plus speakers, administration officials and faculty members who occupied the chapel platform.

A narrow stream called Delaware Run divided our pretty north campus from the handsome St. Mary Church and rectory. Our good neighbor, Father William O'Brian, served the town's Catholic community from there. We always had Roman Catholics among our enrollment at OWU, and at least once a year Father Will was invited to address the student body during chapel services. On one occasion he further endeared himself to all of us by saying, "There really isn't anything separating Ohio Wesleyan and St. Mary except the Delaware Run, and it isn't worth a dam."

Jimmy Flavin was the faithful custodian of Edwards Gymnasium for a good many years. To his regular work he added, by self-appointment, the position of official waterboy for the football teams. This warm-hearted Irishman was fond of denying any conflict of interest by explaining, "You all know my church is St. Mary, but on any afternoon when Ohio Wesleyan plays football there's not a better Methodist in town!"

My chapel seatmate by choice was Bob Jacoby. Occasionally he had difficulty repeating a joke. On one occasion he had been amused by the story about a man who was electrocuted because he sat on a slice of fruit cake and the currant went up his spine. Eager to try that one on his Phi Gamma Delta brothers, Jacoby was baffled at the lack of response when he explained that ". . . a raisin went up his ass."

During our senior year in high school some of us had found college girls willing to date us town boys who drove their own family cars. University students were not allowed to have automobiles on campus unless they were handicapped. It never occurred to us dashing young sports that our popularity with the OWU lovelies was because the cars we drove shown more brightly than our charm.

Occasionally I double-dated with my longtime friend, John Hoffmann, whose dad was Ohio Wesleyan's popular president. John often dated a collegian named Mildred Gillars, who surprised us all by becoming the notorious "Axis Sally" of World War II. She surprised us even more 25 years later. After serving her prison sentence she returned to her college campus to complete her studies and earn a degree.

My introduction to Sigma Chi had been on a quiet Sunday morning when I was 6 years old. My father led me up the street to the new fraternity house, which was still unfinished. He and his Sig. brothers, Tom Sharpneck of West Virginia and E.Y. Mason, an OWU professor, had worked hard to make that building possible.

My recollection includes going with my dad to what was to be the sacred chapter room. In its incomplete appearance it seemed to be the largest room I had ever seen. Eighteen years later, while my father was pinning me with the White Cross of Sigma Chi, I was surprised to note how much it had shrunk. Many years later I was to be privileged to do the pinning for his grandson Stephen.

Many of my college professors were on their way to international recognition, if indeed they had not already achieved it. Among them was a good man who not only was eminent in his field, but appreciated further by students when he arrived late for class, sometimes not at all. The odds of that happening were about even, for the course was taught by the prototype of the typical absent minded professor.

One evening he was on his way to a bridge party. He passed a house and saw through the windows that some of his friends were seated around a card table. He joined them to play until the party broke up. None there, including the hosts, expressed any surprise at this unexpected guest. Nor did our hero realize that he had attended the wrong gathering until his original host called the next morning to find out if he was ill.

On another occasion, while hurrying to class with his busy brain preoccupied, he stopped a passerby to ask what time it was. Told that it was almost one o'clock, he is reported to have said, "Oh, thanks; then I've had lunch."

When our OWU men's glee club won the Ohio state title, we became eligible to compete in the national contest at Carnegie Hall in New York. This trip, although necessarily brief, was crammed with exciting events. We traveled in our own Pullman sleeper and checked into the Grenoble Hotel. We stayed there for both reasons of economy and because this aged facility was diagonally across from Carnegie Hall. We took taxicabs downtown to the towering Woolworth Building, then the world's tallest. We then were escorted by an alumnus of our school on a tour of the frantic-paced New York Stock Exchange. We cut two platters for the Brunswick

GUY E. McLEAN, DIRECTOR

McLEAN DIRECTS OHIO WESLEYAN'S CHAMP GLEE CLUB

Ten Successful Years Of Glee Club Directing Is His Record

Professor Guy E. McLean, director of the Ohio Wesleyan Glee Club, is recognized as one of the foremost glee club mentors in the middle west. Under his capable direction the O. W. U. gleemen have maintained an enviable position for the past ten years.

"Mac", as he is known to the boys, is not only a director and a competent musician, he is a prince of good fellows and a live wire on every club trip.

McLean is a graduate of the New England Conservatory of Music, is a member of Phi Mu Alpha Sinfonia, and of Pi Kappa Lamda, national musical honoraries. He divides his odd moments between Alpha Sigma Phi, his fraternity, and golf his hobby.

Under his direction the Ohio Wesleyan songsters have covered thousands of miles of territory while on tour, have won two state glee club contests, and have been honored by a trip to the Panama Canal Zone as guests of the United States Government, and have recorded Ohio Wesleyan music for the Brunswick Phonograph Co.

Singers Make Records For Brunswick Co.

The O. W. U. Glee Club may now be heard on phonograph records as a result of a recording made for the Brunswick Phonograph Company in New York last March.

"Red and Black" (Alma Mater), and "Drink To Me Only With Thine Eyes" may be bought on a double faced record number 3164 from any Brunswick dealer. "Drink To Me Only" was the number chosen by the Wesleyan gleemen as the light selection to be used in the state contest last spring. The Ohio Wesleyan Glee Club receives a royalty on each record sold.

WHAT THE O. W. U. GLEE CLUB IS NOT

The Ohio Wesleyan Glee Club is not a bunch of "college boys" on a spree. In the event that your contract involves keeping the men in your homes, you will find them courteous, considerate, and refined.

The Ohio Wesleyan Glee Club is not a money making concern. Contracts are designed to pay expenses, the primary object being to promote interest in good glee club singing and to advertise the university.

The Ohio Wesleyan Glee Club is not a troupe of jazz artists. A number of popular or jazz numbers are included in the club's repertoire, but emphasis is placed primarily on the heavier, classical type of music.

The Ohio Wesleyan Glee Club is not the only glee club in the country but it is one of the best. Backed by fifty years of musical tradition, an outstanding university, and a top-notch position among singing organizations of the middle west, Wesleyan gleers offer the best that can be procured in this particular field of music.

The Ohio Wesleyan Glee Club furnishes free of charge all necessary advertising for a regular concert booking.

Newspaper stories, window advertising, and newspaper cuts are forwarded several weeks in advance of the concert. Programs are also included in this advance material.

O. W. U. GLEEMEN WIN OHIO CHAMP CUP IN CONTEST

Place First For Second Time In State Meet Here Last March

The Ohio Wesleyan Glee Club known throughout the country as superior singing organization, enjoys a history which compares favorably with the illustrious tradition of the university under which it functions.

For nearly half a century, Ohio Wesleyan gleers have charmed audiences both at home and abroad with a type of music and a manner of presentation far above the average. The activity of the Ohio Wesleyan Glee Club prior to 1920 resulted in a tour of the Panama Canal Zone under the auspices of the United States Government, a distinction which very few glee clubs had been able to win.

At the present time, the O. W. U. warblers are in possession of the Columbus Dispatch Trophy Cup, presented annually to the winner of the Ohio Intercollegiate Glee Club Contest. Ohio Wesleyan has won this competition twice in the past four years.

The victory last spring enabled the Wesleyan singers to compete in the national intercollegiate glee club contest held in Carnegie Hall, New York City, on March 6. Here, the Ohio Wesleyan gleemen received nation-wide publicity and favorable comment from an audience of 4500 including 300 O. W. U. alumni who attended the concert.

This year's glee club promises to surpass all previous efforts in musical value and in variety of entertainment. A glance at next season's offering as presented in this folder will convince you of the unusually complete entertainment to be had from an appearance of the Ohio Wesleyan Glee Club in your city.

This is the center spread of a promotional brochure published by the OWU Glee Club in 1926, after their Carnegie Hall concert in

JOHN P. HOFFMAN, LEADER

VARIED BILL TO BE FEATURE OF 1926 GLEE CLUB

Chalk Artist And a Magician Are Available Feature Attractions

Several feature attractions will make their debut with the O. W. U. Glee Club during the 1926-27 season. A chalk artist and trick cartoonist premises to be an extremely desirable attraction, while a short magic act to be present by an experienced professional magician will offer an unusual treat for those who enjoy a little mystery with their music.

In addition to the regular glee club concert program consisting of the Glee Club of twenty-five male voices, the Varsity Quartette, a feature pianist, and at least one soloist, contracts this year, without involving any added expense on the part of the party booking the club, will include a choice of the chalk artist or the magician.

DALE BARTHOLOMEW, PIANIST

HOFFMAN PILOTS O.W.U. WARBLERS

Is Named Student Leader In Annual Spring Election

John Hoffman, son of "Prexy" Hoffman, is student leader of the glee club this season. He was honored by his fellow gleemen in the annual glee club election last spring.

Hoffman has proved himself an earnest worker toward the welfare of the club and has won the confidence of the gleers through his ability and willingness to serve. He sings baritone and is a junior in the university.

A resident of Delaware, his spare moments are spent at "Fairbanks Lodge" which is only another way of saying Phi Gamma Delta.

QUARTETTE IS SURE FIRE HIT

The O. W. U. Varsity Quartette, an organization composed of glee club men, has proved a major attraction for several seasons. Not only does the quartette appear on the regular glee club concert program, but may be booked as a separate attraction. In addition to a number of appear-

MOMENTS OF MYSTERY

ances during club tours last year, the Varsity Quartette entertained the O. W. U. alumni at a banquet in Chicago last May. The music was broadcast from a Chicago radio station. Close harmony and mean melody are featured by the quartette.

GIFTED PIANIST IS 1926 FEATURE

Club Accompanist Is Redpath Chautauqua Artist

Dale Bartholomew, accompanist for the glee club, provides a distinctive part of every concert program. He is an accomplished pianist of exceptional ability, playing both classical and popular numbers with equal artistic interpretation.

Intensive practice claims a lot of Bartholomew's time, but he nevertheless finds time to take an active interest in things at the Sigma Chi house. "Sid", is also a member and president of Omega chapter of Phi Mu Alpha, national honorary musical society. He has composed a number of songs for his own amusement and is co-author of a musical comedy to be presented at the annual Ohio Wesleyan "Homecoming" celebration this fall.

Summer season of 1926, he spent with Redpath Chautauqua, where Bartholomew was booked as accompanist for Irene Stolosky, Chicago violinist.

New York City. The absence of identification of the magician indicates that he was the author of the publication.

The OWU Glee Club at the start of the 1926-27 season. I am fourth from the right in the third row from the bottom.

Phonograph Company before attending an afternoon rehearsal at the concert hall.

On stage that evening we noted two marked differences between our group and singers from the East Coast. We and the Kansas State champs were the only men wearing tuxedos, while the easterners were attired in tails. Also, ours was the only club that sang (as Professor Guy E. McLean's men always did) entirely from memory — all other competitors held the music in their hands.

We placed fourth, but when the winner was announced my baritone buddy, Jim Smith, cheered loudly. Then he was reminded that we were not the only Wesleyan on the map; Old Wesleyan from Middletown, Connecticut, had won the cup.

Our night on the town was supplied by former Delawarean Hildreth Riddle. She was then living with her sister, a Mrs. Phillips, and her family in Manhattan. They made our visit memorable by taking our total membership on our first night club visit. The place was called the Rendez Vous, and it promised to be a lively occasion since British stage comedienne Beatrice Lilly and her *Charlot's Revue* were celebrating the conclusion of their Broadway engagement. In attendance also were Mary Pickford's actor-brother, Jack Smith, and Eleanor Painter, a celebrity of the musical stage and close friend of our hostess.

We took cabs to the famed after-theater breakfast address known as Reuben's. With stars in our eyes we dined on sandwiches and soft drinks — those were Prohibition days. I remember riding with our deepest basso, "Bevo" Near, who asked if I had noticed the

amount of the night club check. I had. The total seemed unbeliev-
ably high to us; it was 82 bucks!

At the conclusion of my first college year I had the thrill of going
to Arizona to work on the *Tucson Citizen,* which was owned and
operated by our Jaynes cousins.

Enroute I stayed one night in Chicago. There I saw what ever
after was my favorite of all operettas, Sigmund Romberg's wonderful musical triumph, *The Student Prince,* with its great male choral
sound.

This was at Chicago's historic Great Northern Theater. Many
years later, while a theatrical publicity advance man, I would be
bringing to that theater Alfred Lunt and Lynne Fontanne in *The
Great Sebastians.* I brought singing star Todd Duncan there for *Lost
In The Stars.* And to shine in *Middle Of The Night,* I brought
drama star Edward G. Robinson.

I enjoyed his company in visits
to art galleries town-to-town
since appreciation of art had
turned this stage and film star
into a collector.

Upon arrival at the West
Coast I rode with my cousins in
their Studebaker from San Diego
into Arizona. In those days passenger cars frequently carried
spare water and gasoline containers on their running boards.
The Mojave Desert was crossed
at low speed on a plank road.
Cars could pass only when one of
them pulled onto side aprons
placed at regular intervals. This
was the soft sand part of the

*Edward G. Robinson, star
of* Middle Of The Night.

Arizona desert that Hollywood movie companies favored as the location for filming stories set in the Sahara Desert.

The eastern tenderfoot soon became a dedicated worker at selling
classified advertisements in the West. I even learned from the
Citizen's Lucy Virginia Rule how to operate a switchboard. But I
wondered why so many of my potential customers disappeared between noon and about 3 p.m. The thermometer registered 115
degrees every afternoon. Had I been a better student of Spanish in
my days as a college freshman I would have remembered the

meaning of the word siesta.

On weekends we escaped the desert-level heat by driving to the family cabin atop Mt. Lemmon. Cars could not pass on this steep and narrow mountain highway. All traffic lived by a rule that specified certain hours of travel in each direction. If a driver couldn't adhere to this strict timetable he might have to wait at the halfway fueling station for several hours.

My cousin and I cut firewood, he and I at either end of a crosscut saw. I didn't mind the work but I was puzzled at how soon I tired. He explained that breathing was much more difficult at an altitude of 9000 feet.

In the 1920s, when a coed appeared on campus wearing a fraternity pin, it was the equivalent of a formal engagement announcement. ''Pinning'' was a romantic milestone, and it called for a serenade by members of the man's fraternity.

How well I remember the pleasant scent of smoke in the autumn evening and the rustle of dry leaves underfoot. The windows of Austin Hall held lighted candles, signifying that the girls behind those windows were sisters of the sweetheart who had just been pinned. The sweetheart — my sweetheart — was Ruth Stephens.

Three of the unlucky freshmen members of our fraternity wrestled our piano on a flatbed truck. They lay prone on the bed, each with a vise-like grip on a leg, for the trip to Austin Hall. Dale Bartholomew was at the keyboard and accompanied me while I sang the lovely song, ''Rose of Sigma Chi.'' Then my brothers joined in for ''Sweetheart Of Sigma Chi.'' Frank Dimke brought his trombone and went into a soaring register to play ''I Love You Truly.'' And there in the window stood the girl of my dreams, wearing the White Cross of Sigma Chi. What an incredible feeling that was!

This relationship has endured for well over a half century, and for this vintage Sig each year has been more wonderful than the one before.

My fiancée majored in fine arts with emphasis on interior design. Sallie Thomson Humphreys, director of the department of fine arts at Ohio Wesleyan, had long-range influence on Ruth's career as she went on to expand her ability designing the interiors of office buildings, hospitals, motels, conference centers, university buildings, and even a private railroad car, as well as numerous private homes. As our children were growing up, Ruth did much of the creative part of her work in our home, where her beautiful fabric samples made tents for children at play.

9

THE LAST OF OUR RAH RAH DAYS

Our holiday glee club tour proved profitable and included an amusing incident. One of our members was weary from having spent all of his free time swimming in the pool at the handsome new hotel in Huntington, Indiana. It was New Year's Eve.

We were well into an opening rouser called "Glasses Up" when our enervated singer fainted. Two men caught him as he fell back and promptly pulled him offstage while the singing continued without interruption. There doubtless were those in our audience who wondered if perhaps he had decided to dramatize the song title.

A great fan of ours was an OWU alumnus named George Whitehead. He ran the Columbus office for Redpath Chautauqua, and he helped us line up an Easter week engagement at the James Theater there. Manager J. Real Neth turned the occasion into "College Week" by booking also Ohio State's popular Scarlet Mask Dance Band plus a football movie thriller entitled *One Minute To Play*.

Our working schedule for this assignment was the standard vaudeville two-a-day, with three shows on Saturday and Sunday. As manager of our troupe I was paid by the theater's impresario. It was the first $1,000 bill I had ever seen.

Of this we were able to save $600. Our men stayed at the YMCA and we followed our regular touring policy of giving each glee club member $1 a day for food. It was a standard joke that during my management nobody in the troupe gained weight.

It was a busy college year. I had moved to the fraternity house during a term as chapter consul. I was active in campus politics and became a candidate for the presidency of the student body that spring.

Classmate Paul Anderson was my campaign manager and we carried the ticket, but what I best remember is that on the afternoon when the votes were counted, my dad left the store to join my mother and me at home. This was not so much to celebrate a victory as it was to be with me if I had lost.

In anticipation of our summer tour abroad we had added to our singing repertoire a six-piece dance band, a three-piano novelty act plus Jim Smith, Scotty Gray and Ralph Lloyd comprising what I had named the "Blue Tune Trio." Occasionally on the tour our leader, John Hoffman, would join me in a burlesque mind reading act. We did not perform this for our Eugopean audiences. Many of them might not understand our stage dialogue, whereas music is an international language.

The hospitality abroad was mighty pleasant for traveling Americans in those wonderful days of 1927. Charles Lindbergh's solo flight from New York to Paris had made him everybody's hero. The laconic President Coolidge, when told that Lindbergh had conquered the Atlantic alone, responded, "That's most remarkable, and it would be even more so if he had done it with a committee."

Indeed the mantle of popularity that the handsome young aviator wore with such modesty became a kind of welcome mat spread by Europeans to be shared by all his countrymen that summer.

Our foreign friends and allies hadn't yet begun to dislike us for having proved useful in their time of peril. (That reminds me of the reaction of a man when told of someone who had been outspoken in his dislike for him: "I really don't see why he should hate me," the victim replied. "I never did anything for him.")

Following a triumphant farewell concert on campus during June graduation week, we kept dates at Bryan and Toledo, Ohio, enroute to Toronto and Montreal. We sailed on the Canadian-Pacific steamship *Montrose*. During the passage the first class passengers regularly deserted the ship's official orchestra to dance to the livelier beat of our dance band on a lower deck.

We gave a concert at the Zoological Garden pavilion in The Hague. The pretty Dutch girls wanted to be taught to dance the Charleston. They so neglected their regular orchestra that I decided on a public relations gesture of giving its musicians cigars while praising their prowess on the bandstand.

We enjoyed our engagements in England at the famed Saint

Dale Bartholomew, left, and I composed songs at the Sigma Chi house in 1926 and 1927.

*The OWU Glee Club Dance band is shown during its European
tour in 1927, from left: Ralph Lloyd, Ken Pearce, myself, Scotty*

Gray, Dale Bartholomew, Don Curry and Frank Dimke.

Martin's In The Field church and at the English Speaking Union. The most memorable of our appearances was at London's Savoy Hotel. That commemorated the American Independence Day celebration on July 4th. In attendance were numerous notables including Kermit Roosevelt, who was our ambassador to the Court of St. James. He was the son of President Theodore Roosevelt. Each of our troupe was announced formally on arrival.

Of all our numbers, the best reception was for our rendition of the lively English hunting song, "John Peel." One of the London papers declared at the conclusion of an enthusiastic review that, in listening to us, they finally had learned how "God Save The King" should be sung. We didn't mention to any of our British friends that millions of Americans could not remember the worlds to our 'Star Spangled Banner."

In preparation for the trip we had learned to sing "Oh, Canada" as well as the French National anthem, "La Marseillaise," in both our languages. This was appreciated in both Paris and in Montreal.

Concert attire was black tuxedos with our red and black college colors on a rather wide silk ribbon worn diagonally across our dress shirts. During the second half of our repertoire, with its more contemporary music and novelty numbers, we changed to informal jersey blazers, also in red and black.

While standing in the back of the theater in Montreal, I was startled to discover that the colors of our jackets were black and orange. I was unfamiliar with the stage lighting and the lamps had changed our red so that our men all looked like Princeton Tigers.

A trip into Belgium and down the beautiful Rhine River into Germany was followed by a week in Paris prior to boarding the *Empress of Australia* for home. A distinguished passenger was the Prince of Wales, enroute to his Canadian dominion. Of course our singers enjoyed entertaining the popular heir to the British throne, who would become Edward VIII.

A lively interest in our glee club remained through many years beyond our college days. There were reunions every 10 years during graduation week. In those days it always was referred to as Commencement Week. It usually began with a rehearsal for a brief informal appearance on campus and was preceded by dinner in our backyard on Oak Hill.

Occasionally we entertained at the traditional alumni luncheon. It was after one of these appearances that I received a letter from an alumna who said, "I saw what love is from watching the way you men looked at your conductor."

Indeed his men did love "Mac." After his demise we had a modest gathering in 1977 to mark the 50th anniversary of the European tour. With our vocal prowess seemingly undiminished by the years, we lacked numerical strength for providing the sound for which we had been famous.

An admirer of our McLean-trained glee clubs was his neighbor and the OWU college football coach during the years of gridiron glory. And from Coach George Gauthier our singers received this observation: "The same kind of teamwork that serves us on the field is what has made you winners."

No participation in competitive sports attended my college years. I played some golf with my dad and older members of our Odevene Country Club. Among other golfing friends were Francis Strohm and Paul Bonner. To us it was a rather new game. We welcomed some instruction from Lloyd Gulickson, pro at the Elks Club course in Columbus, and from our pro at the Delaware course. His name was Aitchison and he had a good Scot's brogue to match it.

It was a memorable experience when we saw the great Bobby Jones win the National Open at Scioto Country Club grounds in Columbus. He was in close competition with Joe Turnesa.

I must say I liked the game, although my scorecards were many more upper-40s and lower-50s than a good golfer's should be. Years later I briefly resumed play because I wanted to spend time with our son. He had become interested in the game too, and I was pleasantly surprised to discover that his dad's game was no worse than it had ever been!

During my senior year at OWU my musician-friend Ray Williams and I coauthored a review called *It's All In Good, Clean Fun.* A dance called the "Black Bottom" had followed the Charleston in popularity. Inasmuch as our college colors were red and black, my collaborator named our principal dance number "Red And Black Bottom."

Ruth's brother Harold Stephens and his sidekick, Harry "Levi" Berno, were remarkably effective comedians and Pearl Ward obliged with her customary good job of choreographing. John Hoffman and I were the show's directors and also appeared in some stage roles. One of his was in a skit we lifted without permission from an edition of the touring *George White's Scandals,* then playing at the Hartman in Columbus. We had attended a performance to see if there was anything we might "borrow" to replace a skit that our faculty censor committee had found to be in bad taste.

The offending line was that of a convicted criminal pleading for acquittal because he was about to become a father. Our substitute effort was a scene in which a girl alone in a room with a trunkful of family heirloom silver and a string of priceless pearls was visited by a thief who left with the trunk. Enter now the girl's father, who learns of the theft and reminds her that the pearl necklace is invaluable. Then his daughter explained that only the trunk was stolen; she had thought to sit on the jewelry. Her father's (and the skit's) closing line was, "Good grief, if your mother had been there we could have saved the trunk!"

The head of the school's drama department was famed Shakespearean scholar-director Clarence Hunter, who cast me as the duke in his *The Merchant Of Venice*. Two years hence he used me in a much more demanding assignment as the distraught father in *Much Ado About Nothing.''*

But during my junior year our mentor was on sabbatical leave. His capable assistant and former professional player, L.C. McNabb, was in charge. He tried to increase interest and attendance by the students and townspeople as well.

To tackle this problem we suggested that the season's slate consist mainly of Broadway hits whose stock company rights were available. The result of this decision brought forth student productions of such dramatic triumphs as *Seventh Heaven, The Cat And The Canary,* a mystery chiller; Lulu Volmer's prizewinning *Sunup,* George Kaufman's comedy hit, *The Butter And Egg Man,* and Ohio-born Elliot Nugent's laugh-producer about a track meet between Wisconsin and Ohio State. The hero was cast in the play's title role of *The Poor Nut.*

I was the steady publicist and occasional player for this repertoire, which nearly doubled attendance. I appeared as an unloved sheriff in our Theta Alpha Phi Drama Society's *Sunup* and as the hard-boiled New York producer for the George Kaufman comedy.

From an auto junk yard we found the makings for a passable French taxicab to serve the *Seventh Heaven* requirements. We ran inconspicuous wires from this contraption to the backstage area. There an unseen stage crew could pull them to make the taxicab shudder as though ready to move when the driver out front started its motor by turning an old-fashioned crank.

The problem of a proper motor sound was solved when my obliging fraternity brother, Howard Scaife, loaned us his motorcycle. With it came his personal services in starting its motor on signal. So now, behind the stage set's rear flats and invisible to the spectators, our actor cab driver could turn his prop crank and set into motion a realistically impressive effect.

A sad and rather dramatic event occurred during my last year on campus. Our distinguished fellow townsman was the United States senator and former governor of Ohio, Frank B. Willis. The Republicans of the Buckeye State at last had been able to persuade him to seek the presidential nomination as a favorite son candidate. So now we were marching in a torchlight parade to Gray Chapel where Senator Willis was to announce his candidacy in an address to enthusiastic admirers from town and gown.

An added attraction this evening was the popular Republican Glee Club from Columbus. It entertained the sizeable crowd awaiting the appearance of the senator who was in the office of the university president, adjoining the auditorium.

At the conclusion of the brief concert by the men's chorus, an announcement was made that there would be a short delay because the speaker was being attended by a physician. This news was followed rather quickly by the report that the senator had failed to survive a heart attack. And a little later it was established that death had come while the Republican Glee Club in the auditorium was singing ''The Soldier's Farewell.''

By early September I had a job as a cub reporter for the *Indianapolis Times*.

I had just read of this scrappy Scripps-Howard daily's winning a Pulitzer Prize for a series of articles that helped to send head Ku Klux Klansman D.C. Stevenson to prison on a murder conviction. Then I learned that the paper's fighting editor was an OWU alumnus, Boyd Gurley. So I sent an application that he later told me convinced him I might be good material, because it said that its writer did not think he was the answer to a city editor's prayer.

My enthusiasm for circuses, which was dormant during the busy college years, flared anew during the summer months before the start of my newspaper job. I read *Billboard Magazine,* sometimes called the showman's bible. It carried weekly news of the traveling big tops and the colorful circus personalities. Included was tiger trainer Mabel Stark, who was recovering from a near-fatal encounter with one of her big cats. That had happened when John Robinson's Circus, which starred her, had played Bangor, Maine.

This show was due in Ohio and I visited at its nearby date in Marion. I told its manager I was a soon-to-be newspaper writer seeking to follow his show at my own expense.

My parents had given me a new Model A Ford as a graduation present. I followed the Robinson show through its Ohio and West

Virginia dates for two weeks. The world of red wagons was exciting and the talks I had with the courageous Mabel Stark eventually led to the first of several circus stories I sold to *Collier's Magazine.*

The Indianapolis Times

A SCRIPPS-HOWARD NEWSPAPER

OFFICE OF THE EDITOR

June 1, 1928

Beverly Kelley,
Sigma Chi, House,
Delaware, Ohio

Dear Mr. Kelley:

I think we will be able to give you the opportunity that you ask for to start a newspaper career after you have finished your college course.

Of course you understand that the pay at the start is necessarily limited and the future depends entirely upon yourself.

If you will let me know about the time you wish to start, I will make the proper arrangements with our managing editor.

Yours very truly,
THE INDIANAPOLIS TIMES

Boyd Hurley
Editor

BG/V

This is the letter that started my career in journalism.

10

THE FOURTH ESTATE & THE DARROW DEBATE

I was proud to be even a novice in the exciting working climate of the Fourth Estate, whose patron saints are the greatest reporters of all time. After all, the greatest story was covered by Matthew, Mark, Luke and John. Soon I learned to appreciate the newsman's reliance upon a few common words. Their importance was saluted in rhyme by one of my antecedents, who wrote: "My helpers are six little words; they taught me all in knew. Their names are What and Where and When and Why and How and Who."

My *Indianapolis Times* tried harder because its afternoon daily competitor, the *News,* was older and bigger, and so also was the morning and Sunday *Star.* Still, ours had the greatest street sale, being on the stands promptly at 11:30 a.m. with the first of three lively afternoon editions. We were the least prosperous among all the papers in the Scripps-Howard group, but that is just the kind of place where a cub reporter can learn a lot in a hurry.

He is on general assignment and is expected to cover a wide variety of local events. I wanted to be out on the street where the action was, rather than on a city room desk job. I gladly accepted any and all assignments and often with little time in between, including fires, raids and funerals; high school and college football games in and out of town; plus some features I dug up myself.

Frequently I was accompanied by our one-and-only photographer, Virginia Edwards, with her heavy Speed Graphic news camera. This dedicated lady climbed many farm fences with me, and her willingness to cover stories in rough neighborhoods qualified Virginia for almost any job to which a man might aspire.

My weekly paycheck of $25 was top salary for a cub, inasmuch as most began at $18. My pay was sufficient to feed and shelter a single man in a comfortable room plus garage accommodations for a small car. My rent totaled $5 a week.

During my rather brief hitch as a reporter for the *Indianapolis Times* my principal recreation was bowling with the team headed by our assistant sports editor, Norman Isaac. The lanes were in the basement of the palatial Indiana Theater. On occasion I took in a dance on its Starlight Roof when the big bands came to town.

I was given the school page to handle while the regular editor went out of town on another assignment. During my college newspaper work I had learned to put a page together manually with metal type, making it ready for galley proofing. But when I went out into the composing room and began to assemble my school page, I suddenly became aware of dead silence in a place that normally teemed with the sound of machinery. The workers began to take off their aprons in preparation for leaving, although it was many hours before quitting time.

Finally, our managing editor, Stan Tullsen, appeared to explain that while my interim job was to write and to edit the school page, I was not a member of the typographers' union and therefore could not handle type or perform any work that by contract was the exclusive province of union members.

Soon after this education in union shop regulations, our women's editor took a holiday. I then inherited her ''Advice to the Lovelorn'' column. This challenge I promptly flunked. I couldn't come up with a suitable reply to a letter from a young woman who wanted to marry her brother.

Eddie Ashe, the senior sports editor of the *Times,* had only one arm. He triumphed over this handicap, pounding out his stories with one hand on his vintage Oliver typewriter. For this and his unfailing good nature I much admired him. One early autumn afternoon he both amused and delighted me with the news that my modest-sized alma mater had beaten the mighty Wolverines in a non-conference football game in Michigan Stadium, at Ann Arbor.

What had amused me, and supplied the editor with a good follow-up story, was my recollection that the University of Michigan severed athletic relations with Ohio Wesleyan back in 1897. That followed a contest in which it was charged that Ohio Wesleyan's coach played on his team. I always believed the charge had the ring of truth, because my mother once described an occasion when, as an OWU coed, she had been Coach Fielding "Hurry Up" Yost's date in the stands. That afternoon he suddenly excused himself and was next seen as a replacement for one of his injured players on the field.

The lamps of Indiana's literary giants burned brightly in my memory of Booth Tarkington's *Penrod* books, his *Seventeen,* and Meredith Nicholson's mysterious *House Of A Thousand Candles.* I found those authors to be kind and encouraging to young writers. Tarkington spent most of his time at a working address in New England, but his widowed sister and her son, Booth Jamison, still occupied the beautiful white-and-yellow family mansion on North Pennsylvania Street in Indianapolis. Here young writers and musicians were guests at Sunday afternoon soirees that I much enjoyed. The given name of our hostess was Terre Haute, so I assumed that she probably had been born in Terre Haute, Indiana, and had been named for the city of her birth.

Of his many literary triumphs, Booth Tarkington's first best seller remains my favorite for two special reasons. *The Gentleman From Indiana* is the story of a crusading young newspaper editor, and my treasured first edition was my mother's first Christmas gift to my Hoosier-born dad in 1900. That was three years before their marriage. The book contains her inscription to **her** Gentleman From Indiana.

One of my first interviews was with John L. Lewis. The national headquarters for his United Mine Workers was in our city. After waiting awhile I was ushered into what seemed to be an unoccupied office. Suddenly I saw the famous bushy-browed labor leader standing and glowering at me from behind a huge desk. I felt that he might be posing to intimidate an obviously youthful reporter. Inasmuch as I remained outwardly unperturbed, the chill soon subsided and the interview went very well.

I covered a noontime rally for Al Smith, the 1928 Democratic presidential nominee. He spoke at the Soldier's Circle monument. I felt that this capable New York governor had been poorly advised as to the right kind of campaign for getting votes in the Midwest. This was hardly a salubrious political climate for a candidate whose typical campaign prop was a brown derby hat and whose theme song was "The Sidewalks Of New York."

This hunch seemed to have been valid during the vote counting vigil at the courthouse, where I was on duty. There were 21 million votes cast for the Republican candidate, Herbert Hoover, against 15 million for Smith, and in the landslide victory Hoover carried 40

Clarence Darrow, world famous criminal lawyer.

of the 48 states.

My Ohio friend, George Whitehead, who had been favorably impressed with my management and promotion of our Ohio Wesleyan championship Men's Glee Club and its European tour in 1927, brought my newspaper reporting to an end. He hired me to publicize the Clarence Darrow debates.

The famed criminal trial lawyer, philospher and agnostic was under contract to Whitehead for a series of public appearances. He was to argue the Prohibition issue with senators and other political personalities, and to debate the Mechanistic Theory with prominent rabbis.

The great attorney and friend of unpopular causes was a marvelous showman as well. He liked to enliven courtroom and other stage appearances by pulling aside his necktie and by snapping the suspenders on his rumpled tailor-made suit. That suit had probably cost at least $100 but he admitted to having slept in it on more than one occasion when he was too busy or too weary to undress.

When I joined his road show, Clarence Darrow was still fresh in the minds of newspaper readers. They remembered his contest with William Jennings Bryan at the so-called "Scopes Monkey Trial" in Dayton, Tennessee. Because I worked the towns prior to his arrival, I saw him infrequently. However, I have cogent recollections of some talks with him, and especially in Providence, Rhode Island one night, when we were with Iowa's Senator Brookhart, a prominent Prohibitionist.

On that occasion I mentioned that as a college debater I had followed his trials. He told me that I probably had discovered in debate that one can make statistics prove almost anything. He was an avowed enemy of capital punishment. He felt that the Leopold and Loeb murderers, whom he had saved from the noose during their sensational trial in Chicago, should never be eligible for parole.

Darrow indeed was an actor and the courtroom was his theater. During the debates I noticed that he lost no time in pouncing on the first opportunity to hold his opponent up to ridicule. Once his adversary had been laughed at, Darrow had his battle half won.

My experience in radio broadcasting was limited to the preparation and delivery of some circus talks on WAIU in Columbus, Ohio, soon after the appearance of some magazine stories I had written. The talks were well received and this encouraged me to write to John Ringling about employment as a radio publicist for Ringling Bros. and Barnum & Bailey Circus.

PATRONS ARE REQUESTED TO FAVOR THE COMPANY BY CRITICISM AND SUGGESTION CONCERNING ITS SERVICE   1201-8

CLASS OF SERVICE

This is a full-rate
Telegram or Cable-
gram unless its de-
ferred character is in-
dicated by a suitable
sign above or preced-
ing the address.

WESTERN UNION

NEWCOMB CARLTON, PRESIDENT   J. C. WILLEVER, FIRST VICE-PRESIDENT

SIGNS

DL = Day Letter
NM = Night Message
NL = Night Letter
LCO = Deferred Cable
NLT = Cable Night Letter
WLT = Week-End Letter

The filing time as shown in the date line on full-rate telegrams and day letters, and the time of receipt at destination as shown on all messages, is STANDARD TIME.

Received at 20 East Winter St., Delaware, Ohio. Telephone No. 2392

CZ6 37 NL=SARASOTA FLO MAR 4

BEVERLEY KELLEY=

        40 WEST WINTER ST DELAWARE OHIO=

CAN YOU CONVENIENTLY COME TO SARASOTA FLORIDA FOR AN

INTERVIEW IF NOT POSSIBLE YOU COULD GO TO CHICAGO AND

MEET OUR MR GEORGE MEIGHAN WHOM YOU WILL FIND IN OUR

CHICAGO OFFICE 221 INSTITUTE PLACE=

        JOHN RINGLING

                738A MAR 5

WESTERN UNION GIFT ORDERS ARE APPROPRIATE GIFTS FOR ALL OCCASIONS

This wire started my lifetime love affair with the circus.

My life changed completely while I was working Toledo, Ohio, for the Darrow debates. John Ringling personally responded to my letter. He sent a wire encouraging me to meet with him in Sarasota or his general agent, George Meighan, in Chicago. I had my commitments to the Darrow people so I met with Meighan, who offered me a job promoting radio time for the Greatest Show On Earth. I was eager to accept this, not only because of my enthusiasm for the circus in general, but for an even more important reason. My childhood sweetheart, the lovely Ruth Stephens, had consented to become my bride, and touring for the Ringlings in my Ford in that summer of 1930 would be a wonderful circus honeymoon for my bride and me. Our wedding was scheduled for the coming June.

Meanwhile, I joined the circus during its New York City engagement. On my first try at NBC I was fortunate — that was the start of a lifelong friendship with William Burke "Skeets" Miller, the program director, and Madge Tucker. Miss Tucker was willing to let me tell some circus animal stories on her popular "Lady Next Door" show, an NBC network production for children. Those were big breaks indeed for a young press agent.

11

CIRCUS HONEYMOON

Elizabeth Ruth Stephens and I were married in our home town of Delaware, Ohio, on June 21, 1930, and three days later I proudly walked my beautiful bride onto the circus grounds at Rochester, New York. Her personality then was no less sparkling than it is now, and she immediately became popular with my new circus friends. They added glamour to our first two years of wedded life, until the arrival of our son kept Ruth occupied at home.

Many were the stars in the galaxy of the Greatest Show On Earth in those days, but aerial queen Lillian Leitzel and Con Colleano, king of the tightwire, were absolutely circus royalty.

Each had a private dressing tent in what was called the circus "backyard," near the performers' entrance to the Big Top. Colleano and his wife Winifred occupied half a car on the fourth section of the 100-car circus train, while the other half accommodated Leitzel and her husband, Alfredo Codona. He was foremost among the world's daredevils of the flying trapeze. In their traveling quarters there was a spinet piano, for the queen of the circus ozone was also an accomplished musician.

The triple somersault from the flying trapeze bar to the hands of the catcher was Alfredo Codona's thriller, and the catcher in this act was his muscular brother Lalo. It was said that nobody else could catch Alfredo, who came out of his triple with the speed of a bullet.

The Flying Codonas were not the first to master this feat and others have achieved it in recent years, but nobody before or since Alfredo has done it with his finesse. And his triple pirouette during the return to his swinging bar upon completion of the triple somer-

sault was an even greater triumph. The pirouette was attempted only on rare occasions,
such as when John Ringling was
among the spectators. Seated in-
conspicuously beside the bandstand, the circus owner would
hold up three fingers, and then
the aerialist would attempt the
miracle. It was John Ringling's
favorite trick.

Born to an Australian circus
family, Cornelius Colleano used
his mother's name professionally instead of his legal last name,
which was Sullivan. He thought
Sullivan did not carry the sound
of the circus, and I think he was
right. This artist originated the
famous forward somersault,
feet to feet, on the tightwire.

*This is the way I looked at
the time I joined the RBB&B
circus.*

Most spectators are inclined to think that any trick done backward is
the epitome of acrobatic achievement, but the forward somersault
is far more difficult. The performer must estimate his position because as he is completing the turnover he cannot see the wire. Con
once told me he harbored a lingering fear of decapitation should the
wire snap during the execution of the trick.

All the Colleanos were talented performers, but the only other
member of the family with the Ringling show was Con's sister Winifred, an aerialist whose specialty was her beautifully executed and
highly hazardous twisting heel catch on the high trapeze.

Her friends called her "Little Winnie" to avoid confusion with her
sister-in-law, "Big Winnie." The latter, Con's wife, caught the
toreador capes discarded by her handsome brunette husband as he
performed his Spanish dances on the wire, and lent a contrasting
blonde beauty to the center ring. Colleano's dancing on the wire
was beautiful to behold, for like many another circus headliner he
had studied ballet. When he was a little boy, his father had helped
him to acquire quickness and precision by teaching him to catch
flies with his bare hands.

The senior Sullivan had been a prize fighter whose specialty was
boxing while standing on handkerchiefs. The first man to step off

The radiant circus bride, Ruth Stephens Kelley, is flanked by Johnny Grady, left, and the brilliant aerialist, Con Colleano.

his handkerchief lost the round. Con Colleano's brother Maurice was a vaudeville star famed for his double somersault, feet-to-feet, from a running start. When Maurice Colleano's engagement at the Palace Theater in New York coincided with our circus dates at Madison Square Garden, I went to see this acrobatic genius in action. And when he came out of his second somersault, his head was so close to the stage floor that I was fearful that he would break his neck.

Our ringmaster's introduction to Con Colleano's tightwire act was: "The dancing, tumbling acrobat on the wire; the great Con Colleano!" But the subject of all this rhetoric, who thought the man to be inarticulate, swore that what he really said was: "The nancing, stumbling, awkward brat on the wire; the Greek Con Colleano!"

Despite its Germanic spelling, Lillian Leitzel's professional last name was pronounced LEET-zel. It was a pet name dating from her childhood. She came to the Ringlings from England, where she performed with an aerial troupe called the Leamy Ladies. Her mother was a member of that group. Her real surname was Pelican and her brother Alfred was head of the Art Museum in Milwaukee for many years.

Her strenuous trapeze work gave Lillian the broadest shoulders of any woman among the performing personnel; also, she had the tiniest feet. She had a personal maid named Mabel Clemmens who was a frequent object of Lillian's mercurial temper. The prima

Con Colleano in 1930, executing one of his Spanish dances on the tightwire.

Wedding bells had just rung for two of the Big Top's most talented performers — the trapeze artist Alfredo Codona and the queen of the circus ozone, Lillian Leitzel.

donna fired Mabel almost daily, but always on the day following there would be an apology and usually a small gift.

Leitzel was unfailingly friendly to my bride and me, never once refusing a radio interview — not even the time when I asked her to substitute for another star who had been my first choice for that particular broadcast. This had startled some observers who knew I was going to admit to Lillian that she was second choice. They had assured me that ''She'll bite your head off!''

We were denied the pleasure of her company beyond our initial season with the circus. While Lillian was performing at a winter indoor circus in Copenhagen, a metal ring in her rigging crystallized. This caused her to plunge to her death. It was on Friday, February 13, 1931, and it was a tragedy that rocked the circus world. Ruth and I were both heartbroken. She was, to us, a wonderful and steadfast friend.

It is fun to recall the nicknames worn by some of the circus working crew and the incidents that accounted for their sobriquets. ''Scranton Harry'' was named for a Pennsylvania city. ''Red Sweater'' acquired his label because he was seldom seen without one. And a character who arrived on the show grounds broke and hungry

A Ringling Bros. and Barnum & Bailey "one-sheet" poster of Lillian Leitzel capitalized upon her popularity.

one cold spring morning told the boss canvasman in a voice near tears that he would be "so-o-o-o glad to get just any kind of work." He was known as "So Glad" from that day on.

One of the ticket takers at the show's main entrance was William Downing, whose hearing was impaired. Everyone called him "Straight ahead Willie" because no matter what information might be asked by a customer, Willie always answered "Straight ahead." More often than not it was good advice.

"Chicken Charlie" was a porter on the circus railroad car that carried the ticket sellers and the musicians of the Big Top band. I never knew if he was called "Chicken" because he was soft-hearted or from having been caught raiding a henhouse. Charlie was minus an eye, and he was so popular among the men he served on his car that they took up a collection to buy their servant a glass eye. It was expensive and a good color match too, but when they showed its new owner how to fit it into the empty socket, "Chicken" put his hand over his good eye, shook his head sadly and said, "Ah sure 'nough thanks you all for your kindness, but Ah still cain't see a thing."

The magnificent Leitzel during her exuberant act high above the crowd. Six months later her rigging failed in Copenhagen and she plunged to a tragic death.

The famed George Denman was in charge of the elephant herd. He did not resent being called "Deefy" Denman because he probably never heard it — he was virtually totally deaf. Despite his handicap, he knew every one of his 30-odd behemoths so well that he could be standing at the elephant picket line in the wild animal menagerie tent with his back turned to them and with rare intuition know exactly what mischief one of them might be engaged in.

There were two "Mickeys" on the executive staff. One was Michael Whalen, the veteran boss convasman who affectionately was called the "Whale." His responsibility was to get the Big Top up and keep it up come hell or high water, and sometimes both came. I can still see the "Whale" in his raincoat and hat, which on Mickey seemed to attain the status of a uniform. He would be standing atop a wagon tongue while calling to his crew to guy-out the great canvas auditorium against an expected windstorm or to slack off if the rain came first. He looked for all the world like a ship's captain preparing to sail into a hurricane.

The other Mickey was Michael Graves, the show's boss property man and the best in the business. The secret of operating a big circus, which often had to take on unskilled labor, was competent and dedicated department heads. Mickey Graves belonged to this group. He was no great friend of the English language and this was good for a laugh on more than one occasion.

It was dress rehearsal night in Madison Square Garden. Mickey stood on the vast arena floor and looked aloft at the maze of aerial rigging that he and his crew had erected earlier in the day. Graves always tried for perfection and now his eye was offended by a useless and unsightly rope that should have been pulled up out of sight. So Mickey called to one of his men to put it out of the way temporarily, but what we heard from our prop boss was "Pull it up; pull it up tempermental."

He is remembered also for an observation made late one afternoon in Philadelphia. Mickey was relaxing with some of the performers in the circus backyard. Here, aerialist Vera Bruce was reading a newspaper feature about her in the *Philadelphia Bulletin*. "Isn't it strange," she remarked, "that this writer says I have a unique face?"

Graves obviously thought of the definition of oblique, instead of unique. He shook his head and said in his tender Irish brogue, "You're not to worry, me darlin' — you're not to worry at all. Your face is not unique; it's oblong."

The band played "Auld Lang Syne" at the conclusion of the night performance in Montgomery, Alabama, on October 10, 1930, serenading into circus history the 1930 touring season. Soon after midnight the trains were loaded and ready to roll for Sarasota, Flor-

James Michael "The Whale" Whalen, boss canvasman of Ring-ling Bros. and Barnum & Bailey Circus, shown giving his orders during the 1930 season.

DATE		TOWN	STATE	R. R.	MILES
			11th Week		
June	9	Jersey City	New Jersey	P R R	158
"	10	Newark	"	"	10
"	11	"	"		
"	12	Allentown	Pennsylvania	P R R C R R of N J	95
"	13	Wilkes - Barre	"	C R R of N J	84
"	14	Harrisburg	"	P R R	117
		SUNDAY	**12th Week**		
June	16	Pittsburgh	Pennsylvania	P R R	245
"	17	"			
"	18	Youngstown	Ohio	"	75
"	19	Akron	"	"	60
"	20	Cleveland	"	"	38
"	21	"	"		
		SUNDAY	**13th Week**		
June	23	Buffalo	New York	N Y C	181
"	24	Niagara Falls	"	"	22
"	25	Rochester	"	"	93
"	26	Syracuse	"	"	80
"	27	Utica	"	"	54
"	28	Albany	"	"	95
		SUNDAY -27-28	**14th Week**		
June	30	Pittsfield	Massachusetts	B & A	49
July	1	~~Worcester~~	"	"	107
"	2	~~Salem~~		B & M	67
"	3	~~Portland~~	Maine	"	95
"	4	Manchester — 30-1-2	New Hampshire	"	97
"	5	Springfield -3-4-5	Massachusetts	"	152
				Total Mileage to date	- 4448

The third route slip from the 1930 RBB&B circus. I made the markings to indicate some of the advance travel dates.

ida, where all departments of the physical show would put in four months of intensive preparation for the 1931 tour of the Greatest

Show On Earth.

We had traveled 13,635 railroad miles to visit 112 cities in 24 states and the District of Columbia. The near-miracle schedule called for shows in a new town almost every day, and every day the big show's cook-and-dining department served three meals to more than 1,200 employees.

So now, fond farewells were exchanged and the next morning the circus honeymooners were on the way to our home in Ohio, via Washington, D.C. I planned to stop there for a day and try to convince the *National Geographic Magazine* that the biggest circus in the world, with its complete traveling community of animal and human entertainers from many lands, and its amazing peripatetic timetable was proper story and pictorial material for the world's most prestigious international publication.

We were aware that the magazine never had bought a circus story, but nobody told me that our mission was impossible, and we found the *Geographic's* editorial and photographic people interested in our proposal.

The end result of this effort was that a year later, in October 1931, there appeared the first of our two circus stories sold to *National Geographic* — 17 years apart and reflecting especially the progress made by color photography within that span of time.

I was increasingly aware of the extra dimension of excitement that a good band can add to the pageantry of the rings, the air and the hippodrome track, and when we had resumed the trouping trail in 1931 and spread our tented city in Philadelphia for a one-week stand, I remembered that just across the river in Camden, New Jersey, were the recording studios of the Victor Talking Machine Company.

So, I paid them a visit and made a sales pitch that resulted in the cutting of a pair of excellent two-sided records that sparkled with the luster of the authentic music of the Big Top, representing the very first commercial phonograph records to be made by a circus band.

A decade later, at the acoustically perfect old Liederkrantz Hall in New York City our musicians made their first circus album for Columbia. It is now a collector's item. Meanwhile, I talked to the producers of the Fitch Bandwagon radio program, that presented famous dance bands on NBC every Sunday night. I convinced them that they should include the spangle-clad music of the Greatest Show On Earth.

It took me two years to sell this idea to the advertising agency that represented Fitch Shampoo. Our very first appearance, in 1941,

The man shown here with me is one of the great names of the circus — the veteran bandmaster Merle Evans.

brought the heaviest telephone and fan mail response that the program had ever received.

Radio script writer Ward Byron and I put together the scripts which I narrated. Conductor Merle Evans and his "windjammers," as they are called in circus vernacular, rode the airwaves for seven Fitch Bandwagon programs into 1947.

Our musicians and their colorful conductor Merle Evans enjoyed a rising popularity. Evans never missed a performance during a long and distinguished career on the bandstand. His talking tempo was almost as fast as his men could play circus galops. Their fame enabled me to sell my big Merle Evans feature, "Toscannini Of The Big Tops," to what was then the most powerful magazine in America, *The Saturday Evening Post*. Editor Ben Hibbs and our conductor both hailed from Columbus, Kansas — that didn't make my job any more difficult.

12

TROUPING FOR THE GREATEST ON EARTH

My public relations work for the circus made it impractical for us to ride the show train. I needed to be in a town a day or two ahead of the playing dates to talk to the schools and service clubs and to appear on the programs of the local radio stations. So my bride and I stayed in hotels on our circus honeymoon as we visited every city, large or small, on the circus itinerary. We traveled in our little Ford coupe that performed with near perfection. It was uncomplicated, and the rumble seat could hold as many as four dwarf and midget clowns if transportation was needed to take them to a publicity date.

We were awakened in a Pittsfield, Massachusetts hotel on a Sunday morning by the sound of a thousand hoofs clop-clopping on the pavement. From the front window we saw a moving panorama which neither of us will ever forget. Circling the square were more than 300 magnificent Percheron and Belgian circus baggage horses with their long-rein drivers wrapped in coats against the early morning chill. They hauled the heavy circus wagons to the show grounds from the railway sidings where they had been unloaded at dawn.

In only eight short years the daily equine spectacular that enchanted circus enthusiasts of all ages wherever it took place would be gone forever. A teamster strike in Toledo, Ohio, convinced the big show's management that its handsome work horses should be replaced by motor trucks.

Another hotel incident we like to recall took place in San Angelo, Texas. I became ill there with considerable abdominal pain and called the house physician. As I laid back on the bed with my midsection exposed for examination, a wad of chewing gum fell from the doctor's mouth and landed in my navel. It was a perfect bullseye and I laughed so hard my indigestion cured itself.

In the 1930s, radio had much the same impact that television has today. The radio time which I promoted was arranged mostly by writing ahead to the stations on our route. Talks about circus wild animals and their trainers found their way into established programs aimed at young listeners. Information about the making and care of circus wardrobes, the titanic task of feeding 1,200 circus personnel three times a day, as well as talks about the rearing and educating of small children traveling with their performing parents found favor with women's radio programs. Informative material about circus athletes, their training rules and the risks their tricks involved, appealed to producers of radio sports programs.

In those days we never bought commercial time on the air. The talks were accepted as educational and were not only free, but were many times as productive to the circus as spot announcements would have been. Of course a suitable number of circus passes changed hands in what we referred to as an "exchange of courtesy." We occasionally provided personal attention to the people on whose programs I had appeared. This sometimes included allowing the guests to eat with the performers in the huge dining tent. This was especially enjoyed if our guests were accompanied by children, who would long remember such an exciting experience.

Sometimes on circus day a clown, aerialist, acrobat, bareback riding star or a wild animal trainer would be interviewed at the radio station. Occasionally the stations sent their technicians and broadcasters to the show grounds where the erection of the tented city would be described live, and the boss canvasman and other executives were interviewed.

There was a milestone occasion one afternoon during our Madison Square Garden engagement in New York City when a then-famous broadcaster, George Hicks, and his engineers arrived to interview circus performers for the inaugural use of a short wave "walkie-talkie" by the National Broadcasting Company. Radio newsmaster Lowell Thomas and comedian Fred Allen were among my best friends of the airwaves during the annual springtime circus weeks in New York. Both liked to interview circus personalities, and the fact that I had attended Ohio Wesleyan with Lowell's sister Pherbia did me no harm. He interviewed our star of the big cage, the great Clyde Beatty.

The circus lions were not all from Africa; some were aquatic and were performing sea lions. I have never known a man with more

This is the first use of the new "walking transmitter" by the National Broadcasting Company. The site is the basement of Madison Square Garden in the spring of 1932. NBC announcer George Hicks is interviewing the RBB&B giant, Jack Earl. I am standing next to Madge Tucker — Miss Tucker and the children are from her NBC network show, "Lady Next Door."

patience and kindness than their trainer, Roland Tiebor. I learned from this interesting fellow that sea lions that appear to be so docile are prone to slash a trainer or a keeper when they are excited or angry. Tiebor's family had followed the education of these intelligent performers for three generations, employing endless patience and compassion to teach the sleek-coated actors to balance colored balls on their noses, walk tightropes and play musical instruments. "But they are really shy," he assured me. "Spectators all think that the sea lion is a born juggler, but the first time you toss an inflated colored ball at a sea lion he's scared silly. And if you ever give one a sound scolding he'll sulk for days and be almost totally useless in training. Look at Penny there; you'd think she hadn't a nervous streak in the whole of her, but I trained her for three years before breaking her into the act." Patient Roland Tiebor further explained that while sea lions are not born knowing how to balance objects on their noses, they do have unusually agile neck muscles that are an enormous help in the juggling. Tiebor said that the circus physician could always identify the wound inflicted by a sea lion, for this animal had a double-featured attack which inflicts bites and bruises at the same time.

Our trainer friend said that during World War I, British Admiral R.A. Allenby approved a project that attempted to use sea lions in detecting enemy submarines. The animals were taught to follow the sound of a submarine at various distances and then return to their base ship. However, they were unable to detect a submerged submarine more than 200 yards away, and they were distracted by the appearance of surface craft while they were supposed to be paying strict attention to their undersea quarry. So the experiment was a failure.

For some years before, Tiebor had trained a favorite animal he called "Sparky."

"He worked for me for years and was the star of the act until he became old and resented a younger sea lion taking his place for some of the more difficult tricks that he used to do," his trainer recalled. "We played theater dates in the winter when the circus was not touring, and Sparky always knew the way, sometimes through corridors with turns in them from the dressing room to the stage. Of course some of the other sea lions in the act could do this too, but for the last four years of his life my wonderful Sparky was stone blind."

One of the greatest anthropological attractions of all time was a prime feature of Ringling Brothers and Barnum & Bailey Circus in

The "Big Lips" — saucer-lipped Ubangi women from the Belgian Congo.

both 1930 and 1932. The saucerlipped Ubangi savages "from the deepest depths of darkest Africa" as press chief Roland Butler graphically described them, were imported from the Belgian Congo. Certainly they were the strangest looking people ever to be put on public exhibition and proved to be an immediate sensation.

The "Big Lips" or "Duckbills," as they were promptly nicknamed by the circus personnel, were a troupe of nine — each of three men had two wives. The males knew a few words of English and some French; their women were unintelligible and made only clacking sounds. This was the result of a most unusual tribal practice. Only the Ubangi women had those huge lips. They had been created artifically to make them so grotesque in appearance that enemy tribesmen might be less likely to kidnap and enslave them.

At about age 5, carefully selected girls had their lips pierced with ivory needles and twigs were then inserted in the holes. Soon small

metal discs replaced the twigs and later larger wood discs replaced
the metal ones. Gradually, as the girls grew older, the size of the
wood discs increased as the lips continued to grow around them.
At age 25 the hoop-like lips extended six to 12 inches from the face.
The upper lip was never made to grow as large as the lower one.

Inasmuch as female tribal status increased with the size of the lip,
the chief's favorite wife was, of course, the lady whose lips were the
size of a phonograph record. This attraction was not part of the other
human curiosities in the circus sideshow, but on an elevated stage in
the much larger wild animal menagerie tent where customers
attending the main performance could see them on the way to their
seats under the Big Top.

One of the Ubangi women smoked a pipe; another worked at
weaving grass baskets while still another learned to knit. The men
were musicians of sorts, playing on drumheads made of elephant
ears, and on a crude instrument made of teakwood and calabash
which looked like a primitive relative of the xylophone. Their
"music" was principally sound and rhythm totally without melody,
and only a notch more pleasant to listen to than today's rock music.
Still, they were responsive to and fascinated by bandmaster Merle
Evans' musicians.

Evans' men followed the action and the mood of the Big Top presentations with inimitable skill to a total of 210 cues in each performance. The Ubangis soon learned to imitate the rhythm if not the
tune of some of the numbers, and if asked to play their version of the
music for the highwire act of the Wallendas, they would make ges-
tures to indicate which act it was and then manage to beat out their
African version of the Spanish song, "Estrellita," with a tempo so
accurate that one could recognize the number being played on their
instruments.

Our Ubangis were gracious and friendly toward the spectators,
thousands of whom bought their picture postcards for a quarter
each. They also were affable toward the circus people to whose
day-to-day presence they became accustomed. Gettica, with the
prize-size lips, always had a big smile for me when I walked through
the menagerie tent. Often she would lean forward to shake hands
with a kind of royal formality.

Late one morning in Chicago we were shocked to learn that the
"Big Lips" had staged a strike. Not only had they refused to work,
but proved it by removing all their clothing while in the bus that
regularly brought them from their sleeping car in the performers'
section of the four circus trains. And it was almost time for our prize

attraction to be on the platform to entertain customers arriving for the afternoon performance.

By that time the circus general manager, George Smith, managed to acquire at a uniform supply source enough hospital orderly smocks to cover almost everything below the lips of our Ubangis and persuade them to appear. The trouble seemed to stem from their increasing dislike of the manager, a Belgian national who had brought them out of the Congo to make the circus tour. He was responsible to his government for their deportment, general welfare and safe return. It was rumored aound the show that the Ubangis felt that they were not getting their fair share of the money that accumulated from the sale of the postcards. This amounted to almost a bucketful of coins on a busy day.

Because they were never away from the show grounds except to go back and forth to the trains, they had little use for the money, but it was suggested that because white men seemed to worship money, they might be about to make of the mistake of imitating him. Every evening in their private dressing tents they dined on their special diet which consisted principally of fish, fruit and okra. Before it was time for them to mount their exhibition platform there now came the continuous sound of jungle drums. Some of the circus people familiar with voodoo and other primitive witchcraft expressed the opinion that the Ubangis were putting their curse on their manager.

The drums continued until one night when they were silent. The next day the circus received a wire reporting that their manager, while temporarily absent from the circus, had died of natural causes in New York.

Some of the more superstitious believed that the ominous sound of the drum-beating night after night had foretold his demise. When others expressed sadness and sympathy, the Ubangis only nodded, smiled and played their instruments with a new kind of enthusiasm.

It was during those early years with Ringling Brothers and Barnum & Bailey that some warm and lifelong friendships were founded. Some of them were with animals — and what animals they were! Ringling carried a huge menagerie and under that canvas I found a gold mine of newspaper and magazine publicity. I have always been especially fond of elephants and I have yet to meet the newspaper feature writer who can walk down the picket line and not be impressed with all that pachydermic pulchritude. But they aren't the sort of critters you can put in the back of your car and take to the city room of a daily newspaper. They were a good excuse to get the newspaper people to the Big Top, and I used them whenever it

I was on the Ringling back lot one day when a newspaper photographer turned the tables and asked me to hold my friend, Orangutan Joe. The cutline read, in part, "Kelley's the one with the hat."

would accomplish that purpose.

The apes were another big attraction. They had human-like characteristics and were especially appealing, I thought, to newspapermen. One which was particularly photogenic was an orangutan — we called him "Orangutan Joe." I know that chimpanzees are supposed to be the most intelligent of the species but there certainly wasn't anything dumb about Orangutan Joe. When I wanted him to hug and kiss a hardboiled reporter that's exactly what he did, whereupon the man's reserve disappeared instantly. Some press agents could measure the effectiveness of an attraction in column inches of newspaper publicity. Attractions like Orangutan Joe were good for column yards.

One of the most fearsome attractions of our show was the gorilla whose name has become a household word. With a little help from my boys in the press department, Gargantua could strike terror in the heart of anyone who gazed upon the huge, muscular beast. We all called him "Gargie," I guess in a show of bravado, but those who knew him best were the least likely to get within range of those massive arms.

However, I shall always remember Gargie with great affection, for he was the catalyst for one of the greatest of friendships for Ruth and me. Our show was playing Chicago, I believe in the summer of 1938. I noticed in the newspapers that *Life With Father* was in the same city at the same time, starring two of the most talented and best known actresses of all time, the great Gish sisters, Lillian and Dorothy. They had achieved fame a decade or more earlier and had worn it well. They were equally at home before the cameras or on the legitimate stage.

It occurred to me that it might be worth some ink to pose one of the most beautiful theater stars with one of the ugliest circus stars — Lillian and Gargie. So I got her on the telephone and proposed the idea to her, and she loved it. Lillian came to the lot where I had assembled a contingent of newspaper photographers. I peeled a banana and handed it to Lillian, and she fed it to the great ape as the flash bulbs popped by the dozens. Newspapers all over America picked it up and that helped attendance at our show and hers.

I found Lillian to be a warm and wonderful person, and both she and Dorothy became wonderful friends of ours. Dorothy is gone now but Lillian Gish, now in her 80s, is an honorary member of the Kelley family — has been since 1938 and always will be.

By the late 1930s I had developed a wide acquaintance with radio

This picture of famed theater star Lillian Gish and Gargantua helped publicize the circus. The actress inscribed the photo, "This, dear Bev, with our love and best wishes, Gargie and Lillian, the two G's."

people. Actually, I knew a lot of newspaper people too but the nature of the medium was such that the radio people, particularly those with network shows, seemed to have more fame than their counterparts with the newspapers. Probably the greatest comedian of all time was Fred Allen; there were more than a few mentions of our show on his top-rated radio hour. That was because Allen was an inveterate circus buff — whenever we could cook up an excuse he would come to the back lot and he liked nothing better than the menagerie tent. That probably sounds silly today — how could a mute animal come across on a radio show? But whenever Fred Allen mentioned our circus on his coast-to-coast show, believe me that sold a bunch of tickets and also paved the way for further press attention wherever we went.

In the early years I used to haul our stars of the Big Top to the radio shows, and sports commentators especially liked to talk to the great athletes with the circus. They would talk training schedules with the petite aerialists, those little girls who looked like they might have trouble lifting a full teapot, but who had the strength and the daring to twist in the ozone 60 feet above the gaping crowds. Unfortunately, many with such incredible physical coordination and who were utterly fearless on the trapeze or the highwire, sometimes had trouble remembering their names when they were before the awesome microphones of network radio. More than once I had to step in and help out.

As the years wore on I found myself getting more and more invitations to appear on the radio shows without the stars. In the early 1940s there were hundreds of radio stations across America, and all of them hungered for special feature material. No longer did the homemaker show hosts ask me to bring the head chef who prepared three meals a day for the 1,200 circus workers; they asked me to come on instead. They loved it when I would give them the recipes that started out with, "Take 45 bushels of potatoes . . ."

New York City, of course, was where most of the radio work took place, partly because we were there longer than anyplace else every spring, but also because there were more radio stations there than anywhere else on earth. Furthermore, many of them were clear channel. Their 50,000-watt signals would carry only 100 miles or so in the daytime but at night they could be heard all the way to the Rocky Mountains. With all three networks located there, we didn't have to worry about clear-channel transmission. Land on one of those and the local stations picked us up from Long Island to Long Beach — that was a real gold mine for the professional publicist.

I was photographed during one of several appearances with the noted sportscaster, Ted Husing. His broadcasts were heard daily on the CBS Radio Network. The photo was made in 1941.

One of my lucky breaks was a friendship with Ted Husing, whose CBS sports show originated in the studios of WABC in New York. I never had to plug the circus on Ted's show — he did it for me.

By the mid-1940s I was becoming less active as a radio specialist, for now I has heading what must have been the most concentrated array of publicists in the world. There were seven of us, some with specialties such as our photographer, but most of our people were able to perform well on about any assignment. Because of the skill of those men we garnered reams of publicity and hours of radio time each week. We competed successfully with the news of the global war, politics, and other late-breaking events. Why? Because over the years the press and the readers they serve had become almost as fond of the circus as we were. It has never grown old, to them or to me, and it never will.

Probably the most interesting and underplayed feature of the circus is what is known as ''Clown Alley.'' This is the seat of the action of the ladies and gentlemen who comprise the contingent that brings laughter to the people who pay to see the Greatest Show on Earth. They may stare in awe at Gargantua or the Ubangis or the great elephants or the soaring aerialists, but when they leave the show with their sides aching from laughter it is because of the

Editor & Publisher took and published this picture of one of history's great teams of publicists, the Ringling Brothers and Barnum & Bailey Circus press corps. Front row, from left: William Fields, Allen Lester, Bernard Head and Eddie Howe. Back row: Sam Stratton, myself, Edward Callahan and Frank Morrissey. Callahan was the full-time photographer. I assembled the team and served as their leader. The picture was made in the office of the Hotel Lincoln in the spring of 1947.

clowns. Two and a half hours in front of their skits can do wonders for the tired businessman or the harried housewife. They think they are bringing the kids because it will make the youngsters happy, and of course it does. But the minute they sit down here come the clowns and they find themselves laughing harder than the kids. The cares of the day evaporate as they start to snicker and end up in bellowing guffaws. From shipyard welder to mortgage banker, from dirt farmer to surgeon, from motion picture actress to scrublady — suddenly they are all equals and their laughter fills the Big Top.

I remember so many of those great performers. One of the famous ones was Felix Adler. You could look at him in his street clothes and give him no more than a passing glance. But in whiteface he became utterly outrageous, surely one of the funniest men on earth.

Another of great import is my friend, Bill Ballantine. Bill wrote a marvelous book in 1982 called *Clown Alley*, which describes his experiences with the Big One. I became better acquainted with Bill in later years, after he had become the first dean of the famed Ringling ''Clown College.'' Later, when I realized what a fine cartoonist he was, I asked that he prepare the jacket for my own book,

Felix Adler, one of the most delightful clowns.

Clown-artist-author Bill Ballantine used this 42-year-old photo of me at work to draw the pictorial biography used on the dust jacket of this book.

This man looks like he might be the owner of a small menswear shop; in fact he was the most famous clown in the world, Emmett Kelly.

This face, not the one on the preceding page, was instantly identifiable by two generations of American circus-goers — Willie the Tramp, a/k/a Emmett Kelly.

I was able to use Clown, *the book I wrote about Emmett Kelly, as a vehicle for opening the 1954 season of the Greatest Show On Earth.*

CBS television was helpful in having the great film star Henry Fonda visit the Ringling Brothers show in 1955, to meet with the man he was to portray, Emmett Kelly. The show was a half-hour adaptation from the Kelly-Kelley book, Clown.

"Willie the Tramp" served as technical advisor to Fonda in the television presentation. Emmett Kelly advised on the makeup. Which one is Fonda? The one on the left.

as indeed he had done for his. He took a simple photograph of me and turned it into a pictorial biography.

These two men were great, but there is one clown whose name has become synonymous with the word "clown" all over the world, Emmett Kelly. Emmett was a veteran of the show even before I joined it, and he was the one who originated the sad-faced character, "Willie the Tramp." It made him famous, and I guess he did more than his share to make Ringling Brothers and Barnum & Bailey famous, too. I had fronted some mighty big shows, both on Broadway and traveling around the country, but had gone back to the Big One for a couple of years beginning in 1954. It was shortly before that that Emmett asked me to write his autobiography, *Clown,* which was published in the spring of 1954. That was fortuitous, for it provided me with an ideal vehicle to publicize the annual Ringling engagement in Madison Square Garden that year.

The following year we had another big break, also timed to help the New York run of the circus. CBS Television turned the book into a "General Electric Theater" dramatization which aired on March 27, 1955, and starred Henry Fonda. Henry was a charming man and readily cooperated with the circus and network publicity people in putting the promotional package together. We helped CBS and, believe me, CBS helped us.

13

I LEARNED ABOUT CIRCUS FROM HIM

My memory of Frank Braden, press agent for the Greatest Show On Earth, still grows green. Let me try to set him down in black and white — and in red and gold, the colors of the circus and of the life we lived and loved together.

Frank Wilson Braden made his last town, which was Providence, Rhode Island, a good many years ago. He had been traveling for some days with pneumonia, one of the occupational companions of showmen. He refused medical attention; he insisted on getting to his next town. The most important town to a traveling press agent is **tomorrow's** town.

The first time I ever saw this man I had been working for the Ringling Brothers and Barnum & Bailey Circus for a month. He had a considerable reputation earned from press-agenting other big shows, but he never had been with what the show fraternity calls the "Big One." I was green as grass and running scared. I needed him although I didn't know it then. I had persuaded John Ringling that I knew how to put radio to work for the circus and was hanging on only because the circus knew even less about this medium than I did. Braden knew nothing of radio publicity either, but he did know how to sell the circus and it was the same thing. In those days the circus had several press agents, including Dexter Fellows, Tom Killilea and Floyd Bell. They all went out of their way to help me but I learned from Braden most of all.

His life with Ringling Brothers opened with him sitting on a press trunk, waiting to be interviewed by the boss press agent for the circus, Roland Butler. Braden was middle-aged, bald and short in

Two of the great Ringling press wizards posed with me — Frank Morrissey in the center, and Frank Braden at right.

physical stature. But he walked tall. He had big shoulders and slim legs and a waist so small that from the rear he looked like an inverted slice of pie. Any knowing person would have spotted him as a man with a military bearing, and indeed he had been schooled at Annapolis. Later he served in the United States Army in the Philippines.

Braden was noted for his impeccable attire. The peculiar tilt of his hard straw hat was a point of instant identification in newspaper editorial offices across the country. Once he took a train from Washington, D.C. to New York for no reason other than to have his tailor move a button on his coat. For 20 years and more he was continually annoyed by the sartorial indifference of an unkempt colleague, and at last in desperation called him the three worst dressed men in America.

Braden stayed with R.B.B.& B. for 25 years. When he finally went to the ''Big Lot'' it was no surprise to showmen and to the newspaper fraternity that there was a rash of editorial copy about him. Not since the passing of Dex Fellows a quarter century earlier had anyone been recalled with so much affection by the Fourth Estate.

They missed the natty little guy whose pockets were stuffed with copy about the stars of the big top. (He once said a briefcase was for college professors and business executives.) He promoted Lillian Leitzel, the aerial queen; Alfredo Codona, the triple-somersault genius of the flying trapeze; Con Colleano, originator of the forward somersault on the tight wire; the Great Wallendas of the high wire; Gargantua, the giant gorilla; the Ubangi Savages "from the deepest depths of darkest Africa;" the Zacchini human cannonballs and the giraffe-neck women from Upper Burma. Nobody ever had more stars in his constellation than did Frank Braden.

Newspaper files recall his most spectacular stunt. A circus midget named Lia Graf sat on the lap of the younger J.P. Morgan during a senate investigation in Washington in the spring of 1933, when the circus happened to be in town. The stunt was born during a session at the National Press Club. Braden always said it had not been his idea, but the brainchild of an Associated Press photographer who placed the little lady on the lap of the financier. It happened quickly. Morgan thought she was a child and asked her where she lived. Properly coached, she replied, "I live in a tent." That did it. An attempt was made to kill the picture but it was a publicity sensation, even though it was of such poor quality that it practically had been retouched into a painting before it was finally engraved. Our hero wisely backed off to let the story run its happy course.

Braden's stunts, in and out of the circus business, were numerous. He once fronted a traveling whale show. The attraction was embalmed and traveled aboard a railroad car, but Frank breathed life into it by arranging to have a couple married by a publicity-seeking preacher in the mammal's cavernous mouth.

Frank was always good for a story in which he was the goat. During his Army days he put in for transfer to a post at Fort Brady, Michigan. Somebody had pulled his leg by assuring him that they had a fine polo team there. Braden was a fine horseman and it wasn't until he went out to the parade ground to practice that he discovered that there was not only no polo team at the post, but no interest in the sport whatsoever.

In a social setting Braden invariably lit up the gathering like a lamp. His were not all circus stories either — just part of the total Braden-iana. His father had operated a dry goods store in his home-

This heavily-retouched photograph was set up by Frank Braden and taken by an Associated Press photographer. It shows circus midget Lya Graf seated on the lap of financier J.P. Morgan during a 1933 Senate hearing in Washington.

town of Watseka, Illinois. The second floor of the building was the opera house, and many were the tales Frank told of traveling companies that played one-night stands there during his youth. He attended regularly with a boyhood pal who frequently embarrassed his host with his loud, critical comments. Once when a thespian delivered the line, "A year from now I shall be rotting in my grave," Frank's guest yelled, "You're rotten **now!**" On another occasion, an actor delivered the line, "Petronius, thou art an ass!" This inspired Frank's pal to break up the house by shouting, "A **horse's** ass!"

Frank was proud of having played high school football on a state championship team. This experience, he claimed, enabled him at age 60 to survive a fall from the circus office wagon without sustaining injury. The circus treasurer blamed the fall on the fact that Braden had passed out when his expense account had been approved without challenge.

Frank could write. He turned out stories for magazines and he wrote thousands of priceless letters, usually kidding himself. His conversation was studded with expressions that were pure Braden-isms. He would say that something was "as phony as a 10-cent cornet" or that someone was as fake as a "printed tuxedo." One of the circus jobs he had before joining the Ringling organization had been with Miller Brothers 101 Ranch Wild West Show. Thereafter he always referred to cowboy performers as "rubes in hair pants."

One of the near miracles of show business is that Frank Braden didn't die broke. He was lightning-fast in grabbing a dinner check and was a notoriously soft touch. More than one of his colleagues complained that Braden was solely responsible for the fact that waiters and bartenders and cab drivers coast-to-coast all expected to be overtipped. Once, while he was in financial straits, Braden wrote to more than a score of men to whom he had loaned money. He received one reply and it was no.

At various periods of his long career, he fought the bottle and lost every round. But he stayed on the wagon during many of his last and best years. He always contended, however, that it was a temporary compromise with health and general welfare and that before he retired he would be a two-fisted drinking man again. He died sober; hadn't had a drink in years. Just shows the depths to which a press agent can fall.

This man influenced my career as a publicist. He showed me how to paint color into circus copy — color that not only passed by editors and ended up in print, but color which enraptured the public with the circus. Elephants were not just big mammals; they were "thundering tons of educated mastodonic marvels." Clowns were not simply funny people, they were "captains of caprice, cutting capers incomparably." A featured aerialist was "the epitome of grace, daring and precision aloft," and the high-wire daredevils performed "in the vast upper reaches of the canvas dome, beyond the deep abyss of intrepidity." That kind of prose rarely failed to stir the imagination of the young-in-years and to jog the memory of the young-at-heart.

Braden taught me how to kid a circus story with verbosity and harmless hyperbole — many newspaper editors liked to serve that up as contrast to the more serious issues of the day. That kind of story usually hits the street for sure and that, after all, was what we came to do.

So, from this man who took seriously his high calling and who took quiet pride in being a herald of the impossible, I learned. When I say that circus press agents often promise what seems to be impossible, I am on firm ground. For what prediction carries more fiction among the cynics than that a mobile city carrying more than 1,200 people, hundreds of wild animals, dining facilities for all, a blacksmith shop, hospital, barber shop, post office and even a chapter of the American Red Cross, giving a performance in a town 150 miles away, would arrive at dawn in tomorrow's town and be open and ready for business at 1 o'clock in the afternoon? That is exactly what happened to the "Big One" in my day, when it moved on a hundred railroad cars in four separate trains.

No western sunset was as beautiful to Braden as the sight of his circus stories in printers' ink. He maintained for years that his principal protagonists were people like Charles Lindbergh, the Dionne Quintuplets and Amelia Earhart, whose big stories broke to crowd his circus publicity off the front page.

Frank Braden taught me something else: "Never tell a lie to a newspaper man or to anyone in any medium ready to help you. If you have a preposterous idea for a stunt, spell it out to the city editor so that if he finds it harmless fun, he is your partner. Never try to take him in on a phony story and make him look foolish." This passes for professional integrity among the best of the press agent breed. That is one reason why newspaper men and women loved Braden, that and the fact that he loved them. He had been on both sides of the fence. He had been the city editor of a newspaper in Taylorville, Illinois, when he was just out of the Army. Soon he took

I helped assemble this group of Hollywood stars at the White House to kick off one of the annual March of Dimes campaigns in the early 1940s. Included in this photo are Danny Kaye, Myrna Loy, Vice President Harry S. Truman and his wife Bess, Alan Ladd, Gene

Kelly, Kay Kyser, Monte Woolley, Mitzi Gaynor, Mrs. Eleanor Roosevelt, Veronica Lake, Joe E. Brown, Margaret O'Brien, Jane Wyman, Shirley Temple and Deanna Durbin.

on his first circus job, with the Gentry Brothers Dog and Pony Circus out of Bloomington, Indiana.

Frank Braden also affected my career unwittingly. He went on a binge during a Madison Square Garden engagement of the Ringling show in 1932 and caused the boss press agent to replace him temporarily with a theatrical publicist who loved the circus and was anxious to get tanbark in his shoes. The man was William Fields, and he became my staunch friend. He taught me theatrical publicity and gave me my first job with a great play, *The Green Pastures.* Later, Braden turned down a job to head the public relations department for the National Foundation for Infantile Paralysis when D. Walker Wear was reorganizing this department for Basil O'Connor. Wear felt that perhaps a circus-trained publicity man might supply something needed during the annual fund appeals. The job fell to me during the months when the circus was in winter quarters, and I did this work for three campaigns before becoming director of circus publicity after the great fire in Hartford, no longer with time for anything but circus work.

Braden was a past master at ducking trouble; he could smell it a long way off and he usually managed to be absent when it came home to roost. From my observation of this prudent performance, it was natural to conclude that his first reaction to any and all emergencies would be to think of himself first and foremost. He shamed me when I tested this in circus winter quarters one sunny afternoon. I had arranged with a circus executive to telephone the press office and report the false news that while shifting Gargantua from one cage to another, the gorilla had escaped and was at large on the grounds. My small children were there that day. When the news came in, Braden's first thought was for them. He jumped up from his desk and started for the door saying, "We must find your kids!" I felt an inch tall.

I've waited a long time now to write about him since I stood at graveside in his old hometown. But I didn't say goodbye that day. I said, "See you in the Garden in the spring." That was an expression we used on closing day in Dixie because Madison Square Garden in New York City always was the opening stand of the next tour.

I don't know exactly where the "Garden" is for the likes of Frank, but I hope it is the "Big Lot." Circus people don't fancy pearly gates and golden streets. They prefer a fine, dry lot where you can get the show up on time and watch the flags flying on the halyards of the big top and hear the band play spangled music and inhale the scent of canvas in the sun and the smell of cotton candy on the midway and clean animals in the menagerie tent. They, in their celestial vision, see kids streaming in with bright balloons clutched in their grimy little hands, their faces unforgettable at the entrance to the traveling city of enchantment that builds a new home in a new town every day and vanishes in the night, leaving a memory in the corner of the place that is forever young-at-heart.

I guess that's the circus man's heaven. That's where I'll find Frank Braden . . . if I'm lucky.

I fronted for some of the greatest stars in show business during their charity efforts for the March of Dimes. Here is Mary Pickford, with whom I worked in the early 1940s.

14

THE REMARKABLE FELLOWS

Some decades ago I was riding north from the Florida-based Ringling winter quarters with Eddie Jackson, one of our advertising department employees. Eddie pointed to a checkered overcoat in a seat across the aisle and said, "What does that remind you of?"

The answer, of course, was simply "Dexter." Since Dexter Fellows departed this world for the "Big Lot," no other press agent for Ringling Brothers and Barnum & Bailey has ever worn a checkered overcoat.

It is rather like the fact that circus band leader Merle Evans never again used the last movement of the "Second Hungarian Rhapsody" for any other star performer after Lillian Leitzel fell to her death in 1931. It was Leitzel's music and it was Dexter's coat; it wouldn't be fitting the likes of us.

But seeing a coat of the pattern favored by our old friend evoked fond memories. I met Dexter Fellows late in his life and so I never knew him as the dashing young publicist who rode parade with Buffalo Bill and went to Europe with the Barnum & Bailey show long before I ever saw my first plume from a steam calliope.

He was older than my father, but when Dex and I were together we always seemed to be about the same age. I remember going to his room in the Arlington Hotel in Binghamton, N.Y., where he was working the newspapers, and I the radio stations, during my first

Dexter Fellows, the press agents' press agent.

season with the circus. On this occasion I needed to verify the arrival time of the show the next morning. He stood attired in his long white nightshirt and asked me in. This was 1930 and Dexter clung to that style of sleeping garment (and it to him) until some years later when he finally succumbed to the trend to pajamas.

After Dex and I exchanged some circus talk I remarked that this was my 25th birthday. My friend became nostalgic then, and reflecting upon his own years, recited "Backward, turn backward, oh Time in thy flight; and make me a child again, just for tonight."

He mellowed considerably in his remaining years and he became increasingly temperate, although once he had been a two-fisted imbiber. He was married to Signe Eugene Von Brathos, a girl whose Scandinavian lineage entitled Dexter to a listing in the Swedish *Blue Book.* He often bragged about that. Signe liked to recall the first time she set eyes upon the famous circus agent. He was at a skating rink where he wore a red silk-lined cape and cut a dashing figure.

Newspaper men who should have known better thought that Fellows couldn't write; they believed that he simply talked about the circus and managed to get somebody else to do his work for him.

I soon learned that this was only partially true. Although Dex was lazy, he could write well enough, and I have watched him laboring over his ancient Corona, the original tiny model with curving sides that scarcely left room for both his hands on the keyboard.

He looked like a figure in a Norman Rockwell painting with his classic head, belligerent jowls and straggly mustache. He was intent upon his work and from his vintage machine came the story about the arrival of the big show in the town he was visiting. I soon learned to spot a piece Dexter had written himself because he always referred to small boys as urchins.

Once Dexter's feelings were hurt in the editorial room of the *New York Sun,* one of the traditional strongholds of his vast popularity. On this occasion he was enroute to his home in New England after the closing of the circus tour in the South in November. He decided to stop over in New York for a day of visiting with newspaper pals.

When he entered the familiar city room at the *Sun* on this day there was no fanfare. Nobody rose from his desk to shake his hand; it had not been unusual for almost the entire personnel to rise and greet the foremost press agent of the big tops.

Our hero was stunned. He thought he must have done something horrendous to offend not only the *Sun* crowd, but possibly the total New York City press corps. He was considerably relieved to discover that unwittingly he had made his entrance exactly at 11 a.m. on November 11, the time when the whole nation paused for a moment of silent prayer to mourn the dead from World War I. It was Armistice Day.

Dexter Fellows belonged to the old school; he looked it, he talked it and he felt it. I had a hunch that, although we then worked for the circus of the early '30s, my colleague still lived with the circus he had served before the last glorious street parade turned the corner to march off down Memory Lane. He lived the period of Lillian Leitzel, May Wirth, Bird Millman and Mabel Stark. They were the "Big Four" of the stellar femininity of the circus — in the air, on the horse, on the tight wire, and in the steel arena with the tigers.

The circus changed. It lost a lot and improved a little, but Dexter Fellows worked for the old show he held in his heart. Fortunately the current edition resembled it enough in general character and appearance to permit him this illusion.

Fellows had a funny side. Once, when he was relaxing with his wife at a fancy seaside resort, he acknowledged an introduction to a canned bean tycoon whom he considered a pompous bore: "Oh yes, Mr. so-and-so, I have always heard good reports of your product."

One evening Fellows was attired in his plaid suit, checkered topcoat and gold-topped cane. He was standing under the marquee at the main entrance to the circus, awaiting newspaper guests. Suddenly he was confronted by an irate customer with a tearful lady in tow. Probably mistaking the distinguished gentleman for the show's general manager, the man yelled, "You may believe it or not, sir, but a tiger has just urinated in my wife's eye!"

This situation called for quick thinking and Fellows was equal to the task.

He suspected that the culprit had been the big Siberian cat we called "Whitey," who took a perverse delight in spraying hapless spectators in the wild animal menagerie tent.

Dexter knew too that probably the high percentage of ammonia in the feline urine was responsible for most of the damage and that if he stalled for time it might wear off.

So the circus man distracted the unhappy couple by asking if they had ever heard of Fitchburg, Massachusetts, where his family operated a pharmacy, and then went on to tell them how his people had invented a popular patent medicine called "Fellows Hypophosphate."

The story happened to be true, and the tiger's victims said that they lived not far from Fitchburg and so now their boiling point had lifted a little. Thereupon Dexter assumed his most impressive stance to orate, "And another of our important pharmaceutical discoveries was that tiger urine happens to be one of the best eyewashes known to man!"

The husband looked at Fellows aghast; the circus man looked at the lady, and she stopped crying. Now her spouse burst out laughing to say, ''By golly you're all right! And I only hope that the circus performance is half as entertaining and that your clowns are half as funny.''

The man took his wife's hand and they started into the Big Top while some circus executives who had watched quietly as the little impromptu comedy drama unfolded now realized that they had witnessed the difference between press agentry and public relations.

Dex had a habit of looking under the bed in a hotel room before he retired, fearing that a prowler might have concealed himself there. None ever had, but a couple of villians named Typhoid and Pneumonia awaited him at Hattiesburg, Mississippi, near the end of his final tour.

That was his last town; he died in harness as all circus press agents wish to do, and in the years since there has never been another even remotely like him. He was as different from the rest of us as the present day circus differs from the colossus we worked for then.

15

JUMBO YANKEE

I suppose those of us associated with the circus are a little prejudiced, but as far as I am concerned, there was just one number one — one unquestioned all-time great promotional genius.

Number one is Phineas Taylor Barnum.

Born in Bethel, Connecticut in 1810, he ranks with his friend and contemporary Mark Twain as the best known and most interesting American of his time, save the United States presidents.

Barnum was not born to affluence. In fact, he was a failure at several business ventures early in his career. His talent for showmanship surfaced through his museums in New York City. *American Heritage* magazine published a long feature about that facet of his career, which I wrote in 1953. His success as an impresario was evidenced when he brought the Swedish Nightingale, Jenny Lind, to America and exploited her talents. His genius was underscored by his presentation of the midget Tom Thumb; the Siamese Twins, Chang and Eng; and of the elephant Jumbo, which caused his name to become known throughout the world.

Yet, Yankee Barnum was more than a showman. He was a serious and highly respected mayor of Bridgeport, Connecticut, his home town. He became a member of the Massachusetts Legislature. He was a persuasive temperance lecturer. He was a man of great courage, as witnessed by his rise from the ashes after his New York museums were twice destroyed by fire.

On the minus side, he was not a skilled circus man at all, but he was amazingly lucky in his choice of partners. His identification was with the Greatest Show on Earth, the Barnum and Bailey Circus, and its apparent immortality. Misdirected history long gave

The most celebrated portrait of Phineas Taylor Barnum.

Barnum's partner, James A. Bailey.

him the sole credit for its success, and he accepted it gladly. However, he neither sired it nor built it singlehandedly.

In his younger years he had had some undistinguished and in-
considerable experience with traveling wagon circuses of question-
able reputation. Two Wisconsin showmen named William Cameron
Coup and Dan Castello, fresh from a triumphant coast-to-coast
tour, persuaded Barnum into partnership, mainly for the value of his
famous name. Suddenly he found himself in the big league of the
big tops.

Coup and Castello put the Barnum show together in 1870 at Dele-
van, Wisconsin. That state was to become known as the ''Mother of
Circuses'' because over 100 of them, large and small, started there.
Included was the Ringling Brothers leviathan. They railed the

Barnum show to New York City where it met with great success as "P.T. Barnum's Museum, Menagerie and Circus."

By 1872, Coup had changed circus history by putting the Barnum show on specially-built railroad cars, against the advice of P.T. Barnum himself.

The Barnum-Coup alliance broke a couple of years later when P.T. leased his name to a grafting circus owner. By 1880 the Barnum luck flourished again. His two top competitors, the huge Adam Forepaugh Circus and the Cooper & Bailey Circus were both headquartered in Philadelphia at that time and a royal partnership was about to be formed.

James A. Bailey, whose real name was McGuiness, had been an orphaned stable boy in Pontiac, Michigan. An itinerant circus advance man, traveling by horse and buggy, saw promise in the industrious and attractive lad. He employed him and adopted him, giving him his own last name.

In 1880, Bailey's circus earned national notice when its elephant Hebe gave birth to the first pachyderm born in America.

Barnum naturally coveted this prize and telegraphed a handsome offer for it, but the reigning monarch of flamboyant advertising had met his match at last.

Bailey reproduced Barnum's telegram on his posters and trumpeted: "This is what P.T. Barnum thinks of our baby elephant!"

It is not surprising that a partnership was formed, or that it outlived both men. The Ringling Brothers, who bought it from Bailey's heirs early in this century, operated it separately from their own circus enterprise at first. In 1918 they combined the titles to create Ringling Brothers and Barnum & Bailey Circus and it prospers to this day.

Barnum & Bailey got along well personally simply because Bailey didn't care who received the credit so long as the job was done well. The show's triumphs, such as its initial trip to London and the erection of the first Madison Square Garden, were brought off in spite of and not because of Barnum. The man was aging, cautious and seldom with the circus on tour.

Barnum was not without a sense of humor. That couldn't be better illustrated than it was during a press conference relevant to the famous "White Elephant War."

That fight was between Barnum & Bailey and its arch-rival, the Adam Forepaugh Circus. Barnum & Bailey had a genuine East Indian sacred white elephant that was, in fact, a light gray. All genuine "white" elephants are light gray. Now Forepaugh's con-

Barnum had this etching made to illustrate the gigantic size of his prize elephant, Jumbo. The beast actually was 11'9" tall at the shoulder. The man depicted between Jumbo's legs scales out to be 4'7" tall. It was not for nothing that they called the showman "The Prince of Humbug."

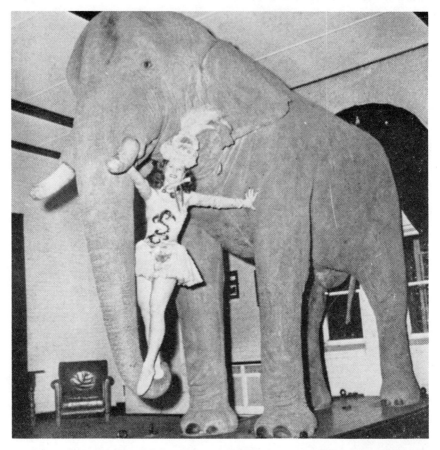

After the elephant's death in a railroad accident in 1884 Barnum gave his hide to the Tufts College museum. It was stuffed and this is the result.

tender was really white, because he had it whitewashed daily. That didn't come to light until a cloudburst hit Forepaugh's street parade, and in his home town, too!

To return to the newspaper session, a reporter for the *New York World* had complained that he and his colleagues felt that Barnum's elephant was not really very white.

"Gentlemen," proclaimed the great P.T., "God made our white elephant, but if either Mr. Bailey or I had had anything to do with it, I assure you it would be white as the driven snow!"

Prominent and popular among Barnum's human curiosities in his 19th century museum was a peaked or pin-headed black called simply "Zip." When the distinguished writer, Charles

Dickens, saw him, he asked, "What is it?"

Barnum thought quickly and answered, **"That's** what it is." And thereafter "Zip" became known as "What-is-it?"

Barnum was out-skilled by his partners as a circus operator. He had been interested principally in his sideshow freak attractions all the way back to his museum days. But as an advertising man, Barnum was a towering genius. Much present-day advertising and promotion in many fields reflect "Barnumism," but even the best of his breed today are dwarfs by comparison.

Not since the peanut discovered the elephant has any Yankee so captured the imagination of so many for so long as did that poor boy from Bethel.

He was sometimes referred to as the "Prince of Humbug" and that may not have been an improper appellation. While "the people like to be fooled" may indeed have been a Barnum remark, this great Yankee never said, "There's a sucker born every minute." The word "sucker," as used to describe the gullible, was not in the language in P.T. Barnum's time.

And I also doubt that P.T. had anything to do with "Barnum's Bible," that collection of passages from Scripture which many an owner has cited to keep from letting anyone in free:

"Thou shall not pass." Numbers 20:18

"Suffered not a man to pass." Judges 3:28

"This generation shall not pass." Mark 13:30

"Beware that thou pass not." 2 Kings 6:9

"No man may pass through because of the beasts." Ezekiel 14:15

"Though they roar, yet can they not pass." Jeremiah 5:22

"So he paid the fare thereof, and went." Jonah 1:3

I am afraid, or maybe secretly pleased, that a little of old P.T.'s spirit might have rubbed off on me during two decades with his circus. One of my treasured recollections occurred when my friend and fellow alumnus of Ohio Wesleyan, the Rev. Dr. Norman Vincent Peale, was my guest at a matinee performance of the circus in Madison Square Garden. He was accompanied by his charming wife and their young daughter.

As the performance wound down and the next-to-closing daredevils of the flying trapeze worked their magic on the crowd, the eminent churchman-author turned to me to ask, "And just what is it that you do here?"

Lacking both time and the inclination for a detailed reply that I thought might well be boring, I answered simply, "Norman, let us just say that it's better than work.'' Later he told me that he thought that was a good working philosophy, and that he preached a sermon about it at his famed Marble Collegiate Church in New York City.

In more recent years, this good friend urged me to write this book, ''because,'' he said, ''Bev Kelley is a raconteur of high order.'' Well, that is a fine compliment and I appreciate it, despite the fact that in anybody's dictionary a raconteur is listed beneath a racketeer, a racist and a raccoon. I neither expect nor deserve top billing. That belongs singly to P.T. Barnum.

16

GIRAFFE-NECK WOMAN

Whenever I was in St. Louis with worry on my mind, I usually could reduce it to its proper proportions by comparing the problem with the one I had when I lost a giraffe-neck woman there in the Melbourne Hotel.

It was the spring of 1933, and a chilly one it was, when the Hagenbeck-Wallace Circus spread its acres of canvas on the nearby show grounds at Grand and Laclede, now the site of the east campus of St. Louis University. At that time Hagenbeck-Wallace was owned by R.B.B.& B., and I had the job of promoting it that summer.

Some of the elite personnel elected to swallow the expense of hotel accommodations instead of shivering in the unheated circus train. At that time all circus railway cars were without heat. This posed no great hardship except in the early spring in the Midwest, and late autumn in the South. During summertime the cars more often than not were like ovens.

The Hagenbeck-Wallace wild animal show in 1933 was one whale of a circus. It featured Clyde Beatty in the steel arena with a mixture of 33 jungle-bred lions and tigers. We had the riding comedian ''Poodles'' Hanneford and his famous family act; Bombayo, the East Indian circus celebrity somersaulting on the bounding rope; The Flying Clarkonians on the high trapeze, and a grounded aerialist who had briefly been a white-face clown but who now had forsaken that happy visage to impersonate instead a forlorn-looking hobo, a character of his own invention.

His name was Emmett Kelly, and I paid little attention to him. One day Billy Cronin, the ticket boss of the show's main entrance,

The giraffe-neck women were one of the most famous attractions in all R.B.B.& B. history. They are shown here in New York City, shortly after their arrival from Upper Burma.

said to me along about the stand in Herkimer, New York: "There is a clown with us who is a pretty good cartoonist. Maybe you could do something with that. His name is the same as yours, lacking one 'e'."

So I went to what we called "Clown Alley" in the men's section of the immense dressing tent. There I had a visit with my namesake. A few days later he had drawn a good montage of our show's principal features, and this I had made into a two-column ad mat which newspapers along our line-of-march were eager to use.

I did not suspect then that within 20 years Emmett Kelly would be the most famous clown of all time. He was the subject of one of my best stories in the *Saturday Evening Post*. Furthermore, I was immensely honored when he asked me to co-author his autobiography.

But I'm off the route. We were discussing the giraffe-neck woman we lost in the Melbourne Hotel in St. Louis, right? Her name was Mu Kau, which was pronounced "Moo Cow," and she was the stellar new attraction of the Hagenbeck-Wallace show that year. Howard Y. Bary, an explorer who tracked down exotic circus features, had traveled to Upper Burma to bring out three of these unusual ladies who were expected to be as strong an attraction as

The three modest and unassuming ladies are pictured together in this publicity shot.

the African Ubangis who had appeared with the Ringling Brothers and Barnum & Bailey Circus three years previously.

Now, two of the Burmese women had become attractions with that colossus of the tented world while our show had Mu Kau and her husband. She belonged to a cult that from their childhood selected its most beautiful females to have brass rings welded around their necks.

More rings were added each year until at maturity their necks

Mu Kau and her husband toured with the Hagenbeck-Wallace Circus in 1934.

might be more than a foot in length. I never learned why they continued to wear the rings; I suppose that if they were removed, the neck bones might be too extended to deliver proper support to the head. The rings were cleaned by pulling thin straws between them and the skin while bathing.

Earlier that eventful morning my publicity associate, Bob Hickey, had taken Mu Kau and a newspaper photographer to a St. Louis hospital to determine if an x-ray picture might reveal what had happened to the neck during the gradual but relentless process of stretching it.

Radiology failed to penetrate the brass. This we suspected, but the newspaper shot of the effort was impressive and that, after all, was the purpose of the stunt.

Late that morning Bary and I went to the hotel to pick up Mu Kau and her husband to take them to the show grounds. He had locked them in their room after their return from the hospital publicity visit, feeling that if they were left free to wander over the hotel without protection they might become frightened and confused. Bary reckoned without the fact that, while they were unable to speak more than a few words of English, they nevertheless had plenty of native intelligence. He unlocked the door and discovered their room was vacant.

At this point, the man who had brought them from Burma by oxcart, riverboat and steamship, and who was responsible for their welfare, became frantic. He ran the corridors of their floor, knocking on doors and shouting, "Mu Kau! Mu Kau!"

Guests of the hotel opened their doors to peer out cautiously, probably thinking we were demented adults reciting nursery rhymes. We finally went to the lobby to report our loss. The desk clerk suggested that we look in the coffee shop.

There we found them, calmly having lunch. They had discovered they were locked in their room and telephoned the desk, asking to be freed so they could behave like ordinary guests. This incident convinced us that they were at least as smart as we were, which I must admit was no great compliment, given our performance of a few moments earlier.

Spending many years with circuses will put numerous unforgettable characters in the memory book. A favorite of mine did his work on four legs.

He was a center-ring horse and his name was Thunder. He had been born during a thunderstorm in Antrim, Ireland. That's where the famed Hanneford Family of circus bareback riders was perform-

The Ringling show artists had a tendency to stretch things a bit —

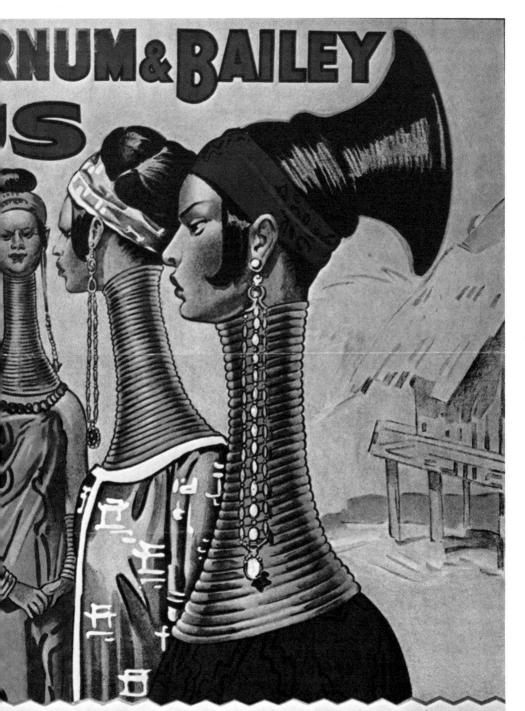

including the necks of the attractions, the number of brass rings,
and the number of individuals on exhibit, in this one-sheet poster.

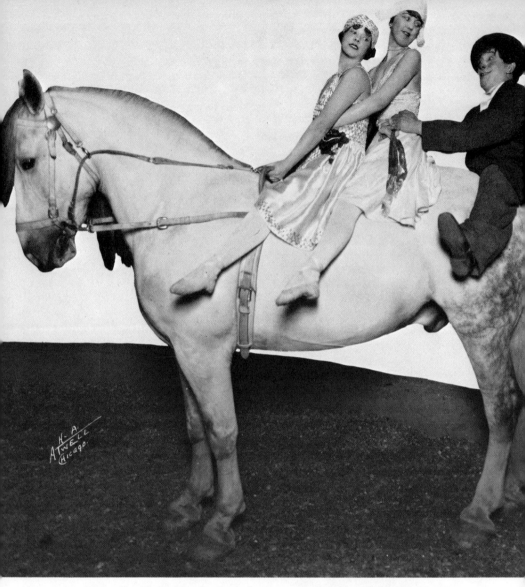

"Poodles" Hanneford and two other members of his famous family act are shown on their magnificent horse, Thunder.

ing at the time. The Hannefords could trace their lineage as a peerless equestrian family down through the centuries, and they rate top billing to this day.

I met Thunder in 1933. He was in America with this family and traveling with the Hagenbeck-Wallace Circus. At age 28 he was acknowledged the oldest equine member of any high-riding act in the world. That means the rider stands upright while performing on a galloping horse.

Generations of Hanneford kids had learned their trade on the broad back of this white percheron. In his youth he had been dapple gray. They said he preferred to carry the girls. Boys practicing on Thunder often found him to be a stubborn and difficult partner in the ring.

The horse lived a full and exciting life. Once, on a cold day following a Boston appearance, he was being run up a ramp to a railroad horse car. He bumped his head so hard he was out cold for an hour or so. An observer quipped that Thunder might have imbibed some liquid lightning, because this particular day happened to be New Year's Eve.

When the act was in Cuba for a winter date, an insurrection broke out and soon the rebels were stealing horses wherever they could be found. The Hanneford mounts were secreted inside an inconspicuous old barn for some days. Finally they were smuggled aboard a friendly freighter bound for the United States.

In his middle years this star of the tanbark circle nearly died of an unexplained ailment, but slowly he was nursed back to health on a diet fortified with milk and raw eggs. At that time the Hannefords had several well-trained younger percherons and no longer needed the dean of the group. They carried him along only because the circus was his life and they loved him.

But in the late spring of 1933 he was retired. It took some time for the old trouper to get the message. He often became restless and tugged at his halter in the horse tents where he could hear echoing from the Big Top the familiar music that the band always played for his family's turn.

That summer he went to the Big Lot. He departed this life as dramatically as he had entered it, in the midst of a thunderstorm. Our show was in Uniontown, Pennsylvania, and that storm was a rouser. The thunder rolled and the lightning flashed; the wind whipped the canvas of the Big Top and set the quarterpoles to dancing dangerously. Torrential rain converted the show grounds into a quagmire. I was already in Pittsburgh, our next stand, when the sad news of Thunder's passing reached me. I couldn't imagine a more dramatic exit and the press release reflected this. Hoping to catch the next edition, I quickly put together a story on the highlights in the life of the loved and loyal trouper. He had been named for the weather conditions at the time of his birth, and his circus career had come full circle to end under similar weather conditions.

The night city editor of the *Pittsburgh Post-Gazette* was invariably affable and generous with circus press agents, especially this one. But as he read my story he smiled, read it again, shook his head and said, "I'm sorry, Bev. It's just too pat. Nobody would believe it."

17

MARIA RASPUTIN

The fame and fortune of Hagenbeck-Wallace were my concern again in 1935, and from its very beginning that season it promised to generate a plethora of publicity because the show's star female attraction was to be Maria Rasputin, daughter of Czarist Russia's incredible "Mad Monk."

Maria, whose photos showed a strong facial resemblance to her infamous father, was a child in 1916, when Gregori Rasputin was murdered by Russian noblemen who were convinced that the "holy man" exerted a demonic influence on Czar Nicholas and his czarina. They had sought Rasputin's help in the treatment of the royal family's little heir-apparent, a victim of hemophilia.

As an adult, Maria Rasputin traveled with a circus that wound up at the famed Cirque de Paris. There a Ringling talent scout saw her in a tiger act with a trainer named Cook. What the scout failed to notice was that, although Rasputin's daughter was billed as the trainer, she only moved props and took bows in the big cage. It was the act's enterprising owner-trainer who actually worked the cats.

On a cold April morning my assistant, Bill Fields, and I went on a tugboat in New York Harbor. We were with several reporters and were to meet our Maria, who was arriving on the North German-Lloyd Line's S.S. Bremen.

As soon as some shipside photographs were taken to serve the afternoon papers, we sped our star to the Hotel Ritz Carlton where

Maria Rasputin, shown in her hotel room shortly after her arrival in New York.

she would stay for a few days. Then we took her by train to circus headquarters in Peru, Indiana. Maria was to take over a mixed group of wild animals in a ready-made act. It had been put together by veteran trainer John Helliott in preparation for the show's opening engagement at Chicago Stadium three weeks hence.

Meanwhile, in Manhattan the Mad Monk's daughter received so much publicity that the press staff of the Ringling-Barnum Circus at Madison Square Garden became less than enthusiastic about our competition, although we were, after all, a Ringling-owned show.

When I arrived at the Ritz Carlton I noted that Maria's luggage looked as though she had traveled steerage class, and I pushed it under her bed before the reporters and photographers arrived. They soon were followed by eager visitors from New York's White Russian colony, many of whom remembered Maria as a child in pre-revolutionary St. Petersburg. Their welcome was effusive and served to dispel any doubt the media people might have had about the authenticity of our star.

Later she told me that most of her guests had come to beg for money, assuming that the prima donna of a big American circus would be highly paid.

But Maria Rasputin had no money to spare; she was a working widow with a young daughter enrolled in tuition school at a Paris convent. By no means was she the high priced show business personality whom her old acquaintances imagined her to be. Also, during her initial workout at circus rehearsals in Peru we soon discovered that while Maria had the courage, she lacked the skill to work wild animals.

In her group were an African lion, a pair of leopards and some bears. One of these bears was the troublesome "Himmie," a Himalayan that already could count the eye of a former trainer among his trophies. Some bears have a favorite trick, which I think they teach one another. This consists of reaching out a paw and tripping the trainer in such a way that he falls flat on his back. In that instant the bear piles on and starts scratching and biting the victim, who lies virtually helpless beneath the animal's great weight. That is precisely what happened to Maria.

Fortunately Bert Nelson, who with his lions and tigers was a circus headliner, attended that rehearsal and quickly entered the big cage to beat off the bear and rescue Maria. She was soon in the care of Peru's Dr. Malouf. He specialized in the treatment of injuries inflicted by circus wild animals and who numbered among his Big Top patients the great Clyde Beatty. This physician had saved Beatty's

I set up this shot of the daughter of Czar Nicholas's "Mad Monk." Maria and the cat posed shortly before she was mauled brutally by the Himalayan brown bear, "Himmie."

life two years earlier.

When Maria was discharged from the hospital we moved her to a downtown hotel. While she was there a telephone call was received, warning us that we should be prepared for an attempted kidnapping. Her publicity value soared.

The call could not be traced and although there was no follow-up, the circus and the hotel people were sufficiently disturbed to station guards outside the doors to Maria's suite day and night.

I suspected that the warning might have been a joke invented by a friend of mine with a rival circus. They were to be our competition during the Chicago run. Nevertheless, we made the most of it, and I liked especially the front page story from an Indianapolis newspaper. The opening sentence was, "In the spring a circus press agent's fancy lightly turns to almost anything that might make the front page." The story's headline was, "Well, This Is Page One!"

Our star recovered steadily from the 30-odd bites and deep lacerations inflicted by 'Himmie,'' but it was clear that Rasputin's brave daughter could not be allowed to return to the big cage in time for our Chicago debut, if ever. Still, we planned an impressive appearance for her on the show's opening night and meanwhile put her into the LaSalle Hotel where the publicity department was headquartered.

There she fell victim to influenza. Our circus physician gave her a supply of pills and told her to take one every four hours. She was unable to read the label and misunderstood the instruction, and innocently swallowed all the pills in one dose. I discovered this about midnight, and was unable to locate either the house physician or our circus doctor. I feared the worst. I had read somewhere that in such circumstances the patient should be restrained from falling into a sound sleep.

So now my wife and the wife of our circus manager spelled me in a kind of marathon that kept Maria more or less awake while we walked her around her bedroom parlor between catnaps for the remainder of the night. Eventually the doctor was contacted, and he said we had done the right thing although the dose our sleepy patient had taken probably would not have been lethal.

The Mad Monk's daughter appeared at the opening performance as advertised, although not in the role for which she had been employed. Instead she took bows from a flag-draped box. She was gowned elegantly. The band played the White Russian national anthem and our trick-riding Cossack horsemen lined up before her

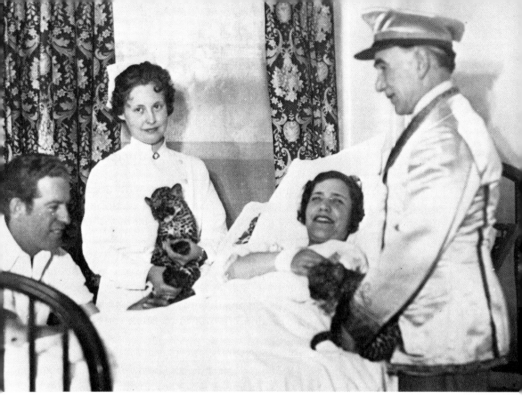

Maria met photographers in a Peru hospital in the summer of 1935, just after "Himmie" had done his dastardly act. At left is Bert Nelson and at right John Helliott, both veteran trainers. I brought the cubs to bedside to add interest to the shot, which was gobbled up by a dozen photographers.

in salute.

Thereafter and for the duration of the tour Maria was relegated to "presenting" a turn in which a male lion rode a pad on the back of a perpetually uncomfortable white horse.

Elephants seemed to dominate my publicity adventures. So, when the excitement attending Rasputin's daughter died down, I thought to enliven our spring engagement in Chicago Stadium by staging an elephant race on Madison Avenue, alongside the building.

For this event our wardrobe wizards made jockey silks in different colors for the keepers, who were to ride their behemoths for one long city block. At the end of the race course stood the trophy, a bale of hay wrapped with a wide blue ribbon.

Sidewalk spectators made bets and cheered their favorites among six lady athletes chosen from the elephant herd, while motion picture news cameramen shot from the tailgate of a swift-moving truck. They were surprised at the unexpected speed of the thundering gray mountains that threatened to overrun them.

Although the "race course" was short, the bladders of our contestants complained at the unaccustomed exertion and this inspired the reporter from the *Chicago Daily News* to finish his story by observing that "At the conclusion of the race, the participants relaxed in a shameless manner."

In the late 1930s John Ringling North came up with a good idea. Frank "Bring-'Em-Back-Alive" Buck had built a national reputation, so we hired him for the 1938 and 1939 seasons. That might have seemed strange at first, because Buck was an animal dealer, not a trainer. He went to exotic lands to bring back wild animals to sell to the circus. But Johnnie North had good ideas and he had planned the greatest of the R.B.B.& B. "specs" that year — a spectacular parade which circled the hippodrome at some point in the show. This one had a Nepalese theme, and Buck rode in a howdah on the back of an elephant.

We also used him to talk a little about "Gargie," our name for Gargantua, the gigantic and fearsome gorilla. Gargie had a special air conditioned cage and it would be wheeled around the hippodrome track slowly, so that all the spectators could see the magnificent beast. A spotlight played on the celebrated animal hunter, who narrated the story about gorillas in the wild and delivered the specifications on our prize example.

I feel the publicity department benefited most of all from Frank Buck. By this time he was almost a legend and there was hardly a person in America who hadn't heard of him. When I called a radio station to suggest an interview with Buck, the question was not "whether" but "how soon can you be here?"

Buck was a little forgetful and for some reason he had trouble remembering my name. I was quite busy whenever the show was in town and couldn't always show up in the backyard precisely at the appointed time to pick up Buck for radio interviews. He frequently would ask, "Where is that narrow-assed agent?"

Buck was hired to present his animal act at the New York World's Fair in 1939. At the same time he bought the rights to a strange concession. He opened a booth where he would sell the right to toss three baseballs at a shelf of empty glass bottles. There weren't any prizes — you got nothing if you broke them all and you got nothing if you broke none. He cleaned up. "Some people just like to break things," he said.

Frank Buck, left, and ''that narrow-assed agent.''

18

"DE LAWD"

Professionally speaking, there have been two great loves in my life. The first, of course, is the circus. That must ever be first, for if it is not, they you really aren't "circus people." But, in my psyche at least, there is room for more than one great love, and the other is the legitimate theater. If you have read this far you know that the affair started back in Delaware, and it has never abated.

Actors traditionally are referred to as Thesians in honor of the ancient Greek theater's poet, Thespis. In 534 B.C. he changed show business by being the first player to step out of the story-telling chorus to speak solo lines in the impersonation of a character. This radical departure from the norm greatly angered a statesman named Solon. He argued that an actor who pretended to be someone else was an outright liar, and that if the practice continued it might soon find its deceitful way into the world of business.

Thespis nevertheless was an immediate smash hit and a new style of theatrical presentation was born. I often ponder that this great innovator should serve also as patron saint of producers and the advance agents of their traveling attractions. Thespis was the first of these stalwarts to take his show on the road.

It may be argued that he had a couple of forerunners. Noah toured his floating wild animal menagerie during 40 matinees and nights, and Moses kept his much larger company on the road for at least that many years.

Still, Thespis remains the first of our ancestral barnstormers. Each time I prepared to front another Broadway show on tour I saluted him, not only in honor of actors I have loved to work with, but also because he knew the territory.

I have a favorite story about this business of shifting from circus to theater press agentry. My old circus friend "Willie" Wilkins from Logansport, Indiana, acquired a job with the small-time repertory company of New England's famed Coarce Payton. Payton billed himself as the "World's Best Bad Actor."

When Willie arrived for work, the circus agent was confounded to discover that he was required to prepare promptly a set of stories about Payton's plays and their actors, and Willie was no writer. In some desperation, he sought to solve his problem by using the same set of stories that had served him well during his summer circusing. Wilkins took the release he had prepared for the dogs, ponies and monkeys in the Gentry Brothers Circus and used it for the players in Payton's theatrical troupe, changing only the names of the performers. There was understandable resentment when the former circus press agent neglected to omit one line. It described his performers as having "almost human intelligence."

Until well into the present century traveling dramatic shows on limited budgets occasionally purchased pre-printed posters. Printing plants sold leftovers from companies that had folded before they could use up their lithographs, or pay for them either.

Usually the posters were handsome pictorials bearing full-color pictures of prominent stage stars and scenes from their plays. These never appeared in the repertoire of these small-time operators. Those troupes presented familiar old melodramas or cheap vaudeville entertainment instead of the advertised attraction.

An advance agent for one of these lesser dramatic tourers was not greatly surprised to find that on the front of the tank-town op'ry house where his show was to appear there appeared an impressive lithograph left over from a recent date. It advertised the eminent Richard Mansfield in his favorite role as Cyrano de Bergerac. Engaging the theater manager in friendly conversation, the publicist finally said, "I see that you played Mansfield here week before last."

"Yes," replied the local impresario, 'the sonofabitch fell out of his trapeze and bent my best footlights.''

It wasn't until the summer of 1932 that I realized what a grip the legitimate boards had on me. Unless one was a performer or had an executive job with the circus, he was out of work from the time the circus headed toward winter quarters in the fall of each year. Four to six months of unemployment each year isn't very appeal-

Ethel Merman, star of the musical Call Me Madam, *fronted by me in 1952.*

ing to a young man, so I was able to hook up with a show that in turn hooked me for life — *The Green Pastures.*

I loved working for that show, even though my initial hitch with this Pulitzer Prize-winning blockbuster was brief. It ended on Christmas Eve 1932. My wife and our 8-month-old son were traveling with me. Our hotel, Chancellor Hall, was conveniently located near the Forrest Theater on Walnut Street in Philadelphia.

We had a one-month lease which I was unable to get the hotel manager to cancel or reduce. In a strange coincidence, 20 years later I booked most of our big *Call Me Madam* company into the same address, and because of this the management gave me a complimentary room. So I did get my money back, even if it did take two decades to do it.

The late Pat Harrington Sr. (along with Ethel Merman), was in that show. We didn't know that Pat was a diabetic until we were notified by a policeman that he was being held in the local station house. Pat had forgotten to keep track of his insulin schedule and had gone into shock. Upon awakening, he wrongly concluded that we had a matinee performance slated for that afternoon. He put on a bathrobe and slippers and set off to find the theater. Fortunately, he was picked up by an officer who knew that everyone who appears to be drunk may not be. They forced him to drink orange juice and brought our man out of trouble. He made the show on time that night. Victims of this disease sometimes respond promptly to the high sugar content of orange juice or soft drinks such as Coca Cola.

Harrington had a similar experience when he played in a production of the same musical at the famed outdoor Municipal Theater in St. Louis while I was the manager. On that occasion the manager of his hotel called me. I suspected it was the same old diabetic routine of losing track of the doses, taking a long nap and waking up not knowing where he was. Harrington recognized me, but thought we were in his home in New York. We forced him to swallow orange juice. A physican examined him and he was able to go on that night. Finally we persuaded him that he must wear a bracelet or a necklace to identify him as a diabetic. He resisted this, saying it embarrassed him to have it known that he suffered from diabetes. He finally consented and this may have added some years to his wonderful life.

Back in the early 1930s *The Green Pastures* was the biggest show on tour, numbering almost 100 people among its cast, musicians and stage technicians. Its scenery and lighting required four baggage cars because one of its spectacular effects employed the biggest theatrical treadmill since the days of *Ben Hur*.

I was in Charlottesville, Virginia, some three weeks ahead of this whopper of a show, when I discovered that the theater we were to play had a stage with only four sets of lines for hanging scenery. Furthermore, there were no regular dressing rooms for the cast.

The show had been sold out three weeks ahead of its playing date; obviously the town wanted it. So I sent a wire to my company manager, Clarence Jacobson, telling him of our space problems. He fired back a snappy "We can play it on a dining room table!" However, after the difficult date had been played successfully, our manager backed off a bit to send me another message reading, "I said a dining room table, not a bridge table!"

There was a mechanical problem on stage left at Miami University in Oxford, Ohio. The players in the exodus scene had to trudge the treadmill in the direction opposite from the usual. Actor Alonzo Fenderson stayed close to his rather slow-witted partner, fearing the worst. And when his companion indeed started the wrong way, he jerked his arm and barked, "Follow me, you dumb sonofabitch!" There was a problem with the treadmill all right, but unfortunately the acoustics that night were perfect!

Finding suitable lodging accommodations for our big cast of Negro actors was difficult. With the exception of hotels in New England, most hotels would not take them in. Only in the larger cities could we find hotels catering exclusively to blacks. *The Green Pastures* received its most enthusiastic reception from both press and public in Dixie. Our star, Richard B. Harrison, was invited to speak from the pulpit of Atlanta's most prestigious church. Yet, I could not get him into a white hotel.

With the help of churches and the YMCA, we usually found accommodations for our people in the homes of ministers, educators, attorneys, and prominent business people in the black community.

But in Big Spring, Texas, where we were booked to play on the stage of a fine new auditorium-theater, I was told by the house manager that the black area homes were not suitable to serve our company's players.

The theater's handsome new dressing rooms were equipped with plumbing, and a big boiler room could be used as a kind of makeshift dormitory for most of the males in our cast. So I offered to rent army cots and blankets for the use of these facilities.

The auditorium manager reluctantly agreed to this arrangement, but later I learned that as soon as I had left town the auditorium's custodian convinced his employer that he could find good lodging

Richard B. Harrison, "De Lawd" in The Green Pastures.

Harrison, left, and Salem Tutt Whitney, who played the role of Noah in The Green Pastures.

for rent among his friends in the black community, thus relieving the theater of the inconvenience of putting up a big troupe under its roof.

The further report I received was that a number of our people lost money and clothing in the primitive rooms they rented, and that one of the young women discovered that the place where she was expected to stay was a whorehouse. For all this trouble the troupe put the blame not on the show's advance man or even the auditorium's management, but upon poor Clarence Jacobson, our company manager. He was handy, being at their beck and call at all times.

The Actors' Equity shop steward for our show wired a detailed report to his New York office. It concluded with the complaint that in addition to all the other problems encountered at Big Spring, the company manager was hostile.

In an exchange of telegrams between our general manager in New York and our company manager on the road, the latter was asked to explain his alleged hostility. A good deal of laughter was generated at the Lambs Club when it was reported that the seven-word reply from Jacobson was simply, "Who ever heard of a hostile Jew?"

It was easy to become fond of our star and I enjoyed Richard B. Harrison's company on many occasions. His starring role was that of "De Lawd." On a lonely New Year's Eve in a Philadelphia coffee shop he recalled to me his days and nights as a Pullman porter on other December 31sts long ago.

I can remember the day I took him on a newspaper interview in a Michigan city. I remarked that this might be the closest I'd ever be to the Deity. And "De Lawd" quipped that it probably was the first time a press agent had been anywhere near heaven.

Then in the winter of 1934, our Canadian dates included London, Ontario. That was the city of his birth as well as that of some other giants of the performing arts, including George Primrose of the Primrose and West Minstrels, and Guy Lombardo, who named his dance orchestra the "Royal Canadians."

Here, in his dressing room backstage, I interviewed Harrison for an article in the *Christian Herald Magazine*. The story's title, "Jes Like A Natchel Man" is in the dialect of the show. God in his celestial "office" has just reminded his "secretary, the angel Gabriel, that "Even bein' Gawd ain't a bed of roses." He has become disenchanted with the ungrateful behavior of mankind in the beautiful world that He created. Now He intends to pay it a visit incognito, walking the earth "jes like a natchel man."

This is the way the story was published only a short time before the sad and unexpected death of the great actor in 1935:

19

JES LIKE A NATCHEL MAN

Sixty-five years span the time between my birth in London, Ontario, the son of fugitive slaves, and the night of February 26, 1930, when I walked out on the stage of the Mansfield Theater in New York to answer the most amazing entrance cue in all stage history: "Gangway! Gangway for de Lawd Gawd Jehovah!"

Some of those years were pretty lean and most of them fraught with adversity of one sort or another, but scarcely one of them passed without contributing something that has helped me in my portrayal of "de Lawd." I believe in a manifest destiny. My own life proves it — at least to my own satisfaction.

For over 1,600 times on more than a hundred stages and in 43 states I've spoken that famous line from *The Green Pastures* — "Even bein' Gawd ain't a bed of roses." Let it be stated here and now that I never meant it!

If the truth be known, being "de Lawd" of *The Green Pastures* has been an inspiration, the fulfillment of a life's ambition — a bed of roses!

Hundreds of times I have been asked how it feels to

play God. In all humility I confess that the part has done something to me. I do not believe anyone could play my role without feeling that he had something alive in his hands — something that transcends its mere physical boundaries. Something that shines like laughter on the face of a happy child. Something that can sear like a flame, then soothe like the still waters of the psalm from which the title of the play was taken.

I feel that we of *The Green Pastures* company are instruments of Fate, chosen to help establish better understanding between our people and white people. And, strangely enough, the medium through which this is being done is a white man's play based on a white man's book about Negroes.

Roark Bradford, author of *Ol' Man an' His Chillun,* the book which inspired Marc Connelly in his writing of the play, *The Green Pastures,* is a Southerner who understands the Negro as do few white men. Consequently, the language of the play is a classic example of simplicity. It is as simple as the religion of the untutored plantation Negro. And it is just as effective. Miss Beatrice Jones, drama critic of the *Times-Picayune,* paid the race a rather nice compliment upon the occasion of the show's visit to New Orleans. Her review contained this paragraph: "These people believe what they are playing. They are not really playing at all. For the time being, they are the children of Israel, or Noah and his family, or the angels in Heaven, and this passionate sincerity gives it the touch of poetry that causes people to compare *The Green Pastures* with a miracle play or other religious expressions of the Middle Ages. The theater alone could not have given us a play like this. The Negroes themselves have added a grace, a child-like charm that is characteristic of their race and that is in itself an art.''

''De Lawd'' appears in sixteen of the eighteen scenes of *The Green Pastures* and it is true that in these scenes I have tried to be a deity who concerns himself with the more important sins and tries to overlook some of the little ones. I have tried to give the character the Negro touch, which is another way of saying I have tried to make it human. I believe in my own heart that the Lord does want to give us humans just as long a rope as he can pay out and that is the way I have tried to play the part.

More than a million people have seen *The Green Pastures,* yet it might not be amiss to say something about its general theme and character as a play. The play is a portrayal of various Biblical events as they might be imagined by thousands of untutored Negroes in the bayou country of the deep South. These unlettered but devout black Christians think of Heaven as one eternal holiday, where elaborate fish frys are plentiful and where "de Lawd" keeps a box of thunderbolts ready for the wicked of the Earth. To these naive minds, the court of "Ol' King Pharaoh" resembles nothing so much as a Negro lodge hall, and the revelry in the city of Babylon suggests that of a black-and-tan night club. The celestial office of "de Lawd" is a replica of a shabby lawyer's business establishment and Noah's Ark looks like a Mississippi River houseboat.

As the curtain opens on the first scene, Sunday School is in session at a little Negro church in the South. A class of pickaninnies listens in awe and astonishment to the pious, elderly superintendent putting his own interpretation on sacred history as revealed in the first two chapters of Genesis. The ideas of this teacher plus the thoughts that filter into the minds of the children, constitute the key to the 17 scenes that follow. From this point, the play deals with the Creation; then runs the gamut of Old Testament history as "de Lawd" himself "walks de earth in de shape of a natchel man" from time to time, conversing with the mighty men he has made.

"De Lawd" creates Adam and Eve; drives Cain "clean out of de country;" reproves his "chillun" for breaking the Sabbath with jazz music and crap games; and makes a magician out of the stuttering Moses so he may force Pharaoh to free the Hebrew "chillun." He helps Joshua win the battle of Jericho and He takes the aged and blind Moses up the mountain to His own particular Promised Land, because as He explains to Moses, "I made you a promise and I ain't goin' to do you out of it." In spite of the rich comedy that threads its way through *The Green Pastures,* the laughter it provokes is never very far removed from tears.

The music of the play, contributed by Hall Johnson's

"Heavenly Choir," serves as the loom on which the pattern of this play is woven. While *The Green Pastures* was in the making, Marc Connelly and Roark Bradford, the authors, spent hours in New Orleans listening to Alma Lillie Hubbard sing spirituals. She sang almost continuously, creating a spell that was broken only when she paused to supply the name of an old Negro hymn which impressed the authors as being particularly suitable to a scene of the play. This laborious and sincere effort on the part of the playwright to mount his gem in a setting of stirring native music has created among his audiences the feeling that *The Green Pastures* is a sort of poetry set to music.

When I agreed to play "de Lawd" of *The Green Pastures,* I little realized that all my background had prepared me for this very thing. Even the hard physical work I had done as a boy had hardened me against the inevitable rigors of such a part. Undoubtedly this boyhood physical training is accountable to some extent at least for the fact that I never have missed a performance of the play.

I think it was from my mother that I acquired a taste for the stage. While a slave in St. Louis, she had attended plays frequently with the young women whom she served. Shortly before I was born, my mother indulged in a luxury she could ill afford and attended a Shakespearean performance in one of the Canadian theaters. It was *Richard The Third,* and so moved was my mother that she named me Richard.

While still in my teens, I made my way to Detroit. There I continued the education which my parents had managed through hardship to provide. Edward Weitzel, at that time drama editor of the *Detroit Free Press,* and a very great influence in the world of the theater, befriended me. Through his encouragement I resolved to turn my footsteps toward the stage.

In 1891, I felt myself ready for a platform debut. For several years thereafter I toured Canada and later the southern United States on Chautauqua and Lyceum circuits, reading in tents, churches and schools. My reading of *The Merchant Of Venice* was said to be the best thing I did and critics were kind enough to say that were it not for the fact that I was a Negro I would have been one of the

One of the great comedic roles in The Green Pastures *was that of*
"Gabe" (the angel Gabriel), as played by Doe Doe Green.

great "Shylocks" of our time.

Success in the entertainment field was not easy for a Negro in those days. Again and again I was driven from my chosen work to some distasteful employment in order that I might eke out a precarious living. At various times I was a bellhop, waiter, and jack-of-all-trades.

Finally, I became a teacher of my people at Agricultural and Technical College in Greensboro, North Carolina. I had been actively engaged there as teacher of speech and dramatic art for seven years when the part of "de Lawd" was offered to me.

The happiest moment in the history of the play came when the announcement was made — on May 13, 1930 — that *The Green Pastures* had won the Pulitzer Prize. I was the first member of the cast to receive the glad tidings, conveyed to me, as I recall, by our stage manager. I rushed backstage to spread the news. It was Wesley Hill, who played the part of the angel Gabriel, that I encountered first. Always vivid in my memory will be his words as he snatched up his golden trumpet from a nearby property table and said, "It's time to blow the horn."

About a year later, I was to have a delightful surprise when the then lieutenant governor Herbert H. Lehman of New York presented me with the coveted Spingarn medal which is given annually to the Negro who is thought to have made the highest achievement for his race during the preceding year. This award was established two decades ago by J.E. Spingarn, author and scholar, and for many years a director of the National Association for the Advancement of Colored People. Among recent recipients of the honor have been Roland Hayes, singer; President Mordecai W. Johnson of Howard University; and James Weldon Johnson, poet.

Of the more than 100 cites that the play has visited, probably the dates the cast enjoyed most were the Tuskegee Institute engagement in the fall of 1933, and the Hampton Institute presentation early in the present tour. There, *The Green Pastures* was presented to audiences comprised almost exclusively of Negroes, representing not only the faculty and student body, but hundreds who had traveled many miles from surrounding towns to witness the show at that particular presentation.

Harrison broke a color line in his native Canada when he was guest of honor at this Rotary Club banquet in London, Ontario, his birthplace.

Many of my Northern friends were amazed that educators and city officials of Greensboro, North Carolina, staged a reception in my honor when *The Green Pastures* visited that city a year ago last autumn. To one who had spent seven years in Greensboro, this honor is not so surprising. The intelligent Southerner more often than not treats the Negro with rare understanding. It has been said that *The Green Pastures* did more to help erase the remaining prejudice of the South than any other agent within the past decade. Roark Bradford, a Southerner who was raised with Negroes on his father's plantation, has paid the following tribute to our race; "The Negro has done things in the past 200 years that the white man hasn't been able to do in 2,000 years. He has created for himself a language of beauty and rhythm more expressive than any language extant. He has created for himself a religion that produces a spiritual peace and rest in his life."

When I have played "de Lawd" a few hundred more times, I expect to return to the Agricultural and Technical College in Greensboro and take up my work where I

left off. Of all the places I have been, I like North Carolina best of all. Yes, I'd still like to play "Shylock" and I'd
like to have a hand in the true Negro opera that is bound to
be produced one of these days. But if I should not live
long enough to achieve these things, still my life has been
happy and no flight of the imagination could have prepared me for the success and satisfaction that have come
to me through my portrayal of "de Lawd."

As I bring this article to a conclusion, I am sitting in my
dressing room at London, Ontario, just a few steps from
the corner where I sold newspapers as a ragged boy more
than a half century ago. Soon our play will be five years of
age — a long life for a theatrical presentation in this day.

In a few minutes the curtain will open on the second
scene of the play and "Gabe" will shout "Gangway!"
Then I'll walk out and create the Earth for the 1,530th
time. Then I think of the stormy night on the Ohio River
when the slave who was to become my father swam the
icy waters to freedom. I remember my mother and the
sacrifices she made to give me a sound start in life. I wish
she were alive to see that what has come to her boy was
perhaps worth the effort.

Now the first scene of the play is finished and the angels
at the fish fry are singing "Rise and Shine." Four minutes
until my own cue. I must go now and stand in the wings.
Something akin to the nervousness I felt on opening night
invariably comes to me just before my entrance. Perhaps
it is to remind me that my role is not merely a part in a
play. For, with all its shrewd stagecraft, its sublime comedy and dramatization, *The Green Pastures* is not just a
show. Each time we present it we lay bare the soul of
a race.

As "Gabriel" standing here beside me, adjusts his
wings and clears his throat in preparation for his entrance,
I remember the remark of an educator who had watched
one of our performances; "I went to the Passion Play
expecting to find God and I saw a show; I went to *The
Green Pastures* expecting to see a show and I found God."

Just a couple of years after my service with *The Green Pastures*
I was asked to front the road company of another Pulitzer Prize-
winning show, *The Old Maid*. This starred Helen Menken and

Two legendary stars of the legitimate theater: Judith Anderson, left, and Helen Menken. They headlined the cast of The Old Maid, *which was fronted by me in 1935.*

Judith Anderson, and I don't think that I have ever worked with two finer ladies. I suppose people might think that I would have my hands full, trying to give equal attention to two of the greatest actresses of the English speaking stage, but it was quite the opposite. They were perfectly cooperative with me and I was proud to count them both as personal friends.

We were playing San Francisco during the run and Judith came to me with distress in her eyes. A local gossip columnist had written that she was involved with an actor and it just wasn't true. She wanted to know what I would suggest she do about it, and I told her to do nothing at all; to not even dignify the allegation with a reply. That is what she did and the matter was forgotten about by the next day.

20

FREAKS?

Long before we began to number circus sideshow personalities among our friends, management had ceased describing them as "freaks." Instead we called our exotic attractions "strange people" or "human curiosities."

Of course they looked different, often to a startling or even shocking degree. But therein lay their drawing power on the midway, and I never felt that circuses and carnivals exploited unduly the physical handicaps and misfortunes of these members of the performing personnel. In a world of so-called normal people there always will be some misfits, but here was a place where their very abnormalities became their livelihood. A curious public would pay to see them, and most certainly they preferred this to accepting charity or to being kept out of sight by embarrassed relatives.

The sideshow entertainers invariably received good treatment by their employers. They were served the same food as the stars of the big top and were respected by all in a warm and friendly world where a glandular whim of nature might have produced a giant or a midget, a "living skeleton" or a "mountain of feminine allure." Excessive facial hair might invent a "monkey girl," thick dermal scales an "alligator boy," or a peculiar skin splotching a "leopard woman." Hair like sheep's wool crowned the heads of two albino brothers presented to the public years ago as "ambassadors from Mars found floating on a raft in the midst of the Pacific Ocean."

In our Ringling Brothers and Barnum & Bailey Circus sideshow

"Cliko," being interviewed in the 1930s by George Hicks of NBC.

there were some genuine anthropological oddities. There was a centenarian billed as a "Wild African Bushman from the Kalihari Desert." And that he was indeed, except for the fact that "Cliko" (called that because of the peculiar clicking sound in his speech) was not wild at all, but of exceptionally good nature. His age and origin were authenticated and his statue graced New York City's famed Museum of Natural History.

During the fours months when the circus was in Florida winter quarters our friendly "wild man" stayed with a family at a rather swank uptown apartment address in Manhattan. His sudden appearance from an elevator often startled strangers. There he was the special friend of the family's little school age daughter. She not only didn't consider him as particularly unusual; she assumed that probably in her own schoolroom there were other little girls who had a bushman for a playmate.

Francisco Lentini had been born with a third leg growing from one side of his hip. Instead of choosing amputation he put this abnormality to work for him. It was stiff and couldn't be used to support his weight, but on his platform in the sideshow tent Lentini used it to kick a football to prove that it nevertheless was a real third leg. Which it was.

Because of her grotesquely exaggerated facial features, Mary Ann Bevan was exhibited as "The Homeliest Woman In The World." Her circus sideshow salary enabled her to send a son through medical school. To her fellow troupers who loved her, "The Homeliest Woman In The World" was the most beautiful person with the show. A magazine story about Mary Ann Bevan brought its author a second check with a letter from the editor stating that the reader response was so remarkable that he felt the writer was underpaid.

Frieda Pushnik from the coal mining region of Pennsylvania was born without arms or legs. A loving big sister carried her about as though she were a clothes basket and never complained, nor did Frieda. Instead, on a raised platform in the sideshow tent, she demonstrated some of the things she had taught herself to do with her mouth, such as using a typewriter with a stick held tightly in her teeth.

An early-day television showing of the circus during its Madison Square Garden springtime engagement included such attractive sideshow personalities as Giant Jack Earl, the Doll Family of Midgets, and others. The program director balked at televising Miss Pushnik as possibly being repulsive to the station's viewers — that

WEEI hostess Priscilla Fortesque interviews the circus midget, Harry Doll.

is, until he was reminded that among the huge television audience would be hospitalized war-scarred paraplegics and countless others tragically wounded who might very well be encouraged by seeing how one so grievously and permanently handicapped from birth had refused to accept defeat.

An artist for the *Philadelphia Sunday Ledger* did a well-received page some years ago that showed circus sideshow "freaks" study-ing with rapt attention and considerable amusement the people in a crowd who had paid to see them.

For years circuses were not permitted to exhibit their human curiosities in Canada, where belief in prenatal influence prevailed. To ridicule this, a sideshow executive of our acquaintance would effect a dourly serious manner and say that, unfortunately, the superstition had been proved for a fact. Then he would tell about the pregnant woman who had been so frightened by an escaped circus polar bear that she had delivered a baby with bare feet.

The best sideshow "talkers," usually misnamed "barkers" by the public, not only are students of crowd psychology, they are skilled practitioners of their calling — to convert midway spectators to ticket buyers.

Once a reporter asked the dignified talker-manager, Clyde In-galls, how this salesmanship is applied in different sections of the country. He replied, "In the East we appeal to the mind, in the Mid-west to the heart, and in the South to the passions!"

In some circuses of the long ago, no sideshow was complete without its hootchy kootchy dancers, presented as an extra-fare finale on a curtained-off stage at the rear of the tent. An appeal by the show's talker to the male customers after some mildly sugges-tive gyrations in a standard sample routine carried the promise that in the private exhibition to follow "the dancers will dance without!"

Then came the request that the customers remove their hats "because, after all, these dancers **are** ladies." The dancers then presented the same routine as before. Then some sucker would yell, "Whaddya mean, 'they'll dance without?' Without **what,** mister?"

The talker then replied, "Why, without your hats, of course, gentlemen; without your hats. Thank you and goodnight."

21

WHAT'S IN A NAME

Because I have devoted countless working days and nights to newspapers and their personnel, I like to reflect from time to time on the names of those papers. To me they are interesting, and occasionally amusing as well.

Of course, there are many *Posts, Dispatches, Couriers, Chronicles, Observers, Messengers, Reporters* and an occasional *Enterprise*. There are *Beacons, Records, Graphics, Calls* and, in state government cities, papers labeled *Capital* or *Capitol*.

I think a rather good-sounding name is Portland's *Oregonian;* across the nation there are many *Leaders, Times, Bulletins,* papers called simply *Press, Democrat, Republican, Telegraph, Pantograph* and just *News.*

Among numerous *Gazettes,* I doubt that there is another that can claim such prestigious longevity as our Delaware, Ohio, daily. It has been in continuous publication by the Thomson family all the way back to the 1860s when it was the *Olentangy Gazette.* Then it was named for the town's river.

Labels like *Patriot, Banner, Statesman, Constitution, Eagle, Sentinel, American* and *Guardian* are not uncommon. And there is at least one *Vindicator,* in Youngstown, Ohio. There are *Globes, Worlds,* and here and there a *Mail.* Unique, I believe, are Cleveland's *Plain Dealer,* the *Toledo Blade,* the *Memphis Commercial Appeal* and *Press Scimitar,* and the *Light* in San Antonio. Occasionally we find spelling differences, such as *Cincinnati Enquirer* and

COLE BROTHERS
★ CIRCUS ★
LIFETIME PASS

"AMERICA" CALLIOPE AT PRESIDENT HARRY TRUMAN'S AND VICE PRESIDENT ALBEN BARKLEY'S INAUGURATION PARADE, WASHINGTON, D. C. JANUARY 20, 1949.

RINGLING BROS AND BARNUM & BAILEY CIRCUS

1954 Radio-TV Working Pass

To Restricted Depts. of Circus

NOT GOOD FOR SEATS - -

Issued to .... Date ....

Place ....

Signed ....

PLEASE
READ
OTHER

RINGLING BROS AND BARNUM & BAILEY COMBINED SHOWS INC.

10 ROCKEFELLER PLAZA NEW YORK

BEV KELLEY

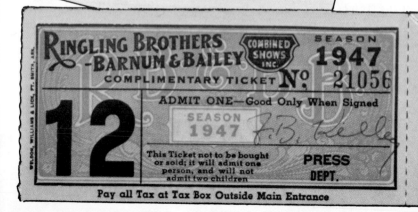

RINGLING BROTHERS - BARNUM & BAILEY

COMBINED SHOWS INC.

SEASON 1947

COMPLIMENTARY TICKET No. 21056

12

ADMIT ONE—Good Only When Signed

SEASON 1947   F. B. Kelley

This Ticket not to be bought or sold; it will admit one person, and will not admit two children

PRESS DEPT.

Pay all Tax at Tax Box Outside Main Entrance

WELDON, WILLIAMS & LICK, FT. SMITH, ARK.

RESERVED SEAT CHECK

To be EXCHANGED when entering Main Entrance for A NUMBERED SEAT

Individual Seat will be held until 2 P. M. and 8 P. M.

12

Philadelphia Inquirer.

I know of only two *Palladiums.* That is a good name for a news-paper. A palladium is a safeguard, according to my dictionary. One of these papers is in Oswego, New York; the other is the *Palladium-Item* in Richmond, Indiana. Astronomy, too, accounts for media names. Many evening publications are called the *Star* and morning sheets the *Sun.* And Battle Creek, Michigan, once had a *Moon Journal.*

Prominent among unusual titles I remember are the *Hustler,* in Pittsburgh, Tennessee; and the *Mesquiter,* which serves Mesquite, Texas. And then there's the *Hungry Horse News* at Columbia Falls, Montana. The editor, publisher and photographer, Mel Ruder, named his Pulitzer Prize-winning weekly for the nearby Hungry Horse Dam, which is near the entrance to Glacier National Park.

I have been in the city rooms of most of the above, planting stories about various circuses or traveling shows. But I never had the opportunity to meet Mel Ruder, although I have corresponded with him for more than three decades. I visited his plant as a circus press agent, and since he was out of town, I hammered out an announcement story. I left it with some photographs and a letter on a huge tree stump that served as a desk in his attractive office.

A few days later I was pleasantly surprised with a copy of an editorial, which observed that the author wished the voluminous press releases sent to him by Washington bureaucrats were half as interesting as that written by circus advance men. This wise observation forever established the editor as one of the world's most preceptive and accurate critics, with me at least.

I've saved the best for last. Many years ago, during a train ride through Missouri, I talked with a passenger whose family published a paper in the town if Linn, in the central part of the state. The name on the masthead is the *Unterrified Democrat.* I did not have time to ask about the origin, but I've always assumed that its owners may have been the only Democrats in a community loaded with Republicans, and they wanted everyone to know that they were not afraid even if they were outnumbered.

Some of the passes, calling cards and tickets I gave out during my career as a circus publicist. The card in the upper left corner was issued in a cloth pouch and handed out to dignitaries and media people as a souvenir. It is made of brass, into which red lettering has been etched.

22

ONE MORE ROUND

One night in New York City during my early years of radio promotion of the circus, I appeared on an interview program. One of the other guests was James J. Corbett, the former heavyweight boxing champion of the world. At the age of 70 Corbett was still the same trim, handsome and articulate personality he had been when he boxed the title away from the slugger, John L. Sullivan. He became known thereafter by sportswriters and fans alike by the appropriate label of "Gentleman Jim" Corbett.

On this occasion he was fielding questions from the studio audience, such as: "What makes a champion?" The reply from the king of the ring required but four words: "Fight one more round." My mind frequently returned to this incident as our circus had to fight round after round against staggering adversity during the years of World War II.

Never before had I felt such towering pride in being part of a battle against odds, for at no other time in its history had the Ringling Brothers and Barnum & Bailey Circus so heroically lived up to its traditional title as "The Greatest Show On Earth."

All the world loves a champion, and our part of the world seems to have even greater affection for a fallen hero who comes up fighting. When our Big Top was destroyed by a fire that took 168 lives in Hartford, Connecticut, on July 6, 1944, the know-it-alls quickly predicted that the circus never could come back. Its proud banners lay ground into the embers of the saddest tragedy ever to befall an American amusement institution. Previous fires, storms, railroad wrecks and all other catastrophies combined paled by comparison to the damage wrought in that one terrible hour.

The prophets of doom forecast that we would be eaten up with debt, torn asunder by lawsuits and broken by friction from within our own ranks, but they reckoned without the stuff that circus people are made of. There are really only two days in the touring calendar of this peripatetic world, today and tomorrow. The citizens of the sawdust trail seldom look back unless it is to profit from a mistake.

There was a trumpeting reply to pessimists who were ready to sound taps over the fallen giant which they predicted never would rise from the ashes of the Hartford conflagration. In a triumphal and unprecedented comeback, The Greatest Show On Earth hid its sorrows, smiled through the faces of its clowns and pointed the tongues of its bright red wagons again toward the open road.

I waited in a police station house through the night of the fire. I wanted to be the first to talk with our top executives when they were released on bail the following morning.

Five circus men had been arrested like common criminals and held in custody on technical charges. These were our chief electrician, the superintendent of seats, the boss canvasman, our general manager, and James Haley. Robert Ringling, the circus president, was at home in Chicago and absent from the show on that fateful night, so Haley, a vice president, was jailed in his stead.

I was in disagreement with our circus attorney who thought that we should prepare a press release that stressed the generosity of our performing talent during years of appearances in hospitals and in support of worthy charity benefit shows. He wanted special emphasis placed on our daily war effort through the giving of free circus tickets to purchasers of war bonds.

I opposed any such position, arguing that this was no time for the circus to be blowing its own horn; that instead, our top executive should make a statement expressing simply and sincerely our heartfelt sympathy to the families of the victims. At the same time I thought we should congratulate the city's police and fire departments, the remarkable non-stop performance of the over-burdened hospital personnel, and the local chapter of the American Red Cross.

By the time our officials were released, I had put into writing an expression of these sentiments and all concerned, including our lawyer, approved my approach as a statement suitable for distribution.

It seemed as though almost everyone in town had suffered the loss of a relative or a friend or knew someone who had. However, there generally was an attitude of sympathy rather than of blame and bitterness toward the circus people.

Hartford newspapers treated the subject with fairness and in sharp contrast to a publication in a neighboring city that front-paged a two column picture of our officials upon their release from custody on that miserable morning after the fire. The caption read, "They Saved Their Animals."

The men were, of course, sleepless, unshaven and distraught, resembling nothing so much as skid row bums. This represented shameless and inexcusably unfair journalism, for it implied that the primary concern of the circus had been for its property rather than for the lives of its guests.

Our people had done nothing to save the animals. The Big Top that caught fire was not far from the wild animal menagerie tent, but whatever breeze there was had spread flame in other directions. Circus employees had all worked to rescue people from the main tent, and not animals from their enclosure which wasn't afire at any time.

The history of the traveling circuses is replete with calamities since 1793, when Gen. George Washington visited John Bill Rickett's circus in Philadelphia. That was the first American circus.

Circuses have burned down, blown away, had railroad wrecks and gone broke. Not until the Hartford tragedy did the attending public suffer the brunt of the blow, and circus people will never get over that part of it. They behaved courageously and won the commendation of the city authorities and that of the Red Cross. The death of children spreads an impenetrable pall over even traditionally optimistic circus troupers and they do not forget.

Following the catastrophe, the circus returned to its headquarters at Sarasota, Florida. There it accomplished in one month the herculean task of converting its physical properties into the kind of arena presentation that can be exhibited in stadiums, ball parks and fair grounds. In this manner it played out the remainder of its touring season under open sky, or, as an Akron, Ohio newspaper man termed it, the "blue heaven circuit."

The circus executives who were charged with technical manslaughter received sentences that were stayed by the same Hartford judge who had handed them down. The sentences were stayed so that these key men could help get the show on its way again.

There was no official comment from the circus itself, but editorial comment around the nation charged that justice would not be served in sending these men to jail. They had pleaded *nolo contendere* (no contest) and thrown themselves on the mercy of the court in preference to standing trial.

Had they insisted on a trial, weeks would have been consumed and so many additional circus executives and performers brought to Hartford as witnesses, that the circus would have been crippled in the midst of its all-out effort to operate successfully and pay off the claims of fire victims.

The circus could have filed for bankruptcy; instead it assumed the obligation of paying off lawsuits of staggering sums, took voluntary receivership to expedite the settlement of claims and agreed to accept the decisions of a special committee in settlement of claims. It required several years to pay off those settlements, which totaled over $4 million.

The circus had announced that it would not exhibit under tents again until it could secure flameproof canvas. There was an effective product made in Baltimore by the William E. Hooper & Sons Company and called "Firechief." It had been used for Army and Navy tents and because of wartime restrictions had not been available for non-military purposes. "Firechief" treated canvas so that no fire could spread beyond the area of flame applied to it. The flameproofing would last the lifetime of the fabric.

When it finally became available without military priority in 1945, the biggest circus in the world needed enough flameproofing to treat 75,000 square yards of canvas. There were 40-odd large and small tents of the traveling city. The Big Top alone was 500 feet long and 200 feet wide.

Our operation stayed geared to the war effort like many another commercial institution. Its four trains traveled under regulations set forth by the Office of Defense Transportation. Our city-to-city effort had been set up with the United States Treasury Department on behalf of War Bond Appeal. The circus had accounted for sales in excess of $200 million over a period of two years.

The trains of the big show were sidetracked for hospital trains and important shipping of war materiel. There were 904 stars in the Ringling Brothers and Barnum & Bailey Circus service flag. The shortage of labor was felt in all departments, for where we once had 960 working men to handle the show's physical requirements, now there were less than 600.

This meant that after the stars of the rings, the air and the hippodrome track had risked their lives under the Big Top, they had to change from spangles to work clothes to dismantle their tent city.

There were 75,000 yards of new canvas treated with flame-proof-ing substance when the circus resumed its performances under the big top.

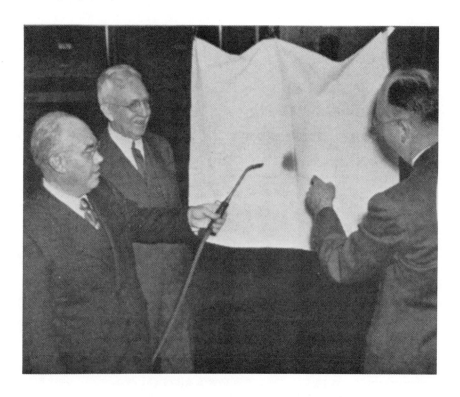

Bob Ringling applies an acetylene torch to the new circus canvas after it had been flameproofed.

The next morning they would help put it up again in another town. Ushers, ticket sellers, grooms and concessionaires "doubled in brass and overalls." The circus people have a phrase for such devotion to duty: "being **with** it and **for** it."

People who are old enough to have seen the great old circus street parades remember how seldom they were on schedule. Waiting for them seemed to last forever.

They had come downtown early to find a good viewing spot, and usually the parades were late. Maybe the show had had to fight rain and mud or wind in yesterday's town, or perhaps the circus train was delayed.

The agony of waiting sometimes was diluted somewhat by a box of Cracker Jack, and maybe a balloon could ease the anxiety. It would have been held in one sticky hand while the other held onto Dad. Father might have pulled a big watch from his vest pocket and looked at its face. The child might look at his almost-new shoes.

Early that morning the mother might have remarked, "The circus people will be wearing their best for us; we must dress up for them."

By now there might be an adult comedian hovering around to tell the familiar circus joke, which opined that the date in our town had to be canceled because "the elephant swallowed the coffee pot and they can't find the grounds!"

Then at long last it was heard, but barely. It seemed a long way off, but the sound was unmistakable — the first faint notes of circus brass that crinkled the air like no other music in the world. And all along the line of march the cry went up, "Here it comes!"

The splendid baggage horses had pulled the heavy wagons from the railroad siding and hurried them to the show grounds a mile or so away in the mists of that morning. Now they had been groomed and arrayed in fine, imported harness. Their plumes nodded proudly as the beautifully-carved tableau and bandwagons rolled behind them, and fast, spangled music spilled into the sun-drenched street.

Along about 1908 I saw my first circus street parade. It was John Robinson's Circus and I remember the spectacle coming up the rise of our main street and passing our furniture store. I was perched wide-eyed on the arm of a large Morris chair in one of the big front windows.

It was almost 40 years later when I stood at the corner of Broadway and 43rd Street in New York City to see the Ringling Brothers and Barnum & Bailey Circus parade for the 7th War Bond drive.

Ringling street processions had been discontinued in 1919, victims of traffic difficulties. The circus was in Madison Square Garden for its annual April engagement and this parade was a special event. Its importance was magnified for me because as the circus publicity director I had helped to make it happen.

When the first faint notes of circus music began to echo in the Broadway canyons, bounding back and forth from skyscraper to skyscraper, I was 8 years old again and oblivious to the fact that I had been a circus man myself for almost two decades. That should have been long enough to have acquired at least the patina of sophistication in such matters as spangled sights and sounds.

But the plumes on the heads of the 10-horse hitch were visible now, bobbing in the noontime sunshine. The band momentarily took a breather, saving its wind for the swing through Times Square. The wild piping notes of the calliope were audible in the wake of the parade's elephant section, more than a mile distant.

The band chariot itself was an object worthy of praise from the best art connoisseurs. The huge, rumbling relic of the vanished golden parade days had been built by the skilled craftsmen of Sebastian Wagon Works in Philadelphia for the Forepaugh-Sells Bros. Circus 60 or more years ago. It had gone to Europe with the Barnum & Bailey show at the turn of the century. In those days it had been pulled by the famed 40-horse hitch driven by alternating drivers James Thomas and Jake Posey. Their shoulder, arm and hand muscles developed far beyond those of even circus acrobatic and aerial stalwarts. The brakeman was a sure-shot with pebbles he kept handy for signaling the lead team way up ahead. Carved on the sides of this bandwagon were the Five Graces of Greek mythology. Their wooden orbs had gazed upon the crowd-lined sidewalks of a thousand cities in half a hundred years.

On that day there was plenty to divert my thoughts from anything as comparatively inconsequential as a circus parade. The German armies were on the run and V-E Day was only weeks away. The circus lately had made me head of its publicity function and the job assumed immense proportions. The memory of the Hartford circus fire was fresh in the public mind and national restoration of public confidence was imperative. At home, the arrival of our third child was imminent.

All these important matters momentarily gave way along the pathway of my senses when circus band maestro Merle Evans lifted his cornet and the bandwagon wheeled into Broadway with the brass wide open.

New York City, mistress of Tin Pan Alley, niece of grand opera

This is the "Five Graces" circus wagon when it was known as the "Golden Chariot." It then was a "telescoping tableaux" wagon. This photo was taken on September 8, 1879, when the Adam Forepaugh Shows visited Northfield, Vermont. The super-structure telescoped down into the body of the wagon.

and second cousin-once-removed of dixieland jazz, hadn't heard music like this since its last circus street procession had turned a final corner a quarter century ago. Behind the bandwagon came the mounted units, open cages and floats carrying people who were my friends. They were smiling and nodding as the newspaper photographers with us fired away.

I was fairly unaware of all this as again my mind lost time and it was 1908. I was squeezing my father's hand in joyous expectation, for he took me to see every circus that came to our town as well as to

In later years the "Golden Chariot" was gutted of its telescoping feature, rubber tired, and turned into a bandwagon. This photo was taken in Manhattan in 1945, as it was being used by Merle Evans in the magnificent Ringling Brothers and Barnum & Bailey Circus street parade.

some of the bigger ones that played Columbus, 25 miles away. I wondered now if my dad might have suspected even then that some years later, when he might reasonably have expected me to be of help to him in his furniture store, I would be answering the Circe-like call of the calliope instead.

My feeling for the circus march in Manhattan during that noon hour was conditioned, too, by something that had happened back home the day before. My Aunt Georgia, pictured on page 37 of this book, had died unexpectedly at age 79. I was a favorite of hers because I had done the very thing she always had wanted to do; I had gone off with the circus.

The town circus grounds in Delaware were near her home in the 1880s. In those times they performed in hand-fashioned dirt ring-banks that were left available to intrepid circus-struck children after the circus left town.

In such a circle my tomboy aunt and her male friends risked their necks on an aging white horse as they displayed their prowess as circus bareback riders.

Some of the boys of that group joined circuses eventually, but Aunt Georgia had to be content with taking over her father's shoe store. She had asked for me in her final hour, and so I experienced the good feeling that on this bright parade day in New York City, my circus-loving relative somehow was within hearing of the spangle-clad music.

As the last of our parade units turned into Broadway, the pride I felt was mingled with memories of the setbacks suffered within the span of only five challenging years. There was the loss of 10 elephants by arsenic poisoning in 1941; the destruction of five more elephants, two priceless giraffes and other valuable display animals when the menagerie tent burned in Cleveland the next year; and then the holocaust in Hartford only two years later.

And I thought of how, instead of bemoaning their bad luck, our people had summoned the heart, mind and muscle needed to come back fighting every time. Then I walked back in time again, about 14 years. Then the veil of the past lifted slowly to reveal a radio station in this city where I had heard "Gentleman Jim" Corbett prescribe a formula for the making of a champion. "Fight one more round," he had said; "one more round." But we had been on the ropes so much of the time and had come up off the floor so many times that how long, I wondered, could even the Spartans of spangleland be expected to keep on coming back to fight one more round? Suddenly now, the answer was there. Forever.

Among the diverse and dedicated family of show people, the citizens of the circus are a special breed. The survival instinct is strong and their acceptance of hardship is realistic. Their battle enthusiasm is spirited, for the bugles of the Big Top never learned how to sound retreat. And that is why they can be expected to face up to such an interminable challenge as one more round. For, after all, **their** show is still The Greatest Show On Earth.

23

A FAREWELL TO RBB&B

I retired from Ringling Brothers and Barnum & Bailey Circus at the conclusion of the 1947 tour. It was my intention to devote more time to the family, to the operation of our furniture store, to the Ohio Wesleyan Board of Trustees (to which I had been elected the previous June) and to the Delaware County Fair. That institution was growing to be a giant oak from the acorn which I had had a hand in planting some nine years earlier.

In our business there are the public relations people, who seem to have super-glamorous jobs with attendant high salaries; and there are the publicists, or press agents — referred to nowadays as "flacks." I don't like to think of myself as a public relations counselor, but then I certainly don't think I was a "flack" either. What's wrong with being a good press agent?

As such, I always seemed to be asking for things from the newspaper people and rather expected a ho-hum reaction from them when I announced my retirement from the circus. I was totally unprepared for what actually happened.

The New York Times has a reputation of being the best newspaper in America. Therefore, imagine my surprise when I opened it on December 4, 1947, to see this:

THE NEW YORK TIMES, TH

Beverly Kelley, Circus Herald, Resigns Without Reaching for a Single Adjective

•

Special to THE NEW YORK TIMES.

DELAWARE. Ohio. Dec. 3—The high priest of hyperbole has settled down in his old home town. Old rocking chair's got him.

Beverly Kelley, long a herald of "The Greatest Show on Earth" and since the autumn of 1944 the chief publicity agent for the Ringling Brothers and Barnum & Bailey Circus, made known today that he had left show business to devote himself the year around to his family and his furniture business here.

Mr. Kelley, whose resignation is effective at the end of the year, spoke in matter-of-fact phrases of his decision to forego the glamour of the sawdust extravaganza and become a merchant of chairs and divans in the Blair-Kelley Company, Inc., but he did admit that the store was "the biggest in town" in furniture or any other line. Delaware, Ohio, has 9,500 souls.

Mr. Kelley, who has been beating the drums for circus and theatrical troupes for the last seventeen years and virtually memorized Roget's Thesaurus in the process, said circus life had become "too arduous" and he felt it was time for a change of scene.

Besides, he explained, he wanted to "give a good hunk of time to the enjoyment of his family and aiding his wife in the rearing of their three children and in the management of a business that has been in his family since the turn of the century. There are a boy and a girl in high school and a 3-year-old girl.

Once a newspaper man himself, Mr. Kelley remarked to a reporter who works nights:

"Doesn't your wife pester you to get a day job?"

Mr. Kelley, now 42 years old, emphasized that he had not given up all thought of returning to the writing business, but for the time being would be content to sit by the fireside and let someone else

Beverly Kelley
The New York Times Studio

be the chief harbinger of spring in New York and other cities.

In addition to press-agentry he has indulged in free-lance writing and is the author of three books, all about the circus.

Two years ago he entertained New York reporters by reciting the following poem about circus tub-thumpers:

"He's a brother to the robin, crying springtime in the land,
"As fact and fabrication lead him gently by the hand—
"And Old Saint Pete will tell him when he's climbed the golden stair
"The City Room is straight ahead —and how about a pair?"

Now whether or not you believe in their editorial philosophy, most people must acknowledge that the editorial page of the *Times* is also one of the most distinguished examples of editorial journalism in the world. Imagine my surprise, then, when on the following day this appeared:

PASSING OF A TROUBADOUR

News yesterday that F. Beverly Kelley had retired at the age of 42 as chief publicity man for The Greatest Show on Earth and would settle down to the life of a small-town merchant in Ohio is hard to take. What are we to think now of all those songs he used to sing, come March, of the joyous, carefree, glamorous life of the circus?

For seventeen years he had been in and out of city rooms, weaving a wordy spell of fantasy about this show and that; he was the envy of the stay-at-homes, an erudite disciple of the open road, a poet patently in love with his work. He was the robin to Manhattan. People who lived in the subways and never saw the light of day learned of spring's coming when he sang of miracles soon due in Madison Square Garden with the advent of Ringling Brothers and Barnum & Bailey. Has all this fine enthusiasm chilled and become now as sounding brass and tinkling cymbal? Is this the man, now winter-ing by the lazy Olentangy, who was lately crying, against a background of calliope, that New York was about to view "for the first time, anywhere, I repeat, anywhere, new spectacles—endearing, enticing, enthralling"? Apparently middle age has had its way.

There was a sort of world-weary philosopher who, with the enthusiastic help of newspaper reporters, had made himself a "character." A college graduate who contributed a learned touch to press agentry, he had made a fine art of cultivating friends wherever he went, in the high tradition of the late Dexter Fellows. He kept book on the names and ages of the children of newspaper men, sent them souvenirs of the circus, remembered them with gaudy poster greetings mailed at Christmas time. Who knows? That boy of 5 might sometime be city editor. We shall miss the fine, hyperbolic, polysyllabic flights of the somber man in the Western sombrero who will now be selling love-seats in his furniture store in Delaware, Pop. 9,500.

Then came the old *New York Sun,* which published this poem by their syndicated columnist, H.I. Phillips, under the title, ''Tell Us It Ain't So, Bev!'':

I

Flash us confirmation, Kelley
Is it true, we now implore
That the Big Top's famous herald
Quits to run a country store?
Kelley there behind a counter
Serving in a mart of trade,
Far from elephant and trapeze
And the old pink lemonade!

II

Kelley, let us have the lowdown;
  When the springtime blossoms swell
Can you stand the merchandising
  Far from any Big Top's spell,
Fussing with a set of ledgers,
  And the day's cash in the till
When no circus starlets glitter
  And no tightrope artists thrill?

III

Furniture's the line you've chosen
  From the papers we now hear
Tables, chairs, desks and knick-knacks
  (Can't you see Gargantua leer?)
Floor lamps, pictures, mirrors, gadgets,
  Carpets, curtains, rugs to spare
Not a wagon wheel acreakin' —
  Not a bareback rider there!

IV

"I want something for the kitchen"
  "Surely, madam, step this way!"
"May I see a cheaper icebox?"
  "We've a special sale today"
Can you really take this, Kelley
  With "Superb!" "Spec-tac-u-lar!"
"Death defying" . . . and "Gigantic!"
  Only echoes from afar?

V

Can a bureau be enchanting?
  Can domestic rugs enthrall?
When those spring scents fill the wayside
  Won't you hear the circus call?
When a lady picks a gas stove
  And is doubtful of its worth
You can't say "This stove's colossal —
  It's the greatest stove on earth."

VI

> Tell me that it ain't so, Kelley —
>   Say it's just a gag instead,
> And that spring will find you coming
>   With the robin just ahead;
> Oh, a country store ain't bad, kid,
>   There's a charm there, too, they say,
> But it's nothing like the old road
>   Where the "steam pianners" play.

One might think that it would be hard to be humble in the face of such adulation. Not so. I simply didn't believe it. And as I look on it tonight, 35 years later, I still don't. They must have been thinking of somebody else.

24

BACK TO THE WARS

So much for my avowed intentions, then. Without so much as a tip of the hat to the sage who said that good intentions are what the streets of hell are paved with, I fell in love again. This time it was with a young female in Texas and it all came about in the following manner.

A friend named R.M. Harvey, who was general agent for a rather new circus called Dailey Brothers, persuaded me to visit the show's winter quarters in Gonzales, Texas. There the circus owner and his wife were raising in their home the smallest baby elephant in America.

"That might make a good magazine story," Harvey said. This circus executive's invitation to come to Texas as a non-paying guest had a further purpose. By the time I realized what it was, I had agreed to organize and direct a publicity department for this rapidly-rising big show.

The importation of wild animals by circuses and zoos had been zero during the years of World War II, and baby elephants were a rarity at any time. But early in 1948 Ben Davenport, the owner of Dailey Brothers Circus, managed to bring in a shipment of pachydermic youngsters, two of whom were destined for circus fame.

The Davenport home was near the big buildings that comprised the show's winter quarters at Nogales. There I met someone I realized immediately could be featured truthfully as the smallest baby elephant in America. Despite her gender, she was named "Little Butch," in honor of the circus treasurer, Charles "Butch" Cohen. She was cute, curious and affectionate after the manner of most elephant babies, and at a height of under three feet she didn't

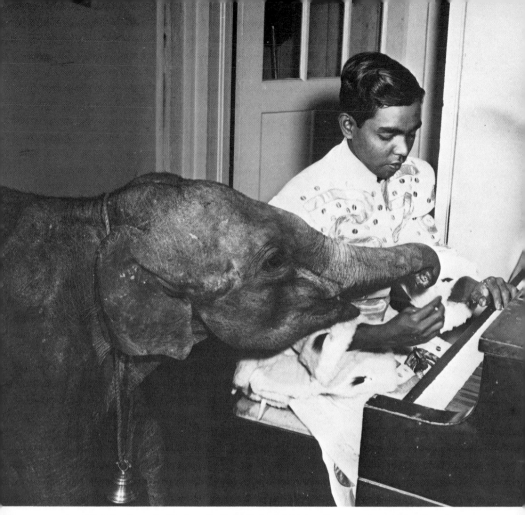

"Little Butch," the delightful subject of one of my articles in The Saturday Evening Post, *with her mahout, Singh. The two were living in the home of Mr. and Mrs. Ben Davenport, owners of the Dailey Bros. Circus.*

overcrowd the premises.

Most of her time was spent on the heated back porch. Occasionally when visitors called she was brought to the parlor by her keeper, whose name was Singh. He and two other Moslem mahouts had come with the elephants from India. For generations their families had been involved in the care and the training of elephants.

The circus owner had been born in West Virginia, and had attended high school and the university in my hometown of Delaware, Ohio. However, I had not known him prior to this meeting. So now I wrote about the Texas family with an elephant baby in its nursery, a good photographer from a San Antonio newspaper took pictures and *The Saturday Evening Post* bought the story. Our national publicity campaign was off to a good start and Little Butch was the stellar attraction of what I chose to advertise as "The All-Star Show From The Lone Star State."

During frequent visits to the elephant herd, I discovered that my attention was arrested increasingly by another youngster whose name was Little Eva, after the circus owner's wife, and almost as small as Little Butch. Admiring her proportions from handsome head to tiny tail, I decided that when she reached her full growth, Little Eva would resemble Modoc, Babe and Ruth — all lovely buxom lady friends of mine in the Ringling herd.

The circus was in upper New York State and well into its tour when *The Saturday Evening Post* picture story about our baby elephant and her family hit the newsstands with a bang that was heard throughout circusdom. Attendance immediately began to soar, but now, amidst the congratulations, our publicity department had to consider, "What are we going to do for an encore?"

Sometimes a press agent gains inspiration from reading about current or coming events, so now I wondered if that day's newspaper might hold the answer. And it did, for this was a presidential election year with the political scene commanding day-to-day attention by all news media.

This morning's big story was concerned with the Republican National Convention scheduled for the summer of 1948 in Philadelphia. Among the pictures of favorite son candidates was one of Ohio's Senator Robert Taft. An accompanying column by a political pundit suggested that while the Buckeye state's senior solon had talent and integrity in his favor, his chances of being chosen by his party were slim, because he lacked color.

As an admirer of Bob Taft and his quiet personality, I was irritated by the implication that compared political showmanship to integrity. I wished there were some way to inject some excitement into the campaign of this hardworking servant of his country. Reading further, I happened to notice that, flanking the photos of the Republican presidential hopefuls was the traditional party emblem, a trumpeting elephant. Well, whaddya know . . .

The pieces in my publicity puzzle started to fall together — National Convention, Taft, color, elephant. Dailey Brothers Circus would provide a living symbol of the Grand Old Party to put action into Bob Taft's campaign and color in his camp! To say nothing of some good national publicity for the circus. But it couldn't be just any elephant.

I knew that Philadelphia's famous zoo, the oldest in America, might have a spare elephant to loan for special occasions and that local Republicans might very well have thought of that.

I could imagine a zoo elephant on the street for atmosphere in front of the GOP campaign headquarters in the Benjamin Franklin Hotel. That was about all that could be done with it inasmuch as any zoo pachyderm would be so huge that it could not go inside the hotel to attend a press conference. But a baby elephant could!

So, as a Buckeye-born registered voter and Taft admirer who just happened to be publicity chief for a circus whose owner was a former resident of Ohio, I contacted the Taft campaign public relations officer. He received my proposal with enthusiasm equal to my own.

For this adventure I reasoned that we should not take Little Butch from the circus and disappoint spectators who had paid to see America's smallest baby elephant. Instead, we would take Little Eva, who was the second smallest. Furthermore, I felt she had even more personality.

Selling the idea to my employer was not difficult. I proposed it on a sunny Sunday afternoon in Sandusky, Ohio, where the show was busy creating its tent town for exhibitions on the following day. Ben Davenport said, "Come with me; we will measure Eva and build a travel crate to fit her, for any airline probably will require it."

Flight preparations were made. Frank Morrissey, who had been with me at RBB&B, now was on the Dailey Brothers payroll too. He went ahead to Philadelphia to find suitable housing for our elephant and her keeper, whose name was Pairu, and to meet them with photographers on arrival. I remained for the preparation of Little Eva's "wardrobe." It was simple enough, but colorful, and consisted of an Uncle Sam hat and blankets. They carried painted inscriptions such as "I'm Little Eva from Dailey Bros. Circus — I'm Simply Daft About Taft;" and "I'm a young Republican from Dailey Bros. Circus and I trumpet for Taft."

Arrangements had been made to keep Little Eva and Pairu at the animal compound of the University of Pennsylvania's Veterinarian College. On the day the circus played Sidney, Ohio, we took Eva and Pairu in a truck to the airport in Columbus where they were given an enthusiastic reception by reporters and photographers from newspapers which we had alerted, and from a cheering group of Young Republicans who also were flying to the convention in Philadelphia.

Flash bulbs popped again a few hours later when Little Eva and her handsome young mahout arrived in the convention city. On our way to the animal compound we made a brief stop at the Benjamin Franklin Hotel, where Morrissey and I were booked, and led our baby elephant and keeper to the front desk in a lobby filled with startled and delighted guests. Eva, wearing her partisan blanket and Uncle Sam hat, and her East Indian mahout in his Moslem red chapeau, were a photogenic pair. The tip of the baby elephant's tiny trunk curled around a pen handed to her by a picture-minded clerk at the registration desk.

At the university's comfortable animal residence, Pairu gave his charge exquisite care and slept beside her, too. Seldom were they apart, and they left the compound only when traveling in a comfortable rented van to make publicity appearances in downtown Philadelphia.

Little Eva's social calendar soon bulged with requests for personal appearances. I doubt that any of her kind had stirred the imagination of the city so much all the way back to 1880. That was the year that the City of Brotherly Love was the birthplace of the first baby elephant to be born in America.

Even small elephants are fearful of stepping on anything that may not bear their weight, but Eva at about 700 pounds was not afraid of riding in elevators until a cruel young operator purposely tried to frighten her with a sudden stop on our way to a GOP reception on the Bellevue Stratford Hotel roof. From then on she had to be prodded.

Also stabled at the veterinary compound were race horses that had been injured at a track near Wilmington, Delaware, and these needed a couple of days to become accustomed to Little Eva's strong elephant jungle scent. Although I appreciated her mahout's devotion to our baby, our communication was limited by the fact that Pairu knew only four words of English — pie, okay and Coca Cola. And I knew even less of his native tongue. However, he could read the notes I wrote when our sign language failed us.

As time approached for taking Little Eva to Senator Taft's press conference in a parlor on the mezzanine floor of his hotel, the promises made to me by campaign bigwigs began to fall apart. First, we could not use the elevator, although I saw a lady passenger who must have weighed almost as much as our plump baby. Fortunately, unlike a horse or a pony, an elephant can be walked up a flight of stairs because its feet are conveniently flat.

So, Eva's keeper and I had no difficulty in climbing with our youngest Republican to meet her chosen candidate. But now the

"Little Eva," the most exciting aspect of the campaign to nominate Robert Taft as the Republican candidate for the U.S. presidency in 1948. A generator of reams of publicity for the Dailey Bros. Circus, she is shown at the Philadelphia GOP convention with, from left, her mahout, Pairu; John Joseph, an official of the Ohio Republican Party; myself; and Frank Morrissey, my assistant.

security man who had assured us he would be there to escort us into the conference parlor was nowhere in sight. So we simply did what one learns to do when people and their promises disappear — one does it himself. Calling in a stentorian tone, "Make way for Little Eva!", I pushed through the middle of a crowded double lane with our elephant and her mahout close behind me. The senator sat in the middle of a long sofa, and I led Eva to him saying, "Senator, they say that elephants bring good luck. This is your elephant.''

Now, with no instruction whatever, Eva pointed her little trunk at him while he smiled and reached out his hand for a trunk-shake. And as soon as the photographers were finished with us, we returned our cute little co-ed to the more relaxed social climate of her university campus.

When New York's Governor Tom Dewey became his party's nominee to take on President Harry Truman in his November bid for a second term, Senator Taft quickly was out of the headlines. But our Little Eva remained a local celebrity. She had been a veritable fountain of national publicity, and now it was time to ship her back to her job, to one of the Missouri cities where her circus was playing.

Suddenly, however, our star attraction was on the front page again, only this time the news was not good. A rural Pennsylvania resident who had been discharged from Dailey Brothers Circus when last it was in the Keystone State, was encouraged by some legal eagle to attach the show's only available property, and of course that property happened to be our baby elephant.

This is what is known as a ''nuisance'' suit set in motion by a plaintiff in the hope of a quick money settlement to avoid the expense and inconvenience of a trial. An attorney I briefly engaged was unable to reverse an order that Little Eva remain in Philadelphia. Aware of our problem, the friendly Philadelphia Zoo offered food and shelter for Eva and her keeper in return for her front-gate attendance value as a guest attraction.

Considering this, but determined to send Eva back to the circus, I remembered that only about 30 miles distant in Wilmington, Delaware, lived my good friend, Don Morton. He was a DuPont executive whose love for the circus knew no limit. If my pal would let me hide Little Eva in his garage until I could fly her to Missouri from Wilmington's airport, I would ''steal'' our own elephant and take her safely over the state line.   .

A telephone conversation with my friend resulted in a promise of his cooperation in my proposed ''elephant-napping'' plot, so now, under the pretense of moving Eva to the Philadelphia Zoo, I hired the van we had been using for her local publicity transportation and explained to its driver that we were going to Wilmington instead of to the zoo.

He did not question the change of destination, so I told Pairu to get his gear and bring Eva to the van for loading. Then, through the open window of the animal compound's executive office I heard a telephone ringing, and immediately had a trouble hunch that was confirmed a few moments later. We were told that an order had been issued to the effect that the elephant could not leave the premises.

I reached our circus owner by telephone and asked for instructions. They were simple and to the point. "Send Pairu back to the show," Ben Davenport ordered. "Without her keeper the elephant will raise so much hell they will be glad to let her go." And that is exactly what happened. Little Eva wore out her welcome in one day of continuous trumpeting and, despite her size, she managed to pull up her stake chain and damage a heavy gate in a frantic bid for freedom. The court order was then lifted.

She was to rejoin the circus at its stand in Mexico, Missouri, but when I went to book passage at the air cargo freight office and make certain that her travel crate was still stored there, I soon learned that our problems had not all evaporated with the release of our unhappy baby from the compound. The freight agent explained that on the flight to Philadelphia our passenger had lost control of her bladder and that now they would not accept her unless her crate was set in a metal tray.

Earlier, there had been a ray of sunshine to brighten this troublesome day. Frank Morrissey, who had been trying to baby-sit for Little Eva since the departure of her keeper, received the exciting news that his son Tommy had been born in Coral Gables, Florida. So, while the happy new father went shopping for a stuffed toy elephant, which seemed to be an especially appropriate gift from his circus dad, I measured Eva's traveling quarters and went shopping for a tinsmith. In South Philadelphia I found a man willing to do a rush job on a metal tray that would serve our purpose. By late afternoon it was on the way to the airport.

The elephant would be walked up a ramp into the belly of the cargo plane where her crate awaited its passenger. Fearing that we might have trouble without her familiar mahout to take her into the plane, I had employed a young man from the Philadelphia Zoo's elephant staff to help us, and soon bid a fond farewell to Little Eva. And I think it was the first and only time in my life that I felt pleasure in saying goodbye to a baby.

Ben Davenport was big and tough and friendly. And because his cookhouse was the best on tour with any circus, he could attract and keep good workers even when the labor market was tight. The boss was hospitable, too. If a valued employee was hurt on the job and his injury didn't require him to be left behind in a local hospital, he was given a berth in his employer's private railroad car until he was able to resume work.

Life aboard the Davenports' private car never was dull. Among its "guests" were a baby tiger and a pet monkey that loved to chase it. This diversion frequently climaxed with the kitten landing on someone's chest.

Davenport's daughter Norma was a talented performer who from early childhood worked with elephants and horses, and her parents owned a good supply of both. The Dailey Brothers Circus performance was presented in five rings, and when simultaneously they were occupied by trained elephants or by circling groups of high school horses, it indeed was an impressive sight.

The show's owner knew that the public often judges the size and quality of a circus by the number of elephants in its wild animal menagerie. Although this show had no formal street parade, in every stand Ben would send his impressive herd of two dozen through the center of town.

On occasions when the legality of this elephant walk was challenged because no parade permit had been issued, the circus employee in charge of the procession would announce that he was lost, and would the officer please direct him to the circus grounds. This maneuver usually resulted in a friendly police escort for the remainder of the march.

When rubber shortages brought gas rationing laws, circus customers often found their tanks empty when trying to leave the circus parking lots after the night performance. In such emergencies, an elephant might be enlisted to push the driver and his family to a nearby filling station. The thrill of having an elephant for an engine was worth many times the modest charge of one dollar, and if anyone suspected that his tank might have been siphoned while he was inside the big top and watching the performance, nobody ever accused the elephant!

In Ben's sideshow tent were two old-time circus games-of-chance for the entertainment and "education" of the customers. There was the shell game, where the gullible try to guess under which walnut halfshell a pea is hidden, and three-card monte, consisting of a fast and skillful moving of the cards. Then the cards are placed face down and the player bets he can locate the ace.

This maneuvering of the cards went by the name of "broad tossing," in the vernacular of the midway — the playing cards being designated as "broads."

I was aware of this grift, as illegal gambling is known among the show fraternity. I never entered the tent where it took place. This was so that if and when I might be asked if Dailey Brothers Circus was a grift show, I could honestly say that I had never seen any dishonest games.

I was told by amused observers that Ben enjoyed watching his customers match wits with his gamblers or "lucky boys," as they were called (because they never lost). One man even bore the legal name of Luck. On such visits the show's owner liked to act as a "shill" or "stick." He posed as a spectator whom the grifters permitted to win so that easy marks might be encouraged to bet. But in this disguise, Ben won no Academy Awards. He looked too much the picture of a circus executive, and the grifters finally discouraged his attendance.

As a young showman, Ben Davenport had been flat broke often enough to fear poverty. Now in his affluence he invented an ingenious way of hiding money against such emergencies as having his ticket wagon held up by gunmen or attached by a local lawman. There were three collapsible steps in a unit that led from ground level to the office wagon's side entrance. When it was time to close the wagon and send it to the circus train, an inconspicuous workman would saunter by, fold the portable steps and carry this single unit away on his shoulder. The top step was more than that. It was built as a box and it often contained as much as $10,000 in cash.

This circus paid its performers and its total labor contingent alike at the end of each day. An exception was the advance agents to whom money was wired, and promptly, upon request. This daily pay system greatly simplified the bookkeeping. Everyone was paid aboard the show's "pie car," where the slot machines and a crap table were located, so a substantial amount of the day's payroll found its way back from the employees who liked to finish off their day with a little gambling.

Circus treasurer Butch Cohen was a delightful old-timer with many years of rough-and-tumble trouping behind him. He had a sense of humor that seldom failed him, although I recall one chilly, windblown March morning when it was tested severely.

Just prior to our meeting at the post office, where Cohen had come to mail the carefully-prepared circus income tax return, he had encountered his employer who asked the amount of the check he was sending. When the treasurer replied, Ben Davenport instructed him to send a sum that was considerably less. This, of course, meant a lot more maneuvering with the report, but Butch managed a sad smile as he said to me, "When I joined this outfit

I wasn't told that my principal act was to be juggling.''

That summer we received the news that the United States was the first nation to recognize Israel's independence. I bought Butch a small blue-and-white flag bearing the Star of David, and he walked all around the show grounds as he waved it and reminded his friends along the way that "At last we have our own flag! Up to now all we ever had to wave was this." Cohen's other hand held aloft a dollar bill.

He even managed to cough up a grin when boarding an ambulance for a brief visit to a hospital, whispering to me that there was $700 in cash in the pocket of the bathrobe he carelessly had left with his wife, "but it probably serves me right for hiding it from her," he said.

Ben Davenport was reputed to have a towering temper when aroused, but I liked him for his numerous good qualities. Also, he was proud of his publicity department, and because a traveling advance man seldom has time for returning to the circus, I always saw our owner on his best behavior.

I was absent when someone convinced him that his trainmaster was over-attentive to Ben's wife. The victim of this unfounded rumore was "Shakey-Leg" Murphy, whose nickname was the result of an accident in a college track meet. Davenport was quoted as saying that he would not simply fire this man; he would red-light him.

In the language of the circus, "red-light" means to push someone from the vestibule of a moving train while asking him to lean out and look for a non-existent red signal up ahead. Deaths and permanent injury were known to have resulted from this form of punishment, but later I was to learn that Ben's better judgment had prevailed at the last minute and that he stopped the train for Shakey-Leg's "resignation" from the show.

Billboard, the bible of show biz, surprised all of us with a feature they did on the Dailey show in their issue of July 31, 1948. Entitled "Dailey Has Growing Pains," it was written by Hank Hurley. The article and pictures which accompanied it are reproduced here:

War-born railroad show comes to front fast and Davenport looks to future — Harvey and Kelley draw owner's praise

BEN DAVENPORT, owner of Dailey Bros.' Circus, admits his show is suffering from growing pains. But like any good doctor.he has the interests of his patient at heart and plans to relieve them as quickly as possible.

Already Ben and his assistants, particularly R. M. Harvey, his veteran general agent, have prescribed quite a few medicines to relieve "that distressed feeling." But more is needed, Ben admits, and the cures are in the making.

Dailey Bros., as a big-time railroad show, actually is just an infant. Technically, it was a war baby, born in 1944, but is expanding so rapidly that it is well past the knee-pants stage.

Snares Top P.A.'s

Davenport's rail show was born back in 1944, but it wasn't until this spring that circusdom felt the full impact of the late arrival. That was in the form of a story that the Dailey owner had hired one of the top circus press agents—F. Beverly Kelley—and surrounded him with a staff of Kelley's own choosing to tell the world about the railroad circus baby. Kelley, for several years, had headed the press department of the Ringling Bros. and Barnum & Bailey Circus. Then came the announcement that Dailey had signed Kelly and two of his Ringling staffers—Allen J. Lester and Frank Morrissey, both of whom are well trained in the Ringling school of press agentry. This truly was the shot heard 'round the circus world.

Will the ex-R-B boys be able to get the national publicity for Dailey that they did for Ringling? . . . How can they compare this new "upstart" with Big Bertha? . . . Those were just a couple of the questions dyed-in-the-wool circus fans started asking the minute they heard the news.

Crashes Public Print

Truth of the matter is, Kelley hasn't made one attempt at comparisons and probably never will. But he hurdled the national publicity problem with ease. His answer to that question was a piece, with pictures in *The Saturday Evening Post* on Butch, the Dailey baby elephant, in particular, and the Dailey show

in general.

A few weeks later he came back with national hits, both in the press and over the air, by sending Little Eva, another of the Dailey midget elephants, to the Republican National Convention in Philadelphia to aid Senator Robert Taft in his battle for the nomination of president of the United States. Dailey Bros. hit the front page of practically every newspaper in the country. Photos were sent out by the wire services, showing the bull complete with a blanket on which the name Dailey Bros.' Circus was prominently displayed.

Needless to say, when Dailey moves into.the towns and cities of the nation now, the populace knows the name and comes out in goodly numbers to see Little Eva and Butch, and, incidentally, the show.

Pays Tribute to Kelley

"Getting Bev Kelley was the smartest move I ever made," Davenport says. "It was Harvey's idea and a good one. Publicity pays off. If I ever needed proof of that, I have it now."

To intimates, Harvey remarked, when he hired Kelley and his staff, "I'm sticking my neck out by going for such an expensive public relations department." But now he says with a smile, "We are more than happy with Kelley, Lester and Morrissey, proud of the work they have done in this short space of time. And they are happy with us. It is an ideal set-up, has paid dividends, and we hope they will be with us for many years."

Ben Davenport and his wife, Eva, aren't newcomers to the circus business by any means and the name Dailey Bros. is an old one. When Davenport speaks about the management of the circus he always uses the editorial "we," which he makes it clear, means himself, Eva and Harvey. Working side by side, this trio knows the ins and outs of the business. Davenport makes it clear, too, that in Harvey he has the best general agent in the business.

Lived, Let Live

Eight years ago Dailey Bros., owned and operated by the Davenports, was a small truck show, making money some years, not doing so well others, but going along living and let living. Harvey was with the org then and he had ideas—expansion ideas. He wasn't going to be satisfied, it was clear even at that time, to let Dailey remain a truck show. Between the Davenports and Harvey there often

BEN DAVENPORT

EVA DAVENPORT

were huddles at which imaginary blueprints were drawn. Little by little things began to take shape, in the form of added stock, larger canvas and more employees.

The year 1943 was the final year for the Dailey org as a truck show. "We had 26 trucks and carried more elephants—12—than any other truck show in the country," Davenport said, by way of leading up to how he finally went on rails. "The war was on, you know, and tires and trucks were hard to get. In fact, they were impossible to get. It was tough going to keep the show moving on trucks. Harvey and I talked it over many times during the season of 1943 of how tough it was getting rolling equipment. One day while discussing the situation, I said, 'Hell, let's go on rails.' "

Keeps Adding Stock

That, in a nutshell, is how Dailey Bros.' railroad show was born. Of course, it wasn't that easy, but thru the tireless efforts of the Davenports and Harvey, not to mention, as Ben says, the many faithful employees of the org who have been with it for years, the Dailey org bowed as a rail show in 1944.

Since that time the show has been bursting at the seams with growing pains. Davenport, a lover of good stock, has been adding to that department and will continue to add to it. It was his idea to go in heavy for good stock, including plenty of elephants. It was his idea, too, to add little elephants to the show and this, he says, has paid off at the gate. For instance, this year the org has added five railroad cars, one of which is an advance. "That advance car was Harvey's idea," Davenport said, "and it was a good one. Before this year we used a truck on advance. You can't give Harvey enough credit in helping this show grow. That's why I tell you he's the best general agent in the business."

Grows Out of Top

Dailey Bros.' big top this year is a 130 with five 40s and seats around 5,800 persons. It isn't big enough, according to Davenport and Harvey, and already an order has been placed for a larger one. The show this year carries 24 elephants (there were 25 but Jap died recently while the show was playing Springfield, Ill.) where last year it had 15. Whereas the show employed about 100 persons eight

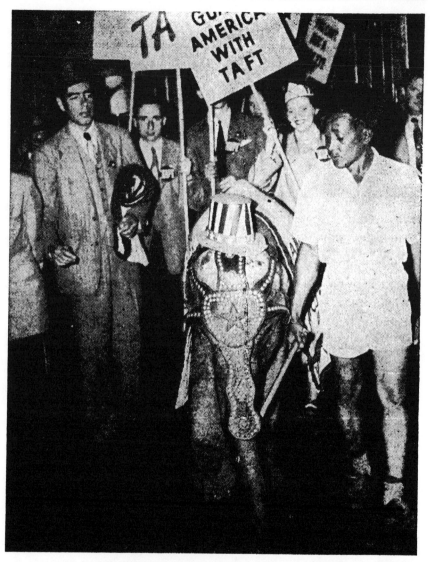

HERE'S **LITTLE EVA IN ACTION at the** Republican National Convention in Philadelphia, accompanied by her mahout who watches over her like a mother hen over her chicks. Note Bev Kelley (with hat on and holding one of Eva's blankets), left, with that look of anxiety in his eyes.

years ago, it now has 325 on the pay roll.

To get the employees' reaction regarding the show, a talk with Ralph Noble will convince you that they are a happy lot. "I started in the circus business 43 years ago with the Norris & Rowe Circus," Noble relates, "and I've been with this one since February, 1944, when it had just 10 cars. We would put it up in about 1½ hours and take it down in 45 minutes.

Now it takes three hours to put up and about 1½ hours to take down. We only had an 80-foot top at the start and now we've got a 130-footer.

Morale Runs High

"You can't beat working conditions on this show. . . . It's more like a big family than anything else. . . . These people can't be beat when it comes to working for someone. . . . Why on this show everyone calls Davenport by his first name, and he knows the first name of practically everyone on the show. . . . He's never too busy to stop and talk to you. . . . And R. M. (he referred to R. M. Harvey) is the same. . . . Everyone loves him. . . . That's why I say it's more like a big happy family than anything else."

Regarding business this year, Davenport says, "To date we are holding our own with last year's figures. Last year was a very good season for us, and I think the great publicity we've received, thru the efforts of Bev and his gang, is responsible for helping us keep even with last year. Whether you know it or not, people have tightened their spending this year and that, coupled with the fact the weather at the start of the season wasn't too good, could have put us below last year. But we are even with last year and that's good, believe me.

Attendance Holds Up

"I'd like to tell you that our at-tendance figures are away ahead of last year, but that wouldn't be the truth," Davenport went on. "I do tell you, and this is the truth, that we are equal to last year and that satisfies us."

Davenport, who started his career in outdoor show business as a groom at $3 per week for Seils-Sterling Circus, owned by the Lindemann brothers, now has one of the Lindemanns, Peter, working for him as contracting agent. The other two brothers are still living. Art is with the Al G. Kelly-Miller Bros.' Circus as brigade agent, and Will, the oldest, is retired.

May Scout Europe

Davenport declares he may go to Europe this fall to scout for new acts. He'd like to get at least one, if not more, good name attractions for the show. Right now, he says, the show lacks a strong name act—one that is different. "You've got to give people something new, something they haven't seen and right now we're working on that. I don't know what we'll come up with next year but you can bet it'll be good. It'll have to be good before Eva, Harvey, Kelley and the rest of 'em will okay it," Ben said with a smile.

Yes, Dailey Bros.' Circus is suffering from growing pains, but the pains have been lessened and Doctors Davenport, Harvey and Kelley are still working on the patient.

25

WIN A FEW, LOSE A FEW

Whenever I visit the magnificent Circus World Museum at Baraboo, Wisconsin, where the Ringling Brothers began their circusing in 1884, I meet an old friend. Her name is "America."

Musically inclined, her specialty is whistling. It stirs my senses as do the wild, free strains of Scot and Irish pipers. Her wardrobe was designed and executed by artisans skilled in wood pictorials. She moves gracefully on beautiful red, white and blue sunburst wheels.

My friend "America" is a steam calliope. Her ancestry dates back to 1885 when a boilermaker named Joshua C. Stoddard of Worcester, Massachusetts, was granted patent number 13668. It was for an instrument producing music by forcing steam or compressed air through a series of whistles.

The great-great-grandmother of our "America" made her debut on July 4, 1885, attended by the inventor's sister Edna. The first tune heard by the Independence Day picnic audience on the town common was 'Yankee Doodle."

Stoddard's idea was to create a steam instrument to replace or supplement bells in calling the faithful to church services. His masterpiece at full strength was so powerful it could be heard for miles, and soon the steam pianos found their destiny in the circuses and riverboats of those times.

The loud and lofty register of my favorite circus coloratura had

The arrow points to me, as I assisted in harnessing the team of eight white horses selected to pull the calliope "America" in the 1948 presidential inaugural parade.

enlivened the street processions of more than one big show during a long and distinguished career. We met first early in 1949 in Louisville, Kentucky, at the winter quarters of Cole Brothers Circus. (I had left the Dailey show at the end of the 1948 season.)

Our first publicity assignment was a big one. The voters had given their hard-fighting president, Harry Truman, an unexpected victory at the November polls, and his inaugural was scheduled for January 20. Moreover, our "America" steam piano was to be the first circus entry ever to appear in a national inaugural parade. It was to serenade our piano-playing chief executive with "The Missouri Waltz" and Vice President Alben W. Barkley with "My Old

Kentucky Home.''

I was no stranger to climbing aboard ready-made national events in the interest of circus promotion. This splendid publicity coup was mine to bring off, but it had not originated with me. It was born in the bright mind of Ed Seiler, treasurer of the State of Kentucky.

His proposal found instant favor with the chairman of all the inauguration events. Soon the America calliope, accompanied by a hitch of eight splendid white percherons, was on her way by rail to the nation's capitol and to circus history.

We kept our renowned musical antique under wraps until a day before the parade. Then we invited newspaper and magazine photographers for pictures of some special inaugural guests of the musical stage. Phil Harris and his wife Alice Faye posed at the calliope keyboard.

Assisting me on the steam calliope assignment was Allen J. Lester of our circus publicity corps. For most of five hours of waiting in the long parade's lineup we were busy carrying water. It was not only for our calliope's horses, but also to prevent our star attraction from becoming dehydrated.

The best known steam calliope player, Tommy Comstock, came out of retirement in Jackson, Michigan, to make the glory ride. Soon the great lady and her virtuoso became the most popular of all the parade units. Our musician was most generous with his talent.

Every time someone in the crowd called out ''Hit it!'' Tommy would oblige with a couple of choruses of his favorite songs. His most frequent rentition, ''I'm Looking Over A Four-Leaf Clover,'' had been the theme song for Robert Taft during his unsuccessful bid for the GOP nomination. That seemed to pass unnoticed by our sidewalk audience.

Our problem as circus press agents-turned water boys was that every two choruses used up 10 pounds of precious steam. The calliope's boiler tank was situated at the rear of the wagon just behind the keyboard and was heated by a small coal fire. When the procession finally began, we had to have a full tank of steam and we had to use it sparingly. We didn't want our star performer to lose her voice before passing the reviewing stand at the White House.

A friendly area druggist let us run up his water bill for countless trips back and forth with cardboard containers of water for our thirsty mistress.

I had planned to grab a taxicab and speed ahead of the procession to a vantage point where I might relax and watch its progress. That idea evaporated when our fireman confessed that he didn't know

Alice Faye, Hollywood film star, posed with Edward Seiler prior to the start of the inaugural parade. Seiler, treasurer of the State of Kentucky, dreamed up the idea of the calliope.

how to read the gauge on the boiler.

Someone had to watch that instrument during the total two miles and I knew it had to be a man on foot. In every circus parade the calliope traditionally is the concluding attraction. So it was on this occasion. We walked slowly and directly behind the open-back wagon, keeping an eye on the steam gauge and calling out to Tommy Comstock so that he would know what to play and when to play it.

To comply with the parade committee's ruling that participating units were not to carry any commercial advertising, we were supplied with some bunting and cardboard replicas of the Democratic

The calliope "America" rolls down Pennsylvania Avenue enroute to the White House during the Truman-Barkley inaugural parade.

Party's rooster symbol with which to cover the name of our circus, painted prominently on the wagon's skyboards. Just prior to parade time that material somehow disappeared, and what happened to it remains an unsolved mystery. In the finest circus traditions, we decided to carry on despite our adversity.

The beautiful "America" rolled past the White House reviewing stand. It was whistling "When You And I Were Young, Maggie," as a special salute to the Truman's singing daughter Margaret. The circus name was in plain view for all spectators and news cameras as well. One may imagine how a *faux pas* such as that might embarrass a circus press agent!

Our steam conservation program enabled our big music box to keep her voice through the last few notes and no more. We tootled past Blair House, the presidential guest quarters diagonally across from the executive mansion. Our problems were not all accounted for. It may seem next to impossible to lose anything as conspicuous as a team of eight white horses hitched to a brightly-painted circus wagon in a city the size of Washington. However, our driver man-

"When You And I Were Young Maggie" booms from the pipes as the calliope passes the White House reviewing stand, where it was applauded by President Harry S. Truman and Vice President Alben W. Barkley.

aged to accomplish this by making a wrong turn on his way back to the railway loading area. Darkness now complicated the search. Three more hours were to be devoted to worrying, watching and waiting before our parade prima donna with her equine traveling companions could be found. They bid farewell to the scene of their triumph and entrained for their old Kentucky home.

But not all publicity ventures turn out so successfully. The following little disaster occurred during my stint as publicist for the road company of *Fiddler On The Roof.* One Sunday afternoon our troupe stumbled cold, weary and unfed into Chicago. We found the city still staggering from the impact of two consecutive blizzards. We had been on an unheated train and were six hours late from Cincinnati.

Taxicabs were almost non-existent. The Greyhound bus I had rented had gone to the wrong railway station. The bus driver finally found the correct address and took my people to their hotels.

Paul Lipson, who played the role of Tevye the Dairyman in Fiddler On The Roof.

I was proud of them for not complaining about the hours of inconvenience and severe discomfort. They had been through so much wild winter weather that they now were taking the rigors of the road in stride, as real troupers do.

We opened our engagement at McVicker's Theater two nights later, in the midst of another snowstorm. Immediately the musical masterpiece burned up the track at the box office. The visit lasted for eight sellout months before *Fiddler* resumed its traveling.

We were not far from March 17 and one of the numerous street parades for which the Windy City is noted.

This time the Saint Patrick's Day street procession would be led not only by Mayor Richard J. Daley. Beside him would be Mayor Driscoll, the popular Jewish-born chief executive of Dublin, Ireland, and in honor of this oncoming spectacular enough dye was to be poured into the Chicago River to make it flow as green as the River

The cast of Music Man *was headed by Forrest Tucker and Joan Weldon, in the center of the back row.*

Shannon doesn't.

I learned that many of Chicago's ethnic groups would have units in the parade on March 17. Once again I could exercise my natural inclination toward generating publicity for my show through becoming part of a prime established event.

Arrangements had been made for a substantial number of our *Fiddler* company to march with their traditional Jewish beards dyed green.

Many of our actors had begun the tour with artificial beards that were discarded as their natural beards grew sufficiently, but none had grown green.

But now they had to go to the trouble of renting theatrical hair and dying it emerald green. We were certain to be the object of considerable attention, especially among the television people covering the parade.

However, as my confidence mounted, so did the muscle of the

Prof. Harold Hill's exuberant pool scene from Meredith Willson's Music Man, *which I fronted in 1958.*

month of March. The weather turned so bitter that I called off our appearance in the parade. No publicity stunt is worth endangering the health of its participants. Furthermore, we ran the further risk of disappointing theater patrons by having to cancel a performance. No way would I become a party to this, so all our work went for naught.

I take a dim view of performance cancellations by well-meaning playhouses, ''out of respect,'' as they usually explain, for a distinguished public figure suddenly deceased. No proper purpose is served by such a gesture. The theater and the producer have accepted the playgoer's money on the promise that he will see a performance. Regardless of a cash refund or the shifting of attendance to an acceptable future date, the deceased is not honored by the breaking of a promise. Reverence and appreciation for the dead are better expressed in a superb performance by the living.

There were some out-and-out bloopers, too. My biggest one was terribly conspicuous. It happened in the sunken plaza at Rockefeller Center. It followed faithfully the traditional pattern of failures which always "seemed like a great idea at the time."

The Ringling show was heading for winter quarters and in that autumn of 1936 my working address was the Center Theater in the Radio City complex. Our playing attraction was an international extravaganza called *The White Horse Inn.*

Scenery and props alone for this Goliath of imported musicals, whose settings portrayed the splendors of Austria's Tyrol, were so spectacular that even the Center Theater's gigantic stage scarcely could accommodate the total production.

The huge cast was headed by William Gaxton and Kitty Carlisle. It included a troupe of authentic Tyrolean male "slap" dancers plus singers led by a famed lady yodeler named Madam Reverelli. Huge and handsome and impressive as was our *White Horse Inn,* most of the city's entertainment excitement was being generated by the World Championship Rodeo in Madison Square Garden. After reflecting on the rodeo's western warblers, rope-spinning experts and lively cowboy band, I sold my employer on a hot idea. It should be good publicity for all concerned if these rodeo entertainers joined our *White Horse Inn* talent at Rockefeller Center. We could have a noon hour jamboree in the outdoor sunken plaza. Thus the sports and pastimes of the American plains could be compared with those of the Austrian Tyrol. The idea was accepted with enthusiasm by the rodeo's publicity people and a date was set.

Our stunt could take no more than a half hour — the length of the lunch break of the crew running a jackhammer directly across from the scene of our action.

The cost of our project ballooned. Management was persuaded by the musical contractor that the full pit orchestra was needed because of its familiarity with the routines of the performers.

It became a full-scale mounting of exceptional talent and beautiful costumes. The perfect autumn weather contributed to the artistic success of our presentation. Alas, there were only a few standing spectators. Nobody had read about it, for no paper ran my story announcing it, and no photographer from any Manhattan newspaper came to shoot our show. It was a complete and expensive publicity fiasco, by far the worst of my career.

Next two spreads: Some of the calling cards given to newspaper, radio and television people while I was fronting for major theatrical productions in New York and "on the road."

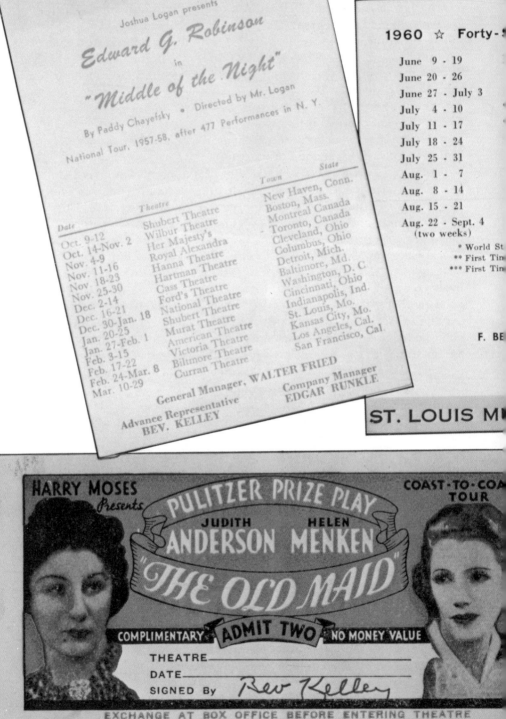

Joshua Logan presents

Edward G. Robinson

in

"Middle of the Night"

By Paddy Chayefsky • Directed by Mr. Logan

National Tour, 1957-58, after 477 Performances in N. Y.

Date	Theatre	Town	State
Oct. 9-12	Shubert Theatre	New Haven, Conn.
Oct. 14-Nov. 2	Wilbur Theatre	Boston, Mass.
Nov. 4-9	Her Majesty's	Montreal Canada
Nov. 11-16	Royal Alexandra	Toronto, Canada
Nov. 18-23	Hanna Theatre	Cleveland, Ohio
Nov. 25-30	Hartman Theatre	Columbus, Ohio
Dec. 2-14	Cass Theatre	Detroit, Mich.
Dec. 16-21	Ford's Theatre	Baltimore, Md.
Dec. 30-Jan. 18	National Theatre	Washington, D. C
Jan. 20-25	Shubert Theatre	Cincinnati, Ohio
Jan. 27-Feb. 1	Murat Theatre	Indianapolis, Ind.
Feb. 3-15	American Theatre	St. Louis, Mo.
Feb. 17-22	Victoria Theatre	Kansas City, Mo.
Feb. 24-Mar. 8	Biltmore Theatre	Los Angeles, Cal.
Mar. 10-29	Curran Theatre	San Francisco, Cal.

General Manager, WALTER FRIED

Company Manager
EDGAR RUNKLE

Advance Representative
BEV. KELLEY

1960 ☆ Forty-

June 9 - 19

June 20 - 26

June 27 - July 3

July 4 - 10

July 11 - 17

July 18 - 24

July 25 - 31

Aug. 1 - 7

Aug. 8 - 14

Aug. 15 - 21

Aug. 22 - Sept. 4
(two weeks)

* World St
** First Tim
*** First Tim

F. BE

ST. LOUIS MU

HARRY MOSES Presents

COAST-TO-COA
TOUR

PULITZER PRIZE PLAY

JUDITH **ANDERSON**   HELEN **MENKEN**

"THE OLD MAID"

COMPLIMENTARY   ADMIT TWO   NO MONEY VALUE

THEATRE_____

DATE_____

SIGNED BY   *Bev Kelley*

EXCHANGE AT BOX OFFICE BEFORE ENTERING THEATRE

TOUR ITINERARY 1955-56

Bev. Kelley, *Advance Agt.*   Edgar Runkle, *Co. Mgr.*

Date	Theatre	Town	State
Oct. 5-8	Hartman	Columbus, Ohio	
Oct. 10-29	Hanna	Cleveland, Ohio	
Oct. 31 to Nov. 5	Victory	Dayton, Ohio	
Nov. 7-26	Nixon	Pittsburgh, Pa.	
Nov. 28 to Dec. 1	Paramount	Toledo, Ohio	
Dec. 2-3	Shea's	Erie, Pa.	
Dec. 5-10	Auditorium	Rochester, N. Y.	
Dec. 12-31	Royal Alexandra	Toronto, Canada	
Jan. 2-14	Her Majesty's	Montreal, Canada	
Jan. 16-21	Erlanger	Buffalo, N. Y.	
Jan. 23-28	Shubert	Cincinnati, Ohio	
Jan. 30 to Feb. 4	Murat	Indianapolis, Ind.	

AND MORE DATES TO COME

Edgar Runkle

the
Teahouse
of the August
Moon

World's Most Acclaimed Musical

Fiddler on the Roof

NATIONAL TOUR 1966-67-68-69

AL. JONES, Co. Mgr.

BEV. KELLEY, Advance Rep.

ROUTE

DATE	THEATRE	CITY and STATE
Apr. 11 - Apr. 16	Civic	San Diego, Cal.
Apr. 19 - June 4	Dorothy Chandler	Los Angeles, Cal.
	Pavilion	San Francisco, Cal.
June 7 - July 23	Curran	Pasadena, Cal.
July 25 - Aug. 6	Civic Aud.	Vancouver, B. C.
Aug. 10 - Aug. 15	Queen Elizabeth	Seattle, Wash.
Aug. 17 - Aug. 29	Opera House	Portland, Ore.
Aug. 31 - Sept. 13	Oriental	Salt Lake City, Utah
Sept. 16 - Sept. 20	Capitol Theatre	Denver, Colo.
Sept. 22 - Oct. 5	Auditorium	Dallas, Texas
Oct. 7 - Oct. 23	State Fair Music Hall	
	American Theatre	St. Louis, Mo.
Oct. 25 - Nov. 5	O'Keefe Centre	Toronto, Ont.
Nov. 7 - Nov. 19	Fisher Theatre	Detroit, Mich.
Nov. 21 - Dec. 17	Palace Theatre	Milwaukee, Wis.
Dec. 19 - Dec. 24	Music Hall	Cleveland, Ohio
Dec. 26-Jan. 7, 1967	Veterans Auditorium	Columbus, Ohio
Jan. 9 - Jan. 14	Shubert Theatre	Cincinnati, Ohio
Jan. 16 - Jan. 28	McVickers Theatre	Chicago, Ill.
Feb. 1 - Oct. 21	Orpheum Theatre	Minneapolis, Minn
Oct. 23 - Nov. 4	Auditorium	St. Paul, Minn.
Nov. 6 - Nov. 11	Clowes Memorial Hall	Indianapolis, Ind
Nov. 13 - Nov. 18	Music Hall	Kansas City, Mo.
Nov. 20 - Nov. 25	Memorial Hall	Dayton, Ohio
Nov. 27 - Dec. 2	Music Hall	Omaha, Neb.
Dec. 4 - Dec. 9	KRNT Theatre	Des Moines, Iow
Dec. 11 - Dec. 16	Municipal Auditorium	Oklahoma City,
Dec. 18 - Dec. 23	6 month engagement	Las Vegas, Nev
Opens Dec. 28	Caesar's Palace	Las Vegas, Nev
Dec. 28 - June 26, '68		

(over)

CABA

the new m

8
TONY
AWARDS

BEV. KELLEY, Advance Rep.

ROU

DATE	THEATR
Dec. 26 - Dec. 31	Shubert T
Jan. 2 - Jan. 20	Hanna Th
Jan. 22 - Jan. 27	Auditoriu
Jan. 29 - Feb. 10	Shubert T
Feb. 12 - Feb. 24	O'Keefe C
Feb. 26 - Mar. 16	Morris M
Mar. 18 - Apr. 13	National
Apr. 15 - May 11	Fisher Th
May 15 - May 18	Communi
May 21 - Sept. 7	Ahmanso
Sept. 10 - Oct. 26	Curran T
Oct. 30 - Nov. 9	Auditoriu
	and Mo

NATIONAL T

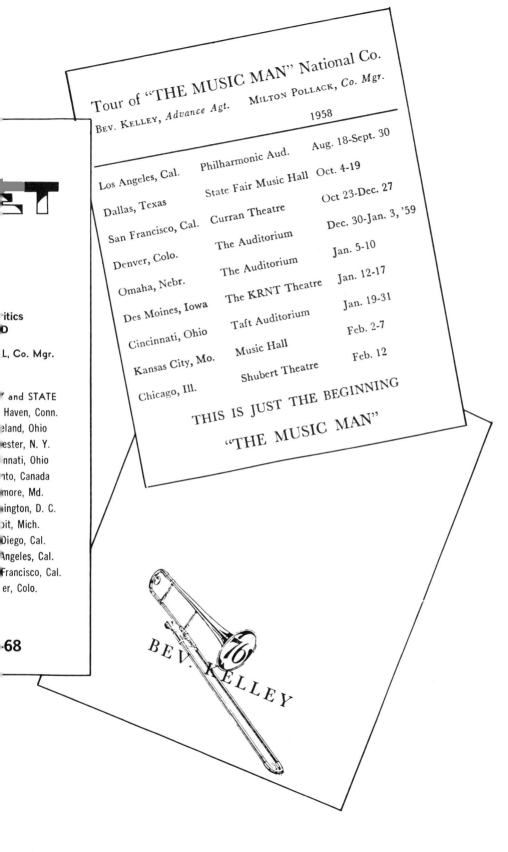

Tour of "THE MUSIC MAN" National Co.

BEV. KELLEY, *Advance Agt.*   MILTON POLLACK, *Co. Mgr.*

1958

Los Angeles, Cal.	Philharmonic Aud.	Aug. 18-Sept. 30
Dallas, Texas	State Fair Music Hall	Oct. 4-19
San Francisco, Cal.	Curran Theatre	Oct 23-Dec. 27
Denver, Colo.	The Auditorium	Dec. 30-Jan. 3, '59
Omaha, Nebr.	The Auditorium	Jan. 5-10
Des Moines, Iowa	The KRNT Theatre	Jan. 12-17
Cincinnati, Ohio	Taft Auditorium	Jan. 19-31
Kansas City, Mo.	Music Hall	Feb. 2-7
Chicago, Ill.	Shubert Theatre	Feb. 12

THIS IS JUST THE BEGINNING

"THE MUSIC MAN"

ritics
D

L, Co. Mgr.

and STATE
Haven, Conn.
eland, Ohio
ester, N. Y.
nnati, Ohio
nto, Canada
more, Md.
ington, D. C.
oit, Mich.
Diego, Cal.
Angeles, Cal.
Francisco, Cal.
er, Colo.

68

BEV. KELLEY

26

THE BIG PRIZE

The gambling fever generated by television's quiz shows reminds me that on one of the ancestors of these memory contests we gave away the biggest live prize ever offered on the air.

This was a network radio program named "Stop The Music," forerunner of a more recent television entry called "Name That Tune." It originated in New York. On a historic night early in the spring of 1949 a surprised housewife in Donora, Pennsylvania, answered her phone and learned she was a lucky winner. Her prize was a pet who tipped the scales at something around seven tons.

The prize was, of course, an elephant. For all her size the name given to her by her keeper was "Baby Mine." And she might have had to bid farewell to 19 other large lady friends in the Cole Brothers Circus herd but for the fortunate fact that the winner of the radio contest had the option of accepting $1000 in preference to her live prize.

The winner chose to do this without hesitation, explaining that she and her husband lived upstairs in a duplex apartment and owned no farm that might accommodate an elephant. And although they emphasized that a check could be sent by mail, we explained that the winners must come to the show's headquarters in Louisville, Kentucky, as guests of the management to meet their elephant and then make their final decision.

Three days later, with newspaper flash bulbs popping and radio interviewers close at hand, the prize pachyderm "trunked" in salute as the circus bought back its property and everyone was happy. The stunt was worth many times the cost in terms of national radio network and newspaper pictorial coverage. There was further comfort in the fact that "Baby Mine" never had to leave home.

About a decade earlier we had climbed aboard another radio contest show named the "Battle Of The Sexes," the first such program with a format that had women competing with men.

That fine show was aired weekly from the NBC studios in Radio City. The program's host and hostess were the musical comedy husband-and-wife team, Julia Sanderson and Frank Crummit. At the Hartman Theater in Columbus, Ohio, I had attended performances of their *Tangerine* and *Queen High* shows, with the songs "Cross Your Heart" and "Sweet Lady." Their popularity was high in the Buckeye State because Frank Crummit had attended Ohio University in Athens and had written "Buckeye Battle Cry" for the dedication of Ohio State's new stadium at Columbus. The band has paraded onto the field to that march ever since.

But to return to the "Battle Of The Sexes," my job in those days was to promote prime time network shows for Ringling Brothers and Barnum & Bailey. That often meant the placing of circus personalities into established radio broadcasts. A problem with the Sanderson-Crummit quiz show was its timetable, for this popular event was aired while our circus performers were well into the evening performances at Madison Square Garden.

We overcame this obstacle by sending to the NBC program our circus sideshow notables. They did not have to be on deck between the start of the arena performance and its conclusion two hours and 15 minutes later. By that time they were on their viewing platforms again for entertainment of customers loitering on their way home.

For several years my able assistant Frank Morrissey and I delivered to that show some of the most exotic talent ever to grace a radio program. Included were a famous family of midget entertainers, a towering giant whose hobby was oil portrait painting, a tattooed "living art gallery" and others, including a lady often referred to by the midway talker as "644 pounds of feminine loveliness." They all were hauled to the studio in taxicabs. The show was before a live audience.

It was customary for me to escort our sideshow fat lady to the radio shows, inasmuch as nobody else was thin enough to share the cab with her. Sometimes she would be Alice from Dallas, while in other touring years she might vary her geography to fit the area where we were showing. Sometimes she was Hattie from Cincinnati, Anna from Savannah, Thelma from Selma and Ruth from Duluth.

Among our radio contestants was a man named Revolvo. His specialty was being able to turn his head almost halfway around. Prior to the airing of each program, its contestants were given the correct answer to the first question so the contest might get off to a comfortable start. Although Revolvo was a remarkable contortionist, he was no memory expert. He invariably forgot the answer he had been given in advance.

On another of our "Battle Of The Sexes" appearances we had a combination strong man and tattooed wonder who could lift heavy weights with rings that pierced his nipples. When he was before the studio audience, entertainer Hal Larson wore a jacket, but on this occasion our program's host was unable to resist seeing how his spouse would react to the sight of such a bizarre spectacle. He invited our walking art gallery to remove his jacket so all might see his "etchings." Julia Sanderson joined in the applause. Later when I complimented her on her composure she told me that she had feared that she might faint.

During one of the springtime circus engagements in New York I received a distress signal from my old college friend, Harry Holcomb. He had achieved prominence at Cincinnati's WLW radio station, where he was the announcer for its popular "Moon River" nighttime program. Now he produced a network quiz show in Manhattan.

Frequently I appeared on radio programs that offered opportunity to get publicity for the circus, but this request was a most unusual one.

My friend explained that their "comedian" couldn't show up for their program three hours from that time. Holcomb recalled from our acting days in college that I was what the theater calls a "quick study," and asked me to tell the story of "The Three Little Pigs" in the vernacular of a midway sideshow spieler.

I accepted this challenge with considerable reluctance because I felt it should be delivered from memory and not read or cued by cards. It went off pretty well. Then my friend said that one of the contestants for that evening's show was too ill to appear and asked if I would take his place. By then I was tired and wanted to return to my office in Madison Square Garden. I was certain I'd miss the quiz questions as fast as they came at me, so I agreed to oblige since it shouldn't take very long.

As fate would have it, I answered every question correctly. I was embarrassed because I felt the program's staff people, knowing that its producer and I were friends, would likely think that I had been fed the answers to the program's questions. Prizes included a lot of merchandise supplied by the sponsor, a portable radio and phonograph, a set of silver table knives, a lot of chinaware and an electric roaster.

Having seen our most recent electric bill, I felt we didn't need an electric roaster so I gave it to Bob and Irene Ringling to use on their private railway car. I felt sure that nobody in our Ohio town would have heard the radio program.

I was mistaken. As I stepped off the train for a weekend visit at home, Ruth's first question was "Where's the electric roaster?" And for some years thereafter, when I was inclined to be less than cooperative on the domestic scene, one of the children could be counted upon to ask, "Daddy, where's the electric roaster?"

27

SOME LAUGHS, SOME LUMPS

If I were to teach playwriting in a college drama department, I believe I would use *Mister Roberts* as a blueprint for the perfect play. It is the best of the comedy dramas; wonderful to watch and gratifying to represent as a touring advance agent. In 1950, that was my job. In Herman Bernstein, producer Leland Hayward had the kind of general manager who employed a front man because he knew the territory. Then he left him to do his work without interruption from the New York office, unless he asked for assistance in solving some local theater problem along the route. Our company manager was Clarence Jacobson, my pal of *The Green Pastures* tours, and again we shared some lively and amusing situations.

Such as the time somebody literally "got our goat" during the Cleveland, Ohio, engagement. We had a nanny goat tethered outside the stage door at the rear of the Hanna Theater. She was returned the following morning and didn't miss a performance; the incident did make a good news story especially since it happened on Halloween.

Another time, a New Orleans playgoer showed up one morning with a goat he had found wandering in the neighborhood. He assumed that we had lost the goat which he had seen on our stage the night before. However, a search revealed our four-footed actress safe in her traveling crate. Her single walk-on part needed no understudy, so our stage manager asked the Humane Society to get the stray.

One of the advance agent's duties was to rent a goat in each of the towns on the *Mister Roberts* itinerary. While the French alpine and Nubian varieties are more impressive because of their horns, our preference ran to the female Toggenbergs. They have a gentle disposition and lack the strong odor usually associated with the traditional billy goat. In the course of my goat-getting, I rented one belonging to a farmer in Syracuse, New York. He told me that drinking goat milk steadily for a year had cured an arm rendered almost useless by arthritis. He had stopped all medication. The milk, he said, is homogenized naturally in the animal, tastes like cow's milk and has no offensive goat scent if the billy has not been allowed to run with the nannys.

Stagehands sometimes appear unexpectedly in a scene where only the play actors are meant to be. Sometimes when working onstage and unable to disappear before the show starts, stage technicians often can hide in a window drapery or duck down behind a sofa. At one of our *Mister Roberts* matinees in Washington, D.C., our revolving set turned to reveal a new scene, including a man they had never seen before. He wore an old hat and a raincoat and later explained that he was a visiting stagehand who had come backstage to collect some money owed to him by one of the theater's employees. He had managed to get caught when the revolving set moved. He didn't panic, but simply stood in a convenient corner while the actors ignored him as they played out the scene.

It was during this same engagement in May 1950 that President Harry S. Truman and his family attended an evening performance. In the nation's capital, where President Lincoln was shot by an actor in 1865, security is so tight that the attendance of a chief executive at a theatrical performance is never announced in advance.

Although the theater management expects its distinguished guest, it does not receive offical confirmation until just before he leaves the White House. During the daytime hours preceding the presidential visit a number of quiet but capable-looking young men examine the playhouse very thoroughly all the way from the basement to its lofty gridiron. Several rows of seats on the main floor are "killed" both in front of and behind the row in which the president and his guests will be seated.

After the conclusion of the performance it is customary for the president to leave his guests for a brief backstage appearance to congratulate the players. The night when it fell to me to escort

John Forsythe played the lead in Mister Roberts.

The famed goat from Mister Roberts *is the one on the right.*

President Truman, his popularity had dropped appreciably because he had just fired Gen. Douglas MacArthur for insubordination. Our players were lined up to shake hands when the president arrived on-stage and said, "Thank you, boys, for giving me a wonderful evening." But one of our actors who was a MacArthur fan withheld his hand. Sensing the reason for this, the president simply smiled. Then the player contributed to the overall embarrassment by saying, "All right, I will!" and they finally shook hands.

We took our acting company in a charter bus to the United States Naval Hospital at Bethesda to give a complete performance for the veterans there, and this was a heartwarming as well as an amusing event. A young chaplain who assumed I was in charge of the troupe quietly said that he hoped we would not omit any of our play's rough and authentic language. "Even our nurses will love it," he explained.

The players had saved some time by donning costumes prior to boarding their bus. Because they portrayed officers and men aboard a cargo ship in the South Pacific during World War II, their so-called "wardrobe" was treated regularly with chemicals to make the stage uniforms look realistically sweat-soaked and otherwise disreputable.

I was walking behind the last of our actors as they marched down the long corridor to the end of the building where the stage had been prepared for the performance. We passed a large ward where an orderly reacted in surprise. He turned to a companion and asked, "What the hell is this?"

"Damned if I know," replied his friend. "There must have been a shipwreck somewhere."

Theater people usually hold the citizens of the circus in high esteem, but the enthusiasm of stage star Alfred Lunt was monumental. I became aware of this first in the autumn of 1941. The Broadway hit, *There Shall Be No Night,* starring Lunt and Lynne Fontanne, played Atlanta during the engagement of the Ringling Brothers and Barnum & Bailey Circus there.

Alfred Lunt attended our circus matinee performance, but it was a sad occasion because eight of our elephants were dying from a mysterious arsenic poisoning. On the previous day in Charlotte, North Carolina, the herd had been allowed to graze on the show ground, where we feel the vegetation had been poisoned with waste from a nearby chemical plant. All the circus company mourned the demise of our noble beasts, and the great stage personality wept openly at their quiet suffering.

Alfred Lunt and Lynne Fontanne, superstars of the international stage, as they appeared in The Great Sebastians.

A week later in Norfolk, the touring Lunts and the circus met again. It was a cold and windy Sunday when the big show labored to erect its tented city in preparation for performances on the following day. I invited my illustrious theater friends to watch the circus at work. Lynne begged off but her husband accepted at once. On a busy circus lot, Alfred's interest was captured by the six-man team of stake drivers swinging their 12-pound sledges in rotation.

Fascinated by this precision performance, he soon asked, ''Could I do that?'' I asked permission of our boss canvasman, who noted the muscles of my tall, well-built guest. (They were developed during his early years on a Wisconsin farm.)

''Sure,'' he said, ''but be careful; it's almost as dangerous as the flying trapeze.'' The actor smiled, thanked him and joined the circus workers, substituting briefly for one of the regulars. He didn't miss a beat or get a hand mauled either.

After dinner in the circus dining tent, we returned to the hotel. Alfred cried out in excitement as he entered their suite: ''Lynnie,

Lunt and Fontanne posed with me in San Francisco's Huntington Hotel.

they let me drive a stake!'' I have known actors to show less enthusiasm at being given a Tony award.

Later I had the pleasure of working for a show that starred the two, who were the theater's most distinguished husband-and-wife team. *The Great Sebastians* was a cloak-and-dagger kind of comedy which I fronted for their coast-to-coast road tour. Alfred was worried over a promise that he had made to address a school group on the subject of acting. Public speaking was not in his line of experience and he sought the help of his wife. ''What can I say to them, Lynnie?'' he asked. ''It's simple enough,'' she replied. ''Just tell them to speak clearly and not bump into other people on the stage.''

The Lunts were international luminaries and one of their best friends was England's famed actor-playwright, Noel Coward. He shared Alfred's interest in gourmet cooking. In his later years, when Lunt lost most of his sight through neglect of glaucoma, he asked Coward if he thought it might be possible to continue his cooking. "I think so," encouraged his friend. "Just remember when you cook whitefish don't serve it on a white plate."

My wife and I enjoyed our visits with the Lunts at their beautiful home, "Ten Chimneys," at Genesee Depot, Wisconsin. Alfred had helped his widowed mother raise his sister on that land during his boyhood. He sent his mother $30 of the first money he earned as a young actor in Boston. She used it to purchase the single acre that grew to be the palatial place of the present. I asked him how much he thought that first single acre might be worth on today's market. "Why, it's worth $30," he replied, "because it's not for sale!"

Dear Alfred is gone now, but his Lynne still lives in Genessee Depot and Ruth and I stop to see her whenever we visit our good friends at the Circus World Museum in Baraboo.

It was a genuine pleasure having our children and their mother on the road with me from time to time. They came to New York City for some of the annual springtime engagements of RBB&B in Madison Square Garden, and also to attend the 1939 World's Fair. When our son Stephen and his sister Pat were age 9 and 7, respectively, they traveled with the circus for several of the convenient Ohio stands. Our circus photographer recorded their day-to-day adventures to illustrate the book I was writing at the time, *Circus Holiday*.

Our son's love of animals both wild and domestic was apparent at an early age. One day when his mother found him seated on our side porch with his cheek against the nose of a stray dog of uncertain parentage, she told thim that he should not get his face that close to a strange dog.

"But he's not a strange dog," Stephen protested, "I told him my name."

That same little boy grew up to become superintendent of the fine Columbus, Ohio, Zoo. He and his wife had the honor of being babysitters for the first gorilla to be born in Captivity in America.

I was fronting the national touring company of *The Teahouse Of The August Moon* in 1956 when Ruth brought our Kathleen and Rebecca to join me in San Francisco. Our younger daughters then were 11 and 4, respectively. They traveled by rail from our neighbor city of Marion, Ohio, to Chicago for a connection with the Union Pacific train that would bring them to Oakland, California, where we would ferry across the bay to San Francisco.

A good railway friend of mine was Bill Klomp who served the

Stephen and Pat Kelley admire the Ringling Bros. "Giant Couple," Mr. and Mrs. Fred Fischer, as the youngsters toured the circus for my book, Circus Holiday.

Patricia and Stephen Kelley talk shop with their new circus friends, Paul Jung and aerialist Elly Ardelty.

The Kelley kids are handed by their father to their mother, as they board the circus sleeper for another Ohio stand during their Circus Holiday.

Chicago, Milwaukee and St. Paul Railroad for many years. I had enlisted his assistance in planning the western trip for my girls via the scenic Royal Gorge route. But their train from Ohio ran late going into Chicago, where they had to change stations.

Their California-bound train was ready to roll as they arrived at Chicago's Union Station. In trouble now, Ruth wisely thought to use the name of Bill Klomp in order to have the train held for five minutes as she, the little girls and their redcap ran through the station. Then, safely aboard and bound for the West, Kathleen said, "Mother, I knew we would catch the train because I prayed that we would." Her mother's reply was an example of the practical philosophy which I still treasure: "Praying is important, dear, but always remember that you still have to run like hell."

During their return trip we took our daughters to visit their great aunt, Ruth Kelley, for the first time. She was long retired from a teaching career and then living in Long Beach, California. She lived into her 90s and I like the way she anticipated the phenomenon of death — as a welcome adventure, or like a child eagerly awaiting an invitation to a party or a pleasant trip.

28

OUR FAMOUS, FUNNY FRIENDS

My circus and theater work kept me on the road almost constantly during the 1940s and 1950s. There were some long weekends made possible only when I had hoarded time by working almost around the clock.

But Ruth never complained. She traveled with me during the early years of our marriage and she had become familiar with my work and the time required to do it. Later, however, the rearing of our children kept her at home. She was embarrassed often by having to attend social functions without me. This worried me some, but I finally concluded that perhaps our friends and acquaintances were about equally divided. There were those who felt sorry for my wife because her husband was away so much and those who thought that for the same reason she might be the luckiest woman in town.

Her own career in the field of interior design was at its zenith. She gave more and more attention to the carpet and drapery requirements of our Blair-Kelley Furniture Company and to our gift department which she had created and stocked. When our timetables permitted our being together at home we were rarely without visitors.

Among interesting guests who came calling was Edith Ramsey, editor of *American Home Magazine*. She wrote an excellent pictorial about the handsome and practical new kitchen my talented spouse

Ruth Kelley in 1959, at the height of her career as an educator and interior designer.

had designed into a remodeling of our home.

Steven Dohanos was an Ohio-born illustrator for the *Saturday Evening Post*. I had worked with him in New York on his idea for a *Post* cover. This depicted an unhappy boy trying to be brave in a second-floor dentist's chair while the clown bandwagon of a circus parade was passing in the street. I had supplied the bandwagon and live clowns for models.

Stage star Cornelia Otis Skinner shared honors with Ruth Draper as a queen of the one-woman dramatic presentations. She came to us from an evening of playing *The Wives Of Henry VIII* at the University Auditorium. Whenever we met during the 40 years thereafter she never failed to ask if my wife still made the world's best hamburger sandwich. And the answer has always been a truthful "Yes."

Circus kings John and Henry Ringling North, my employers at that time, indulged their curiosity in seeing the hometown I had talked so much about. Their brief visit coincided conveniently with the Big Show's playing date in Columbus, only 25 miles away.

One morning we were visited by our Columbus friend, Mary Katherine Noland. Ruth had asked her to be on the lookout for a cleaning man who might arrive while she was doing a quick errand. The workman failed to show up at all that day; instead we were delighted by the surprise visit of the New York newspaper celebrity and circus buff, Fred Woltman. Fred, his wife Virginia and their chum, the musical stage and screen actor Ray Middleton, were traveling together by automobile from the West Coast.

All of us except our Columbus friend talked show business. Middleton, who was Ethel Merman's co-star in the powerhouse Broadway musical, *Annie Get Your Gun,* is not at all pompous or conceited. However, he seemed to be less than amused when Mrs. Noland said to him, "I thought you were the cleaning man."

A few years later Woltman suffered a paralytic stroke that left him unable to speak coherently, to read or to write. He made a good recovery after 24 months of continuous heroic effort. During that long two years he never lost his sense of humor and frequently referred to himself as "the only Pulitzer Prize-winning reporter who can neither read nor write."

Freddie Woltman invariably was assigned to cover the circus during our Madison Square Garden engagement. In the years when "Bo" McAnny was the great city editor of the *New York World-Telegram.* Freddie showed up on the afternoon of the show's opening night when all the performers were in dress rehearsal and I

The brilliant actress, Cornelia Otis Skinner.

couldn't produce a single star to be interviewed.

Finally, at the outside lobby snack stand I spotted the famed Doll family of midgets: Daisy, Harry, Gracie and Tiny (in order of age and altitude). I steered Fred Woltman to them. For a few minutes they talked about their motion picture appearances, beginning with Harry's role of the cigar-smoking tiny bad man with Lon Chaney in *The Unholy Three*. They discussed their home in Sarasota, where all the furnishings were custom built to suit the special physical requirements of the family. I thought of an interesting fact that I felt our reporter friend might not know. To our miniature marvels I said, "Isn't it true that in your family there are four midgets and four children of normal height, and that you were born alternately?"

Whereupon pretty little Daisy Doll responded, "No, we were all born in Germany."

Another Buckeye-born friend and ex-reporter was the famous librettist, Russel Crouse. He brought to our home the distinguished Howard Lindsay, his collaborator for the Broadway triumphs *Anything Goes, Life With Father, Arsenic And Old Lace* and *The Sound Of Music*. At the time they were working on a new comedy they called *Tall Story,* about a basketball star. Researching college life and the general vernacular of the era, they had chosen Ohio Wesleyan. They knew that it was in my home town.

We all spent a couple of enjoyable days on and off campus. I mentioned that while both the Kelleys and the university were honored by their presence, the really basketball-crazy state was Indiana. Buck Crouse replied that he knew this, "but there we would not be able to enjoy Ruth's great cooking!" And indeed this was a wise observation, for my wife not only is the best cook I have ever known, she taught our three daughters to cook and to sew just as Ruth's mother had taught her. Her brother Harold and Alfred Lunt were the two best male kitchen magicians I can recall, but neither can compare to my Ruth.

It was while we lived on Oak Hill that ex-President Herbert Hoover came to Delaware to deliver the principal address at the inauguration of Arthur Fleming, the new college president. Fleming had served in federal civil service posts for years. Later he was appointed secretary of health, education and welfare by President Dwight D. Eisenhower.

Fleming had been my contemporary during college days. Now he had moved his family into the Oak Hill home that was traditionally a residence of college presidents. Hoover was, of course, their house guest. I walked our two older children there to meet him. I wanted

From left, Russel "Buck" Crouse, Edgar Runkle and me, during the run of Teahouse of the August Moon.

them to be able to say that they had met and talked with Herbert Hoover, the man for whom their dad had cast his first presidential election ballot in 1928.

My admiration for this public servant increased through the years. He was unjustly blamed for the Great Depression of the 1930s and denied a second term. Instead of pouting in embittered retirement, Herbert Hoover continued his service to his fellowman by heading the Boys Clubs of America during the remainder of a useful and dedicated life.

29

NED ALVORD — MASTER OF BALLYHOO

Frank Braden, Dexter Fellows and even old P.T. Barnum were giants in the field of circus publicists, but they had their counterparts in the ranks of theatrical press agents. I was fortunate to have been able to serve about equally in both capacities. The circus was more enjoyable, I thought, but there were lots of thrills in the legitimate theater too. And some of my predecessors were also gloriously colorful folks indeed.

A certain flowing tie, cutaway coat and hard hat were preening for the trail and they all belonged to the same man: Ned Alvord.

In Broadway's late summer, one of the signs of the upcoming new touring season is the stirring of road agents from their summer-long hibernation.

Their getting-ready-to-leave-town appearance as they visit and talk shop in the high-wattage shelter of theater marquees presages the advent of autumn as surely as the first circus poster heralds the coming of spring. And among this itinerant fraternity Ned Alvord was by many lengths the most colorful.

I had heard a great deal about Alvord for years before I finally caught up with him. In many a town, while I was doing advance work for traveling plays and for circuses, I'd miss Ned by a few hours or a few days.

We met for the first time in the Forrest Hotel on 49th Street in New York. Ned was seated by the window of a small, neat room. His hair sported a stiff G.I. cut. The wardrobe consisted of seersucker pants with wide, white old-fashioned galluses; armor-plate shirt with detachable cuffs; a corncob pipe; high-button shoes and a green eyeshade.

In Alvord's bathtub floated a thermos jug containing the kind of butter he liked. Ned explained that he carried the jug to restaurants with him, and he had cheese too, in neatly-arranged tins on his closet shelf.

When he arose to go out for dinner, he ceremoniously donned a formal cutaway coat made out of seersucker for summertime use. A similar coat made of more traditional material was reserved for winter weather. No matter what the season, Ned always wore a flowing tie.

Alvord, the best-known of all the theatrical road publicists, always had an eye out for the bizarre. That fixed a picture of him in the minds of the local playhouse managers, the newspaper people and others with whom he had business in the town. In Texas, for example, Ned wore a derby hat, but in the eastern cities his standard finery included a ten-gallon Stetson and a rattlesnake belt. "At the start," he said, "the idea was to look as striking as my dad on the day when he was inaugurated mayor of Eldora, Iowa, in 1887. A different kind of outfit made folks talk then, and it still does."

Often Alvord, in pursuit of his publicity and advertising chores, was mistaken for a preacher, until something happened to annoy him and he cut loose with his customary purple language. And the unusual wardrobe saved Ned's employers money from time to time because when he went to the display advertising department of a newspaper, they'd quote the church rate to the soft-spoken, reticent and courteous gentleman in the evangelistic attire. The church, or "charity" rate, was about half the rate that was charged to traveling shows, and there'd be hell to pay an hour later when the same gentleman of distinction returned with a set of lively girl-show "art."

A theater manager who never had seen Ned Alvord met him on the street a few minutes after the advance agent had stepped from a train and said, "Hello, Ned."

"How do you know my name?" asked Alvord.

"Well," the theater man said, "I figured that since I ain't expectin' no gambler, and since no minister would be lookin' for me, and since I had a wire from Ned Alvord, I figured it had to be you."

Alvord once played hookey from his traditional costume and donned a pith helmet in Manila. Wally Anderson, manager of the Manila Hotel, took one look and said, "Ned, just what are you anyhow?'' Alvord was hurt.

"You know damn well I'm an American showman!''

"I wasn't sure,'' replied Anderson. "You look a lot like a Limey tourist.'' Whereupon Ned and his tropical helmet parted company forever.

The colorful Alvord was not featured in stories about Broadway press agents. He was a road man entirely and the whole wide world was his Broadway. Like others among the itinerant members of his fraternity, Ned looked down on publicity people who think that the west wall of show business is the Hudson River. He was properly proud, moreover, of being an Iowan, from whence came such stalwarts as the Ringling brothers, Buffalo Bill Cody and player-producer Corse Payton, who called himself "America's Best Bad Actor,'' and proved it every performance.

By his own estimate, Ned Alvord was a showman. "I reckon I must be,'' he mused. "I've been through bankruptcy once, divorced once, stranded more than once, jailed once, broke several times and generally hated by actors. What else could I be except a showman?''

Alvord used to say that he was Yankee by descent, Jewish by theatrical influence and Scotch (with soda) by choice. His favorite reading was the Official Railroad Guide, and his favorite vista was an empty ticket rack at curtain time.

Ned could work up girl-show advertising calculated to put ideas into the head of an octogenarian, and this talent often cost him no small amount of trouble.

Once the staid members of a community demanded the immediate covering of semi-nude figures that graced one of Alvord's theatrical billboards. He tacked long johns on them instead and the publicity response to the stunt sold out the house.

An oft-used stunt of Ned's once backfired in Dixie. He occasionally pumped steam into a publicity campaign by writing irate letters to newspaper editors. He signed some illegible name with a rural address difficult to trace, and asked the paper if it was going to permit such a sinful show to exhibit in the town. If the newspaper printed the letter, which it usually did, hell frequently broke loose in the ministerial meetings. The resulting fanfare proved to be of considerable help at the ticket windows of what usually was a pretty tame performance. And so it was that in a large southern city Ned's letter to the editor was so effective that it set in motion a movement that **did** keep the show out of town!

Although he spent his declining years there, Ned disliked Los Angeles. Indeed he claimed that the most beautiful sight in town was Union Station, "because its trains can take you the hell out of there!" His antipathy for L.A. may have stemmed from an unhappy experience he had had there during World War II, when Alvord put together a lecture and rented an auditorium. His thesis was that the Japanese came straight from the gorilla without a missing link. However, he was no great shakes as an orator and he made the mistake of playing his ace first. He showed his slides and then tried to put over his point.

As soon as the pictures were finished, the disappointed spectators loudly demanded their money back. Our hero was not so fortunate as was the thespian Duke in *Huckleberry Finn;* Alvord had no confederate to help him do a run-out. Instead, he refunded on the spot and the adventure cost him $1,200. "That experience taught me something," Ned said. "To stick with press agentry!"

An experience in 1934 had been the genesis of Ned's dislike of the Japanese. That was the year he toured the orient with the famous Marcus Show. It mopped up in Hong Kong, Canton, Singapore, Manila, Shanghai and Osaka. In Tokyo, according to the press agent, customers paid $3 top price to see what he called a 50-cent show. The run lasted seven and a half weeks. Then jealous business interests in opposition theaters brought such strong official pressure that Ned and his attraction were thrown out of the country on the trumped-up charges that the performances were nude and immoral. "But it wasn't too nude and immoral for seven and a half weeks," Alvord remembered, and he stayed sore.

The ingredients necessary to produce the strange concoction known as a press agent, according to that oracle, are: the hide of a rhinoceros, the sangfroid of Sydney Carton on the guillotine, and the heart, if not the trigger fingers, of the brothers James. If business is good, the management says, "We have a great show." If business is bad, or whatever else goes wrong, "it's the fault of the advance agent."

Once an attraction that Alvord was fronting had actor trouble. The manager sent for the press agent to return to the show and fill the gap. Ned bravely attempted the role of Wally in *Caprice.* After two performances, the director-owner sent for the press agent and told him to remain up ahead of the show no matter what emergency might take place. Then he exploded: "Why, damn it Alvord, you haven't brains enough to be anything **but** a press agent!"

Ned once owned part of a Viennese operetta called *The Gay Musician.* The show was tottering until, in an Illinois town, the theater manager said, "Ned, this ain't a burlesque show, is it?"

"Certainly not!" Alvord replied with indignation. "You know I wouldn't be associated with a burlesque show! Why do you ask?"

"No offense intended," the theater manager replied. "I just thought it would do more business if it was a burlesque show."

"It is!" snapped Ned with enthusiasm. And soon *The Gay Musician* became *Champagne Belles,* featuring "La Twisterita."

Alvord's tour with this one ran a year, but the company seldom was a stranger to hunger. The hot breath of the town sheriffs kept Ned's neck from chapping. When at last the show folded in Manhattan, Kansas, Ned's backer wired him as follows: "Good thing I didn't loan you $200 instead of $100; you would have kept that show out for **two** years!"

Alvord always advocated playing to a lot of people at low prices rather than to fewer at higher prices. He managed a variety theater in Terre Haute, Indiana, in 1907. Al Jolson played the house for three days, receiving $28.92, which figured out at three-sevenths of his $75 weekly salary less 10 percent booking commission. The highest paid act that season was "The Five Columbians," a dancing act that was paid $350 a week and featured a pretty little juvenile ballerina named Marilyn Miller.

Ned Alvord started out to be an actor as a child, and this delighted his mother. However, his father casually remarked that "Every woman thinks her young one and her sewing machine are the best in the world." A few years later, Ned recalled, his old man broke his wife's heart by having the lad's curls cut off. A friend had said innocently, "Ned, that's a mighty pert little gal you have there."

The family moved to Wisconsin when the Alvord son was in high school. There the budding showman became lessee and manager of the town music hall. All went well until the youthful impresario booked an attraction peopled by obvious tarts. Their extracurricular activities caused the community's leading madam to complain to the authorities. She felt that it was unfair competition for transients to derive profit from the sale of services which could be had in hometown establishments.

This episode nearly ended Ned's theatrical as well as his high school career. In time it blew over and he continued at the Music Hall. In dull season he worked on the coal docks as a hatch tender at 22½¢ an hour.

Upon graduation from high school in 1902, young Alvord did a hitch on the town newspaper and acquired his taste for writing advertising copy. It became his forte and years later he had a reputation for creating the most provocative girl-show advertisements extant.

He always felt that he owed his flair for showmanship to his father. The elder Alvord employed ballyhoo to persuade housewives to use Pillsbury's Best flour. He pioneered the use of balloons which contained prizes for the finder, a stunt copied widely by motion picture theaters in later years.

For three years, Ned Alvord was a boss billposter for the Ringling Circus. He distinguished himself and his crew in New Orleans by "ragging," or tacking circus muslin banners, on a historic shrine that was the home of the pirate patriot, Jean Laffite. A storm of protest raged within the parish historical society and the newspapers took it up, Finally, Ned's men took down the banners. The fact was that they had been put up in five hours, whereas five full days were used to get them removed. In the meantime, thousands had gawked at the bright circus advertising and ten times that number at the resultant publicity surrounding their removal.

Ned recalled that the greatest hoax and crowd phychologist of his experience was Grady Galvin, who sold gen-yew-wine Egyptian eye ointment at a dollar a box. Galvin would select a myopic member of his "tip," or audience. He would run his hand carefully through well-oiled hair in a casual gesture, transfering the grease to the lens under the guise of examing the glasses of his mark. Replacing them, he would ask the chump if he could see, and of course, he was more blind than ever.

Then he removed the glasses and set them aside. An attendant slyly wiped them with a clean silk cloth while the eyes of the spectators were on the good "doctor" and his monkeyshines. He was fastening a blindfold over the sucker's eyes. A few drops of the gen-yew-wine dope were put on the bandage. Removing the cloth quickly and replacing the glasses, Galvin would ask, **"Now,** can you see?"

"Fine! Fine!" blubbered the chump. "Better than ever before!" as he gratefully reached for his money and bought two bottles.

Ned's friend gravitated naturally into politics in later years and Alvord recalled seeing him acquit himself with distinction in a Texas primary. Galvin's opponent had just told the people what a terrible person old Grady Galvin was. The object of the verbal attack arose then and with great dignity replied, "What the distinguished Demosthenes has told you of my character is, alas, all too true!" Then he thundered, "But, my friends, do you think for one minute that the great minds of the Democratic party of the great State of Texas in all their wisdom would send **other** than a man like me to stand on the same platform with a son-of-a-bitch like that?''

Alvord's fame as a road press agent was not premised solely on effective advertising and stunts; he could compose good copy. He belonged to the old school of writing agents whose typewriters turned out more rhetoric than boiled-down cutline text. Here is Ned's description of Buffalo Bill's Wild West Show:

> I still can feel the lump in my throat and quickening pulse as I picture the handsomest figure of man and horse ever seen — tall, majestic; his face distinguished with mustache and imperial; his long flowing locks crowned by a wide-brim sombrero; his athletic body clad in elaborately-beaded buckskin, sitting in his saddle straight as a ramrod astride a magnificent dapple-gray stallion with mane and tail as God made them, and galloping across the arena as spot lamps singled him out from the motley entourage of his centaurs from the four corners of the earth.
>
> Then, as though he knew full well the honor of his position, the noble charger executed a graceful curvet and kneeled on his forelegs as the great scout waved aloft his Stetson and there came the clarion intonations of the announcer: "Ladeez and Gentlemen, I have the honor to introduce Col. William F. Cody, Buffalo Bill, and his Congress of Rough Riders of the World!"
>
> In the crescendo of a thousand throats mingled the yippees of the cowboys, the fierce blood cries of the Cossacks from the steppes, the gutterals of the Uhlans and the battle cheer of the famed Seventh Cavalry from the ensanguined plains beyond the Missouri. And, above all, the terrible war whoops of the Sioux, even as might have sounded in the ears of gallant Custer at the Battle of the Little Big Horn. God Almighty, what a show!

Alvord authored three plays. "None," he barked when telling me about them, "went farther than saloon (and I don't mean 'salon') presentation."

As a publicist, Ned Alvord once was embarrassed by the absence of luminaries in the Marcus Show which he represented. So, he wrote to a drama editor and eulogized the musical's owner for his avowed unwillingness to give one of his performing artists more prominence than another in the big company. "Mr. Marcus does not believe in the Star System," penned Alvord.

A typical example of advertising in the Alvord manner was his pitch for that minor extravaganza. He wrote, "The Marcus Show is not the Ziegfeld Follies, it is not George White's Scandals, it is not a New York Winter Garden revue, and it is not Earl Carroll's Vanities. It is, however, the biggest attraction in the theatrical realm ever provided at two dollars for the best seats. It is not designed for the blase, satiated, self-appointed Jovians of the press (Ned never liked critics very much). It is purposed solely for the amusement of those ruddy-corpusculated citizens who revel in abdominal guffaws and who contemplate with ecstatic delight the loveliness of American girlhood."

One critic penned a single-sentence review of Ned's show: "You're right, Mister Press Agent. It's not Earl Carroll's Vanities, it's not George White's Scandals, it's not a New York Winter Garden revue and it's **not** the Ziegfeld Follies."

Alvord got into a brawl with a theater manager following the demise of a tour that Ned was agenting. There was hard talk and finally blows backstage and Alvord was jailed for one night, charged with rioting. Then his attorney reminded the judge that the law read, "When three or more persons shall conspire to incite a riot . . ." Then he argued that, inasmuch as Alvord was only **one** person, he must be falsely accused. The judge squirted a stream of Mail Pouch at a wood box filled with sawdust and said, "Reckon yer right, counsel. Case dismissed."

During the trouble with Pancho Villa in 1916, Alvord wanted a theater concession at Fort Bliss, on the United States-Mexico border near El Paso, Texas. He spent 10 days in Washington and was shoved around considerably, but only 10 minutes with Gen. Frederick Funston at San Antonio. Then he got what he wanted. He had been tipped off that the general was the only person who could do it for him. "My subsequent experience with the military and with politicians," said Alvord, "always has been the same."

Alvord toured Army camps during World War I and on one occasion started a premature Armistice celebration by issuing a handbill with big black headlines that read **Kaiser Drops Dead.** What readers did not tumble to was the smaller-print subheading which explained how "Kaiser **Gloom** was so overcome with laughter at seeing Kitty Francis" in Alvord's little theater masterpiece "that he dropped dead in his tracks."

On one occasion Alvord let his enthusiasm get the better of his judgment. He jumped a touring show 1,500 miles by rail to fill a one-week contract and then saddled his comedian, Milton Shuster, with this label: "The funniest man in the world! The last and only one of his kind! When he is gone the race is extinct!'' Ned and the show went broke.

Alvord appraised the failure thusly: "The smarter a showman thinks he is, the less he knows.'' Still, in the depths of the big Depression of the 1930s he managed to gross $12,000 for a single performance of *Crazy Quilt* at the old Ryman Auditorium in Nashville, Tennessee. He did it with the old Alvord-style ballyhoo.

The show starred Fannie Brice, and because the antiquated building had no regular dressing rooms, Ned arranged to use a restroom as her dressing facility.

The next morning Ned tried to duck his star but she confronted him anyway. "Ned," Fannie yelled, "I know you are going to apologize for what you had to do to me, but I'll dress in a crapper any old time for the kind of money we took in here last night!''

The gregarious and eccentric knight of the old show biz trail had friends all over, but the real love of his life was his boyhood dog Duke. That animal always had eggs for breakfast and the first piece of apple pie as Ned's mother took it from the oven. "Duke lived a dog's life, but **what** a dog's life,'' Alvord recalled.

Duke died from the dread blackmouth malady at the age of 13, and his loving master's epitaph went like this: "Duke was a good dog, a good friend, a gentleman and a Republican!''

Just prior to the time when Alvord took the Marcus Show to the orient, he asked a Chinese friend to draw him a calling card in Chinese characters. Ned handed the cards out all over the map until, near the end of the tour, someone translated the message for him. "It says that you are exceptionally honest, very brave and a great man with the ladies.''

"Hell,'' snorted Alvord, "I'd steal a stove that didn't have a fire in it, I've been frightened by rabbits, and the only gals who go for me now went out of style with the *Police Gazette,* and I mean the **old** *Police Gazette!''*

This one-of-a-kind kaleidoscope among showmen worked hard and played hard most of his life. At our last meeting he was retired and living at the Elks Club in Los Angeles. Still wearing a derby hat, he recalled being employed by a carnival called "The World Of Pleasure Shows.''

He over-imbibed one night while fronting that attraction. During the night he received a telephone call announcing that the show had closed unexpectedly. He rolled over and went back to sleep. He had no recollection of the call the next morning and proceeded to book it into nine more towns before learning it was in the barn.

''All of which illustrates,'' he said, ''that while raising hell never made me forget to do my chores, there came a time when it made me do too much!''

30

GIANTS ON THE TROUPER TRAIL

Now and then when I come across an unusual name I think about George Alabam Florida. And that was his name, or anyhow his professional moniker. George, a theatrical publicity agent, lent color and distinction to that group of showmen who wear no spangles, whose form and face no spotlight ever bathes, who hear no applause and who take no bows.

George Alabam Florida took his unique name when he awakened on a railway station bench early one morning while awaiting a late train. Staring at him from a rack of timetables was one labeled "The Georgia, Alabama and Florida Railroad."

"I decided that maybe that timetable was telling me something," the showman recalled. "I didn't have a colorful name, I wanted one, and it even sounded a little like my real name."

So for the remainder of a long and flamboyant career George was known to his friends as George Alabam. His real name was George Florita. He had been born to a New England circus family with a flying trapeze act.

Because George was the youngest child he performed while dressed as a girl. One day his catcher, an older brother, accidentally dropped him into the treacherous "safety" net. That sent George to look for work in a less dangerous branch of show business.

Many years later people thought that George sounded like W.C.

Fields, but actually it was Fields who had affected a voice like George Alabam Florida, who happened to be his friend. Fields had done some vaudeville trouping with him before building an act of his own which featured trick shots on a billiard table. He appeared with one of numerous editions of the *Ziegfeld Follies*.

Florenz Ziegfeld had Fields performing his specialty on the table with a huge slanted mirror behind it so that the skill of the performer with ball and cue could be seen by spectators on the lower floor of the theater. Ziegfeld wanted Fields to talk while he performed.

"All right," Fields told his employer, "I'll try to work some comedy into the act by talking like George Alabam Florida."

When not on stage the voice of W.C. Fields sounded totally different than when he was entertaining with his marvelous control shots. Later he took his borrowed professional voice with him into film fame.

As George Alabam aged, his eyes became clouded so that he had difficulty seeing at night. Charles Washburn, a fellow theatrical press agent, was having trouble seeing in daylight. He suggested they try to rig a travel schedule that would put them in the same towns at the same time so they could help one another accommodate their handicaps. This seldom was feasible so other friendly publicists who were working their towns helped steer both Charley and George Alabam to the necessary newspapers and radio stations while they made their rounds.

Charles Washburn, too, was a theatrical legend in his own time, providing color and talent to this traveling fraternity. He had been a reporter for the *Chicago Tribune*. A colleague, who happened to be the father of Westbrook Pegler, had collaborated with Washburn on a play that was produced at the opening of a new theater in suburban Chicago.

Recounting this event, Charlie recalled that his own paper's drama critic was jealous of the playwright-reporters and that he reviewed their melodrama in a single sentence. Having praised the physical appearance of the theater profusely, he added, "The opening fare is a play entitled *Little Lost Sister*. It is said to have been written in two weeks and looks it."

Eventually Washburn wrote a book entitled *Come Into My Parlor*. It was about the notorious Everleigh Club, a famed Chicago sporting house operated with great success by sisters with that name. They retired to wealth and respectability on the East Coast in later years. They liked Charlie and his book and they willed him their upright piano.

By then Washburn had moved to New Jersey. He made room in his home for the bordello's piano until he, too, gave it away. A young woman came to ask if it was true that he had a piano for sale which had seen service at the famous Chicago "club." Washburn verified that and then asked why she wanted this particular instrument. "My father used to play it there," the visitor responded, whereupon Charlie presented it as a gift.

Soon after I became a fledgling circus publicity agent in 1930, a senior fellow townsman, Robert McCabe, spoke to me about a notable Delawarean named Whiting Allen. Allen had put in some years with the Barnum and Bailey Circus around the turn of the century.

Allen had been a reporter for the *Journal-Herald* in our town, and during his circus years he wrote magazine articles on that colorful subject. He went to Europe to herald the coming of The Greatest Show On Earth in 1897 and in his later years became a press representative for the Metropolitan Opera Company in New York City, in 1912.

My old friend Dexter Fellows remembered Allen as a talented and often amusing character. He once "starred" in a little comedy drama that took place in the lobby of the old Morton Hotel in Grand Rapids, Michigan, just before the circus came to town.

Whiting Allen had made many friends among the fraternity of newspaper reporters. Now he relaxed with them over several rounds of spirits in his hotel bar. Also in residence was a convention of undertakers. Their rather elaborate burial paraphernalia was on display in a corner of the hotel lobby.

Whiting imbibed to such a degree that he passed out, and his newspaper pals tenderly laid him out in one of the exhibition coffins. It was from this bed that he awakened the next morning, and the world missed what must have been one of the greatest comedy scenes of all time.

This grand practical joke was appreciated by all participants except the star performer and his employer, James A. Bailey. The boss was a teetotaler and reprimanded him severely. I feel our fellow townsman deserved better; the shock of awakening from a night of peaceful slumber in a white satin-lined casket should have been punishment enough.

I've enjoyed good working relationships with many company managers for the touring plays and musicals, and none amused me more than Edgar Runkle. (His picture appears with that of Buck Crouse and me on page 233.) I'd known Edgar during my college days. He preceded me into the theatrical world by many years, and before we were ever teamed for a traveling attraction he had become a teetotaler. That followed a decade of more or less steady imbibing which was why he often said he wasn't trying to get ahead in the world; he was trying to get even!

In Chicago he had been responsible for much excitement. Late one afternoon he responded to a distress telephone call from a pal unable to pay his bar tab at a joint on the Near North Side. Runkle not only satisfied his friend's indebtedness at this place, he joined him in a few additional libations. Suddenly he realized that he was overdue at the theater.

Short on time now, he dashed out to the curb and mounted a horse that happened to be tied up there. He rode it downtown to the side alley next to the Erlanger Theater and there he left it. The episode upset the manager of the theater so much that he shut Runkle into a room behind the second-floor office — he knew the borrowed horse was the property of the Chicago Police Department. I have no idea how the difficulty was resolved.

Later in New York City and unhappy over a broken marriage, Runkle was drowning his sorrows at a favorite East Side watering hole. He fell backward from his bar stool and lay flat on his back, out cold. The bartender who had been a party to this sad state of affairs pointed to the unconscious press agent and said to another customer, "See the nice little guy? He knows when he's had enough."

Runkle was my company manager when I fronted *Teahouse Of The August Moon*. The cast included a good actor, John Alexander, in a major role. Now John was one person at the Lambs Club, where he was my brother member, but John the Actor was quite another during the show's tour.

My problem with John was due to a "billing clause" in his contract which stated that all outdoor advertising on theater marquees must have his name on a line by itself. This occasionally was impossible, in cases where there was too little space on the marquee, unless we sacrificed the proper prominence of the play's rather lengthy title. Sometimes we had to put Alexander on a line containing the names of other players.

Finally, at Shea's Theater in Erie, Pennsylvania, John blew his top. He complained so bitterly that Runkle sent me a telegram saying, "Please try to stick to the actor's contractural demands; it is harder to fool John Alexander about his billing than it is to sneak sunrise past a rooster!"

A press agent named Sam Stratton was in my publicity depart-

ment for Ringling Brothers and Barnum & Bailey. He also fronted
theatrical tours between jobs on the sawdust trail. Another agent,
Al Butler, liked to invent nicknames and because Stratton was tall
and thin he became "Centerpole Sam." Butler's own sobriquet was
"Silent Al" because he so seldom was.

So during a circus hiatus Sam Stratton found himself doing publicity for an aging John Barrymore on his final tour. The play was
My Dear Children, and that is also an appropriate expression to
describe this incident.

Stratton persuaded the star to appear on stage after a matinee, to
be interviewed by editors of elementary and high school newspapers. These were both boys and girls, and there were also several
teachers there who wanted to meet this giant of the theater. These
were the waning days of his magnificent career and Barymore was
not at his best either onstage or off. Nevertheless, he fielded questions until he was overcome by thirst and boredom. One of the
little children asked why he had left film work to return to the legitimate stage.

Barrymore closed the session with this response: "In a dream my
sainted grandmother, Mrs. Drew, came to me and said, 'John, you
old son-of-a-bitch, what the hell are you doing in Hollywood?' "

Not all the friends and acquaintances in my trouping days were
press agents. "Doc" St. Clair was manager of what circuses traveling by rail called a bill car. Its personnel might consist of two dozen
billposters and their supplies, a pastemaker, contracting press
agent and a porter. The car traveled three weeks in advance of the
show's playing dates. It had been in New Orleans for two days during a eucharistic congress (which Doc described as a "eucalyptus"
congress). He said that he was thrilled by a visit to a church where
". . .a quartet of 10 orphans sang a solo and all were dressed like
French pheasants."

On another occasion, pointing to a high-flying airplane, he remarked that the pilot ". . . sure has some attitude!" And after reading a letter from home, he remarked to a close friend on the car that
". . . my wife has something the matter with her virginia."

At the Lambs Club we had what we called the noisy table. That
was where theater managers, agents and box office personnel often
got together for lunch. A member named "Lep" Solomon often was
good for some laughs at that table. Lep was an intelligent and effi-
cient treasurer; also, he was an improvisor of the English language.
We never laughed at what he said until he had left the table, fearing that he might cease to entertain us.

Once he remarked that he didn't like the numerous beggars on our street, ". . . but I never turn down a man with a sightseeing dog." Another time he told about having to "eat" (in theatrical parlance that means not being able to sell) a pair of tickets he had agreed to hold for a customer friend in New Jersey. This was during the *South Pacific* engagement. He explained his complaint: "That no-good so-and-so not only failed to show up; he didn't even have the affrontry to phone me and cancel!"

One Monday noon we were regaled with Solomon's report of a weekend when he had been a guest at an out-of-town mansion. "They didn't serve coffee in cups like we do here at the club," said Lep. "They brought it out in a whole big silver urine!"

It should be noted that the performance of publicity work for circus and theatrical attractions on tour has not been, at least in this century, a function for males exclusively. Comparatively few women have represented the peripatetic realm of the big tops in this capacity.

The first official lady circus press agents were a New York City reporter named Nellie Revelle, who also was the author of a play with a circus theme; and California newswoman Stella Karns. Following in the trouping footsteps of these distaff publicity pioneers were Indiana's Klara Knecht, a writer of popular circus books for children and the sister of famed Hoosier newspaper cartoonist Karl K. Knecht; and Canada's publicist Floree Galt.

Now the list of ladies adding talent and charm to traveling publicity programs for Broadway plays and musicals, as well as ballet and ice-skating companies on tour, is much longer. It includes such stalwarts as Anne Ford, Gertrude Bromberg, the team of Phyllis Perlman and Marian Byram, Lorella Val-Mery, Lillian Libman, Mary Bryant, Shirley Herz, Shirley Carroll, Joan Loomis and Betty Lee Hunt. To be noted also is the greatest of the production stage managers, Kathleen Anne Sullivan.

31

ROADWAY OF THE STARS

The publicity agent for a traveling theatrical attraction usually doesn't begin to grow horns until the show finishes its opening stand.

Prior to then and especially during rehearsal period he helps the players concerning their program biographies, interesting personal highlights such as a theatrical family background, hobbies, pets, past triumphs and amusing stumbles.

During this period the stars and supporting talent usually are friendliness personified. Each expects to receive at least transient immortality. They want more than newspaper advertisements — the players' contracts take care of that as to both size and position. They expect aired and printed publicity, complete with pictures, and the better the reputation of the publicist, the more acclaim is expected.

Now the test is at hand: "If our advance agent is any good he'll see that I have some real media attention in the next town!"

By then the top star, especially if female, is receiving a plethora of print, a rash of radio and a ton of TV. Unless, of course, she adheres to the practice of some stars of ducking any and all in-person assignments. But these deities are rare, and for the most part the publicist is occupied with begging his lesser luminaries into prime publicity dates.

So very soon now he may expect to take his choice of three reasons why ''I'm not getting my share of publicity: (1) our advance man is a two-faced bastard, (2) he's drunk most of the time, and (3) he spends his days chasing town broads.'' I know of no working publicist who ever fit that pattern but we all might as well — we'll be blamed for it anyway.

Sometimes an almost obscure member of the troupe may be a most interesting subject. Suppose he's a former All-American football star; you couldn't keep him off the sports pages. And what if a small-part actress once was a Miss America or is wise enough to want to be known as the oldest chorus girl in show business? That's lineage on the hoof.

The media, after going for the show's top stars, not infrequently will skip the next-in-rank to write about a minor-role gal who once figured in a major scandal and doesn't object to talking about it. Perhaps they will interview a member of the acting company who's written a new cookbook — food editors love a story like that.

It wasn't difficult to get publicity for our *Cabaret* orchestra's percussionist, who held both USA and Canadian records as a blood donor.

Suppose some member of the company has a unique hobby or whose culinary prowess is good enough for the publicist to enter her in a local cooking contest. And suppose she takes the cake. The creator of those events is helping his show, but he gets no merit badges from those cast members who have yet to be written up.

But if the publicist is a real pro, he'll not resent it. He knows how important personal media attention may be to a player, and he fervently wishes that all the materials he prepares about his individual actors would see sudden daylight.

Among his more conspicuous failures may be his swings-and-misses at getting important attention for his producer, especially if that person is interesting, articulate, highly placed in the profession and revels in personal publicity.

The press agent is lucky if he can grab more than a column item about his employer. Media people want to talk about the actors — isn't that what show business is all about? So it will be something like, ''Sorry Bev, you know I'd like to help you, but let's face it, stories about producers, directors, authors and composers don't sell newspapers.'' Come to think of it, they don't sell theater tickets either.

But the worst misfortune that can befall the traveling publicist is to have someone write a story about him! That not only never builds a fire in the box office, it certainly will fire up the actors and top brass who think we ignored them to satisfy our personal need for recognition.

One member of our craft seems to have said it all and with considerable word economy. Agent Joe Shea had worked briefly for the circus, but he had had many years of theatrical publicity experience when he was asked by a television interviewer to explain the difference between working for the circus and for the stage.

Joe thought for a moment and then replied, "I never knew an elephant to complain because her picture wasn't in the paper."

Possibly the responsibility for any and all failures that attend a traveling theatrical company is epitomized in this tale. A troupe once carried an elderly leading man who slipped on the ice in a railroad station when they arrived on a winter morning. He nearly broke his neck, but all he could think to say was, "God damn that press agent!"

32

BIRTHDAY OF AN OLD SWEETHEART

When my circus alma mater touched the century mark in 1970 I wrote a letter that was syndicated by Central Press. It reminded other vintage beaus that it was time for us to be lighting candles to the memory of our grand old girl. Here is the text of my letter:

HEY GRANDDAD! Your old sweetheart (the flashy one) has 100 candles on her birthday cake! That's right — one hundred.

Remember the first time you ever saw her? It was only for a few hours, but you couldn't forget her. From then on, right after mother and maybe a favorite teacher, she was tops.

Probably you had to wait a couple of years to see her again. But she always let you know she was coming. The poster on the barn or the store building or the long board fence said Barnum & Bailey Circus — The Greatest Show On Earth.

Your old sweetheart wore many forms and faces. Sometimes she danced on the broad bare back of a splendid white percheron and sometimes she somersaulted from a high trapeze into the hands of the catcher and you held your breath.

One special time you remember is when she was all alone in a cage full of tigers and she made them do tricks. One jumped though a hoop of fire. Once she lay on the ground and let an elephant walk over her. Sometimes she wore the faces of clowns, and all those things she did to the kind of music you just never heard anywhere else!

You used to get up at dawn to keep a date with her. She came to town on long trains. And you'd watch her hard at work in any kind of weather — getting breakfast for her family of 1200, building her house of canvas where you sat later that very same day and noticed that she had put aside her working clothes and was dressed in red and gold and covered with spangles. And maybe you had helped her water her elephants or carry her grandstand chairs and had earned a pass to the circus!

After 1919 your girl had a longer name. And it's been Ringling Brothers and Barnum & Bailey ever since. But the Barnum part is 100 years old now. And by 1919 she had a nickname. Her sons who'd left her to serve the country in 1917 came back and started calling her "Big Bertha" after the biggest cannon in World War I. And in the tough and tender fraternity of the big tops that name stuck as tight as a guyed-out tent.

There came a time when she kind of lost her glamour for you as you became interested in school and in sports and in a special girl. Then you were married and one day you took your kids for Big Bertha to see. And there she was, waiting for you just like you'd never been away.

She was prettier than ever and she knew a lot of new tricks. She cooked popcorn and peanuts as good as ever and her pink lemonade still was the nectar of the circus gods. Big Bertha's family was so huge now that you heard she needed more than 100 railroad cars in four separate trains to help her keep her appointments across the map.

Then almost before you could say Gargantua the time had come for you to keep another special date with your old sweetheart because you had grandchildren. Only now Big Bertha had moved into the big arena buildings because the towns she visited didn't have convenient space for her 41 tents anymore.

And she had a kind of magic power you had not noticed before. She could look at your party and see one more kid than you thought was there — you.

This was 1969 and John Ringling North had sold the Greatest Show On Earth to Irvin and Israel Feld, Washington, D.C. promotors, and to Judge Roy Hofheinz of Houston, Texas, where he had built the famous Astrodome.

Those fast-stepping and imaginative showmen put together another complete Ringling Brothers and Barnum & Bailey Circus so that now, with two shows of equal size and called Units Red and Blue, the travelingest belle of total show business can visit twice as many people in twice as many towns. And Irvin Feld roams the world to find the best circus talent just as Big Bertha's owners always had done.

So, Granddad, don't be wishing too hard that your little guests could have seen the great Lillian Leitzel and Alfredo Codona in the air and Con Colleano on the tightwire and the towering Wallendas on the highwire; Dorothy Herbert on her rearing and waltzing stallion and Bill Heyer on Starless Night; Poodles Hanneford and the Cristianis in the rings and Mabel Stark and Clyde Beatty in the big cage.

Big Bertha's stars shine bright as ever they did. Only Barnum's Jumbo is missing and the chances are 10 to 1 you never saw him anyhow. He died in 1885.

Just look at your old girl's birthday cake! One hundred candles! A hundred elephants in salute, her bands play galoptime and in her ears is the sweetest music of all — the laughter of children echoing through the big tops of 100 years.

Now she peeks around the corner at a year marked 1971 and primps quickly in the mirror of tomorrow as she prepares to march her spangled legions into the second century of The Greatest Show On Earth.

You see, your old sweetheart never did have much time for looking back. She usually had a date in another town tomorrow morning.

33

ALONE IN ITS GREATNESS

In 1959, while working for the national touring company of Meredith Willson's Broadway blockbuster *The Music Man,* I was invited to become general manager for the famed Saint Louis Municipal Theater, oldest and largest starlight musical playhouse in the world. It came by its slogan honestly: "Alone In Its Greatness."

Many notables took their first giant strides on the way to stardom on its enormous outdoor stage. Included are such celebrities as comedian Red Skelton, the great dancing team of Marge and Gower Champion, stage and screen stars Queenie Smith and Cary Grant (then fresh from his native England and known as Archie Leach), St. Louis native Mary Wickes, Irene Dunne, and a young Bob Hope.

This job would be a challenge inasmuch as I was a publicist and promoter rather than an administrator. But I was touched when I learned that my theater friend of many years, the late Paul Beisman, had recommended me to succeed him. He then was losing his long battle with lung cancer. He had brought the St. Louis "Muny Opera" to international eminence. The Muny was regarded with respect and affection not only by its home city, but by all of show business. For me this was the theatrical equivalent of The Greatest Show On Earth.

A further and important consideration was that this assignment offered an opportunity to have Ruth and our daughters with me while I worked in a city I long had liked. Our Patricia, by this time an accomplished actress, soon would be closing in her New York musical hit, *Red Head*. Our son Stephen and his family would remain in Ohio where he was employed by the Columbus Zoo. Our Kathleen and Rebecca would continue their schooling in Missouri.

Since its inception in 1919, the St. Louis Municipal Theater had produced its own editions of the greatest Broadway musical hits. Its gigantic stage has a 90-foot proscenium opening, a depth of 110 feet, and includes a huge revolving turntable upon which special effects are presented. The theater has 12,000 comfortable seats, of which 1200 are available at no cost to the public at every performance. The Muny is cut into a hillside in beautiful Forest Park, where the greatest of all the worlds fairs had been held in 1904.

The Muny is overpowering when seen for the first time. When our actress daughter arrived to join the singing chorus, all she could think of to say as she saw this theater's immense proportions was, "Play Ball!"

The playing season of the Muny Opera ran for 91 consecutive nights from June until Labor Day. During that time 11 separate musical spectaculars were presented. Each production required 120 or more people, including stage and screen stars and principal supporting players, a season-long permanent chorus of 70 singers and dancers from many states, and our regular orchestra of 50 skilled musicians, most of whom were members of the St. Louis Symphony Orchestra.

From my predecessor I was fortunate to inherit our production director, John Kennedy; musical conductor Edwin McArthur; scenic designer Paul McGuire; and William Zalken, publicity chief. My assistant was Edward Steinhauer, who also was manager of the American Theater, a legitimate house in downtown St. Louis.

There was other exceptional talent in key office positions, in stage construction and in the wardrobe department. The support of a dedicated board of directors made it possible to offer king-size productions that frequently surpassed their original New York stage or their Hollywood film productions.

During our six years in St. Louis the theater presented five world stage premiers. Included was *Around The World In Eighty Days*. It was realistically executed with live elephants. Adventurer-hero Phileas Fogg and his comic sidekick Passepartout floated in the basket of a huge balloon which was maneuvered by a construction crane.

Our daughter, Pat, whose professional name is Kelley Stephens, was chosen to star in the title role of *Molly Darling* by the show's St. Louis authors. The play was about a historical feminist whose

I found myself with a desk job during my years as head of the St. Louis Municipal Theater, the "Muny Opera."

achievements included the founding of the nation's first kindergarten in her home town of St. Louis.

The splendid production of *Meet Me In St. Louis* featured a moving street car filled with passengers for the popular "Trolley Car" song. A magnificent fireworks finale saluted the opening of the Worlds Fair in the play — the real fair took place on that very location in 1904.

Customer complaints usually arrived on my desk, where they properly belonged. Ordinarily they were not numerous but they came in great waves after our all-night dress rehearsal of this wonderfully exciting show. Traditionally, dress rehearsal for each new production began at midnight on Saturday and usually concluded at about 4 a.m. The script for this show called for a finale which filled the sky with showers of colored stars. They burst over Forest Park and the surrounding residential area at 3:45 a.m. Many were aroused from their slumbers and a few were convinced that the city was under enemy attack. I was not surprised that my office telephone was lively all the way into the opening of the new musical on Monday. Then our good neighbors realized that the trial run which had disturbed them early Sunday morning was in fact a sort of rehearsal for them, too. That loud and lovely pyrotechnic spectacular had six more nights to go!

In a happier memory of those days and nights I see again the delight on the face of New York character actor Clarence Nordstrom, who portrayed the lovable grandfather in our *Meet Me In St. Louis*. There was a tender moment when our little Becky, whose grandfathers were deceased before her birth, went backstage unannounced to ask if he would please be her grandfather too. Their mother and I were especially pleased when our school girls joined their big sister to appear in small roles for such handsome productions as *Song Of Norway* and *The Great Waltz*. Daughter Kathleen had a proper appreciation for the performing arts, but showed early a further practical interest in her father's responsibilities. For when I returned to the apartment at the conclusion of the performances in the park, she rarely asked how they had played. First she asked, "Daddy, what was the gross tonight?"

The theater had many accomplishments, reflecting the effort of many hearts, minds and muscles. I think I was proudest of the fact that during our years there the color barrier was broken.

There was never a set rule about it. Many Negroes had appeared in star roles and in principal parts in the years prior to then, but none had ever been employed for the season in the singing or danc-

The three Kelley daughters (from left): Patricia, Rebecca and Kathleen, in 1959. They were costumed for their roles in Song of Norway *at the Muny Opera.*

ing choruses.

Among my assistant's numerous responsibilities was that of hiring and training the theater's many ushers. It was on Ed Steinhauer's recommendation that we hired our first young Negro usher who soon proved to be one of the best. Soon there were others, and it wasn't long before a St. Louis Negro girl earned her way into the singing chorus. This, we felt, was progress and possibly even noteworthy, but before any trumpets were sounded about it I thought back to a time in 1950 when I was the traveling publicist for a Broadway musical called *Lost In The Stars,* with the great Negro baritone, Todd Duncan, in the starring role.

I was able to use Todd Duncan, the great baritone, to desegregate Louisville's Auditorium Theater.

In Louisville, Kentucky, the mayor was planning to honor the distinguished Kentuckian by presenting him with the key to the city. The manager of the city's Auditorium Theater and I decided that this might be a propitious occasion for desegregating the house for the first time. The traditional pattern called for seating white and colored spectators on opposite sides of the center aisle of the main floor. The integration was accomplished with no advance notice and it worked out to the acceptance and well-mannered performance of all concerned.

So now, in our St. Louis situation, we considered the progress that might be accomplished without a lot of fanfare. That is the manner in which it was done. The city's major daily newspapers and the editor of the principal Negro paper concurred with our position.

There were some offhand remarks about the Muny Opera's manager trying to become the Branch Rickey of the theater. All I felt was pride in being compared with this distinguished friend from my own Ohio Wesleyan. Rickey was remembered in St. Louis for having led its baseball Cardinals to fame in years gone by. More recently he had scored a triumph for racial integration by hiring Jackie Robinson to play for his Brooklyn Dodgers, thereby making the national sport a fairer and better game.

In the summer of 1965, after six years and 60 Muny Opera productions, I resigned to resume publicity work for traveling Broadway plays and musicals. Reflecting upon our St. Louis repertoire year-by-year, I drafted a list of 10 all-time shows for a dream season. In terms of both artistic quality and public appeal such a season might include these musical gems: *The Sound Of Music, The King And I, Oklahoma!, The Music Man, Guys And Dolls, The Student Prince, Show Boat, Brigadoon, The Wizard Of Oz* and *My Fair Lady.*

Of a total of 62 musicals presented during our six years at the Muny Opera, all except two were cast, mounted and rehearsed by our own artistic and technical staff. One was a ready-made touring production of *Porgy And Bess.* We imported this show because we felt that with principally local casting we could not do justice to this splendid operetta. No, not even with the assistance of our friend, the eminent Ken Billups, whose superb Negro choral ensemble served the Muny Opera on numerous occasions. Our *Porgy And Bess* importation starred the ebullient Cab Calloway and was a solid success.

The other exception was an excellent Mexican dancing troupe called *Ballet Popular.* For our presentation I changed the title to *Mexican Holiday.* It had been recommended to me by a Texas friend who had presented it at the Casa Mañana Theater in Fort Worth.

To spread a welcome mat for our friends from south of the border, I bought a Mexican flag which flew beside Old Glory outside the hotel that housed the company. That hotel liked its foreign guests so much that it gave them a farewell party upon their departure from a highly successful one-week engagement. That party, however, almost didn't take place.

Not long before our playing date with the Mexicans I learned that New York impresario Sol Hurok had booked into the Pacific Northwest a more formal Mexican ballet troupe called *Folklorico.* The playing dates and locations of these companies were totally non-competitive. Reflecting on the business tactics of some New York entrepreneurs, where even the shadow of competition was concerned, I decided to play safe. I bought what is called a performance bond from the insurance office of the city's mayor-to-be, A. J. Cervantes. This would guarantee the appearance of the troup for which we had contracted. More important, it would cover thousands of ticket-sale refunds if for any reason the performances couldn't take place.

And they almost didn't! Only the fact that our friendly Texan booker had good diplomatic relations in Mexico City blocked wily Sol Hurok's last-minute effort to prevent the troupe from boarding

Ruth and I are shown during our Golden Wedding Anniversary celebration in June 1980.

its scheduled flight for St. Louis.

I like to think back upon the non-stop busy days and nights of serving the splendid St. Louis Municipal Theater. It enjoyed great success during our six years there. We formed many lasting friendships in the Show-Me State. I feel that the best blessing of all was the addition of Robert Schotten Vogt to our family as the husband of our Kathleen. Ruth and I have shared their home and handsome growing children since our retirement in 1977.

In June 1980 our offspring staged a wonderful celebration of our Golden Wedding Anniversary. Here they came — all four of our children and their families. Included were an even dozen grandchildren, ranging in age from 1 to 21. Almost 50 years had passed since that beautiful bride and her nervous groom bid their wedding party farewell in Ohio and drove away in their new Model A Ford to join the Greatest Show On Earth.

But now the shadows lengthen with the march of time. The hand of memory weaves pictures of the past while treasured events increase their beating on the drumheads of the mind. Heard again is a stirring trumpet fanfare leading bandsmen into "Ringling Brothers Grand Entry," and the rich, soaring Negro voices of the Hall Johnson Choir bringing lovely spirituals to living splendor. A fiddler makes music on a roof as time segues to the marching majesty of "Seventy-Six Trombones" and a steam calliope is whistling again on Capitol Hill.

The heart remembers a wedding day when a church organ softly played the strains of "Sweetheart Of Sigma Chi." In the magic mirror of the past I see the stockings of our children hanging from the mantel on Christmas Eve. Through the corridors of time there comes again the echo of a college dance orchestra playing "Home Again Blues." Perhaps that song title is prophetic, designed to lift the spirit and tempo of one's hope that there will be loved ones waiting at the Gate.

The poem used as the opening statement of this autobiography was written by me 35 years ago, in contemplation of the end of an old trouper's career. Suddenly I am that old trouper, and now I guess it applies to me.

And Norman, my reply to your question about show business is as valid today as it ever was: It **is** better than work!

Appendix A

FOR BETTER OR VERSE
The poetry of F. Beverly Kelley

FIT FOR A QUEEN

The Gown her mother sewed with love
for May Day when she played her part
seems smaller as the Mays fly by but
Still fits nicely 'round the heart

KATHLEEN'S RUDOLPH

Saint Peter, part of a child's heart — a warm, soft-
eyed, fun-loving, wriggling part — wags his small tail at
your bright gates tonight. Please watch that gate; don't
let it slam too soon! A dachshund is a long, low dog,
you know. And so he won't feel lonely and look back,
please let him rest awhile in some child's lap when he is
tired from chasing squirrels in Paradise.

Saint Peter, that small bark outside is Rudolph.
Please let him in and lead him to Lord Jesus who must like
to pet a puppy now and then.

For even though no artist's brush, no written word
recounts that faithful dogs were friends of His on earth,
it just may be that on one sunny afternoon when He said,
"Suffer little children to come unto Me,"

Some little girl or boy climbed happily upon the
Master's knee, contented puppy clasped in loving arms.

DANIEL BEARD, FOUNDER OF BOY SCOUTS OF AMERICA,
TAKES GENERAL GEORGE WASHINGTON
BACK TO VALLEY FORGE
- June 30, 1950 -
National BSA Jamboree

The double shadow cast upon the camp
Splits topside to reveal two hats —
One cocked, one peaked in silhouette against the moon.
The image of the figures on the knoll
Reflects on silent, sleeping tents below.
The cocked-hat giant turns his head and speaks:

"Why bring me, Dan, to puzzle at this place
Where once I knelt in prayer long ago,
While winter winds screamed cruelly down the rows
Of log-built shelters in the blood-smeared snow?
What means this camp that sleeps so peaceful now —
I see no cannon and the sentires walk unarmed."

Then Dan Beard squares his shoulders and replies:
These 'troops' are boys, my General, Americans
Whose homes are far beyond the wilderness
You scouted and surveyed when just a lad.
Such names as Steubenville, Pulaski, Lafayette
You'll understand, and some called Washington.
But places named Fort Worth, Topeka, Butte,
And Sacramento, Lincoln, Jackson, Grant.
They learn to live like Indians — and some are
Descendents of the red men that you knew,
And some are boys whose oriental kin, and African
Were half across the world when you stood here.
They learn to sail, and — since my time — to fly;
And General, I would not have you think
The iron vein runs out thinner in this Youth.
Their people flew your flag at New Orleans,
At Soissons, Normandy and Iwo Jima, Rome,
And if we have to do the job again
That you abhored but knew you had to do,

This breed of white and black and brown and yellow, too,
Will prove again that it is all red-white-and-blue.
For when we started Boy Scouts some years back,
We used the perfect blueprint that you left.
And while they don't forget the role you played
At this once bleak and holy place,
They do not think of you so much as 'General';
No, George, these boys and children o'er the land —
The land you fought to give them — call you 'Father.'
This is the harvest of the crop you sowed —
The seeds of Liberty and Brotherhood.

The tall man ponders, sighs, inhales

The warm, remembered scent of Pennsylvania hay,

And puts his arm around the master of the Scouts, replies:

"This might well be my rendezvous with Destiny,

And, Dan, perhaps my greatest victory of them all.

'WAY OUT WEST
(in Ohio)

His bike is a paint cow pony;
The rolling eastern road
Is level desert mesa
For peddling the grocery load.

Old Pal's green mane is flying
Through breezy mountain pass,
And who would think of trying
To call it asparagRAS?

The trading post's back yonder
As anyone can see,
And who would think of trying
To call it the A. & P.?

And here's our cowpoke's ranch house
Where faithful, cycling Pal
Can spend a peaceful evening
In his garage corral.

HAYSEED

They stand and watch the evening eastbound train
Scoop up the visitor, and end
His summer reverie with one hoarse chug;
Aunt Sally with her quiet, farm-bred ways,
And Bob with myriad freckles crowding all
The lively features on his face,
And Peg and Sarah, with two front teeth out —
They all have come to see the city cousin
Carried to some magic urban place
By clicking wheels and whistling, smoking train.
September's hazy golden curtain drops
to separate the summer farmer boy
From city ways now crowding from afar;
And even his straw hat — proud badge
Of rural freedom — wears a look
Of strangeness as its owner boards the train.
They wave, and he smiles bravely at these folk
Who share his blood, but not his winter ways;
And even as the engine labors out,
His thoughts are busy with the months ahead.
Still, there is hayseed in his trouser cuff,
And forty years from now when he is half
A hundred, and his country relatives
Have heeded the insidious call of towns,
That hayseed tardily will sprout, and then
Our city boy goes back to buy the farm.

BEDTIME

Sycamores retire quite early,
Nod and off to slumber go;
Oaks that try to stay up later
Yawn and break a date with Snow.
Cedars, fir and spruce go gadding
With J. Frost to see the sights —
Waving green-clad limbs at Winter,
Dancing through the long white nights.

YOUNGSTOWN

Youngstown is a girl whose clothes
Smart the eyes and soot the nose.
Proudly, though, she puts them on
Every working day at dawn.
Sundown — ah, a different story!
Crowned in redhued, firelit glory,
Flaming plume against the sky —
And every night the Fourth of July!

SPRINGTIME IN DEEP DIXIE

God's bustin' out a bright new rosebud vest
To wear atop his dogwood-flowered shirt:
This time o' year He always dresses best:
Green suit and shoes of rich tan Georgia dirt.

THE PRESS AGENT'S LAMENT

Nobody seems to marvel at the show's publicity
or wonders at the thousands who are lining up to see
our bright and spangled product, for a well-known circus law
is "The title draws the public" when we seat 'em on the straw.

But when it's empty in the seats, the troupe from boss to clown
says "That lazy circus agent didn't tell 'em we're in town!"

The whole show knows the agent never carries any lumber;
he stays in good hotels and has the finest food and slumber,

And when they wish to praise his work, the more considerate
say "He does it all with passes and remains illiterate."

Still, he's brother to the robin crying springtime in the land
as fact and fabrication lead him gently by the hand,
and Old Saint Pete will tell him when he climbs the golden stair:

"The City Room is straight ahead, and how about a pair?"

WHEN YOU CAN'T GO HOME FOR CHRISTMAS

When you can't go back home for Christmas
And you start feeling blue from the start
Don't forget that this day is a treasure
You can keep all year long in your heart
When you yearn for the folks around the table
And you picture the wreath on the door
Don't forget that this day is a blessing
That you hold in your heart forevermore
There's a lift in this morn when the Savior was born
There's a song for your soul in the air
Everything is all right when they sing Silent Night
Anyway, anytime, anywhere
Then you miss the tender kiss of your loved ones
And the kids with their toys on the floor
But remember that Christmas is a blessing
You can hold in your heart forevermore.

REQUIEM FOR PIANO (steam)
While remembering the way it used to be

Sound the strong notes; play them for one hundred railroad
cars — on some tours more; some less, but thereabouts a
hundred in four trains.

Press down on white-hot keys — a requiem for Percherons and
Belgians, three hundred twenty-five full-strength; of bands
and red and gold and blue upon the streets.

Now make a symphony for canvas — twelve thousand yards of 8-
ounce drill; compose a melody describing sight and sound
and smell, and children's faces lighted with the thrill of
watching it all billow into tents.

Touch keys to musically describe the cookhouse, and then try
to conjure up the magic of the late, late afternoon, of
shadows slanting on the backyard card games and on acrobats
rehearsing and on sleeping clowns.

Capture now the midway as the first faint star is born, and
spread your blistered fingers to extole, in bright-toned
steam, the warmth of charcoal buckets doing service on
chilled nights in autumn Dixie.

Lastly, now, reach back and find a chord to hold forever
there, in reverie, the sound of hoofs on pavement late at
night, the hub-cap rumble and the corner flare.

Appendix B

CHRONOLOGY
of the life of F. Beverly Kelley

July 15, 1905, born at St. Marys, Ohio
1924, graduation from Delaware (Ohio) High School
1927, managed European tour of Ohio Wesleyan Glee Club
June 1928, graduated from Ohio Wesleyan University
September 1928, reporter for *Indianapolis Times*
1929, fronted the Darrow Debates
April 1930, joined Ringling Brothers and Barnum & Bailey Circus
June 1930, married Ruth Stephens
1932, fronted *The Green Pastures*
1933, joined Hagenbeck-Wallace Circus
1936, fronted *The White Horse Inn* in New York City
1938, rejoined Ringling Brothers and Barnum & Bailey Circus
1947, retired from RBB&B
1947, joined Dailey Bros. Circus
1948, joined Cole Bros. Circus
1950, fronted *Mister Roberts*
1952, fronted *Call Me Madam*
1954-55, rejoined RBB&B Circus
1958, fronted *The Music Man*
1959-65, managed St. Louis Municipal Theater
1967-79, fronted numerous Broadway hit shows, including *Fiddler
        On The Roof, Cabaret, Hello Dolly!, George M!,
        Applause, The Royal Family* and *My Fair Lady*
1978, began work on this autobiography
1980, celebrated golden wedding anniversary
February 1983, publication of *It Was Better Than Work*

THEATRICAL FRIENDS
with whom we have worked along the way

Richard B. Harrison, Ethel Merman, Edward G. Robinson, Signe Hasso, Pearl Bailey, Douglas Fairbanks Jr., Todd Duncan, Edward Mulhare, Anne Rogers, Kitty Carlisle, Luther Adler, Dolores Wilson, Mimi Randolph, Eva Le Gallienne, Jack Albertson, Sam Levine, Paul Lipson, Bill Carroll, Alfred Lunt, Lynne Fontanne, Mary Pickford, Lauren Bacall, Bert Lahr, Chita Rivera, Harry Hickox, Cliff Hall, Iggi Wolfington, Gene Autry, Shelley Berman, Taina Elg, Anne Driscoll, Melissa Hart, Benny Baker, Judith Anderson, Helen Menken, Martyn Green, Joel Grey, Forrest Tucker, Lary Parks, Margery Steel, Thomas Gomez, Shirley Booth, Gig Young, Carol Beasley, Sid Caesar, Cornelia Otis Skinner, Andy Devine, Maggie Smith, Leo Fuchs, Patricia Morrison, Sam Kressen, John Forsythe, Nancy Andrews, John Raitt, William Gaxton, Billy Daniels, Carol Shelley and Arthur Treacher.